MW00396639

The Awakening of the Heart

Merry Christmas '99
Mom -
I love you
Terri (SANTA)

Savage PRESS
Box 115, Superior, WI 54880 (715) 394-9513

First Edition

© Copyright 1999 Jill Downs

Cover Illustration ©1999 by Diane Schafer

All rights reserved, including the right to reproduce this book or portions thereof, in any form, except for brief quotations embodied in articles and reviews, without written permission from the publisher. The opinions, observations and historical references herein are those of the author alone.

Places, names, characters, organizations or incidents are products of the author's imagination or are used fictitiously. Any reference or resemblance to "real" people, places, organizations, living or dead, is purely coincidental.

ISBN 1-886028-42-7

Library of Congress Catalog Card Number: 99-64916

Published by:

Savage Press
P.O. Box 115
Superior, WI 54880

715-394-9513

e-mail: savpress@spacestar.com

Visit us at: www.savpress.com

Printed in the USA

The Awakening of the Heart

The Soul's Journey from Darkness Into Light

by Jill Downs

Acknowledgments

My heartfelt gratitude goes to countless persons, but especially to the following: John and all in spirit who helped guide me; the late Reverend F.W. Hutchinson for his continued encouragement; Sister Mary Richard Boo, my editor, whose patience and assistance were invaluable; and Mike Savage, my publisher, who was a joy to work with.

— Jill

Dedication

To all my family, especially my parents, my husband Tony, and my daughters Cindy and Leila; and many friends whose loving support helped sustain me throughout this project.

In Memoriam

To Diane Schafer, who so beautifully captured my vision for the cover.

Introduction

No matter how far advanced we are on the spiritual path, in our conscious desire to heal ourself and others, we are continually challenged in our faith, patience, love of self, ability to forgive and many other areas of life.

It is my desire, born out of my own life experience, to assist others in their healing process; hence this book on spiritual growth. The information contained here was inspired by a higher consciousness and came as well from my own inner truth and evolvement. It is my belief that we come to greater self-awareness and acceptance as we learn to trust our own processes. Thus we empower ourselves, facilitating our own healing in a loving, healthy manner.

Life can be an exciting adventure when we learn to view problems as challenges and difficult lessons as opportunities for growth. As we open our hearts to all that surrounds us, we become aware of the magnificent gifts—like the opening of a flower or the song of a bird—that come to us in seemingly insignificant ways.

In my own journey, much time has elapsed since the first writing of this work. The intervening years were necessary so that I might process and integrate the information contained in the book. Upon my return to the manuscript, I felt it was as pertinent today as it was when I initially wrote it.

It is now my hope that these essays will offer the reader an opportunity to explore his or her own feelings, attitudes and beliefs on various aspects of spirituality, and that the concepts contained here will prove helpful to others in their journey into light.

Transformation

I've invited the darkness to join me
So that I may heal my past
Together with angels of light
I'm given a choice at last.

How I respond to life
Is entirely up to me
I may follow the angels of darkness
Pretending I do not see
Or I may go in faith and courage
If my wish is to be free

I may judge myself and condemn my faults
The choice is up to me
Or I may look within the mirror
And honor what I see

The way is never easy
If your belief is strong
For the tests will be intense
And the journey will be long

I've invited the darkness to join me
Instead of pushing it away
So that I may clear my doubts and fears
Not keep them just at bay

And though I sometimes wonder
At the purpose of it all
I know God has a plan
For those who can recall
A time when they were troubled
And things seemed more than they could bear
To lift the hearts of others
And show them that they care

Some come to pave the way
For those who come behind
But to take the road less traveled
Leaves questions in the mind

“Why me?” we sometimes ask
“Why not?” the Voice replies
God, with His sense of humor
Our self-pity He denies

And so the darkness lifts
As the angels of the night
Do their dance in the shadows
Of the angels of the Light.

— Jill Downs

BOOK ONE

ON FORGIVENESS

Forgiveness is the key that unlocks the door to positive change within us and plays a major role in our growth process. In learning to forgive, we must first forgive ourselves for all real or imagined mistakes, just as we know God forgives us. This is the first step in our becoming whole. Then, as we learn to accept who we are and find that deep sense of peace within ourselves, we can look upon others with compassion.

Like forgiveness, spiritual work begins at home. At any time that we're having a problem, it helps to look at our part in it, no matter how tempting it is to blame something or someone else. It is our perspective that can make any situation a problem, so we must always ask ourselves, honestly, where we fit in.

"Why am I having a problem with this person? What is my role?" We must remember that people act as mirrors for us, telling us things about ourselves that we don't always like to hear. We might ask, "What is this person or situation reflecting back to me that is troublesome?" In this way, we learn a great deal about our personalities and what we may need to correct in order to make our path smoother.

Often people reflect that which we would rather not see within ourselves. But without that mirror's imaging our own faults and shortcomings, we would know little about who we are and would be unable to grow and become all we are meant to be. We would not be able to fulfill our potential if we did not have people and situations around us, projecting all we need to know about ourselves.

For example, if we notice someone behaving in a way that is bothersome to us, we need to ask, "Why does this person's behavior upset me?" Perhaps they are doing something that we secretly wish we had the courage to do. Again, perhaps their behavior is indicating another truth about ourselves that we find hard to face. Could it be that they are right, even though we do not like their manner of approach in a particular situation? Could it be that they have a point?

It's never easy to face all the truth about ourselves, but as we learn to get honest with who we are, we become free. The truth always sets us free, no matter how it may hurt to face it initially. We must always treat ourselves gently so as not to harm or destroy our self-worth or sense of who we are. We must never tear ourselves down: it just takes time to build ourselves back up again, and berating oneself is a totally unnecessary exercise that has no purpose in spiritual growth.

Learning to be gentle with oneself is a great attribute. We must remain positive about ourselves. It is only from that standpoint that we can grow and fulfill our potential. Can we build a house on a crumbling foundation? We must create a strong foundation, then we can safely proceed with the rest of the building. We can make it stately, functional and beautiful, allowing it to become whatever we choose—whatever we design it to be.

We need to remember that forgiving ourselves, loving ourselves, and accepting our mistakes is a beginning in constructing that foundation—a prelude to a wonderful ability to forgive and accept others as they are. We ought to remember, too, that it is only as we forgive that we are forgiven; if we are unable to forgive someone for something, we will also feel unforgiven. We cannot fully attain our freedom until we have totally forgiven others for their mistakes, real or imagined.

We must keep in mind that sometimes we invite, unconsciously of course, certain actions on the part of others that will help us to grow. Therefore, from that point of view, their behavior, undesirable as it may appear to us, is really there to help us. In this way, our enemies become our friends: they play a major role in helping us to become all we were meant to be. They help us to achieve wholeness. Without them, we would remain ignorant of our potential as human beings.

Forgiveness and gratitude go hand-in-hand. For as we forgive others and ourselves, we say, "Thank you for the lesson. Thank you for bringing us to this new place of greater understanding and awareness." By this sincere act of gratitude, we take another step up the ladder. Each new step we take brings us closer to our goal of self-actualization.

ON SPIRITUAL GROWTH

What do we mean by "Spiritual Growth?" We are made up not only of our physical body that we can see, touch and feel, but of a spiritual body as well. Our spiritual body is an exact duplicate of the physical body.

When we die, we take with us our spiritual body, which is characterized and strengthened by all that we have allowed ourselves to become in the physical lifetime. In other words, it's the sum total of everything we have acquired and experienced. This is what we refer to as "learning." This accumulation of experiences or learning is not important in itself, but makes it possible for the soul to gain greater awareness. The soul is the eternal life-spark that is connected to God and never dies. Therefore, all life experiences may be seen as good because they give the opportunity to expand the soul—that divine, eternal light of God that we are.

We can see, then, that it is both unnecessary and undesirable to make judgments about others and ourselves. Why should we judge our ability to learn? If we don't experience life in all its many aspects, we learn very little, and our spark remains small and underdeveloped. We shine only after having had many experiences, both positive and negative, which merge into a larger whole, creating an immense light capable of bringing much good and healing into the world.

We need not fear this growth. There are times, it is true, when it seems to be painful. The pain is there simply to let us know we are indeed growing. We learn lessons as well through love and understanding. Learning through pain is a choice we make, like a child putting his hand on a hot stove. Eventually, we learn, through discomfort, not to send out certain thoughts or engage in certain activities because they bring pain to us.

This brings us to the law of "Karma," which is a universal law meaning, "That which we send out, either positively or negatively, in thought or in deed, is returned to us." How helpful this can be to our understanding: whenever something happens to us, we can know that for one reason or another we have invited the experience. Often we won't know why, and we don't necessarily need to know. We only need to understand that we have drawn the experience for our growth. Subsequently, it is our reaction to it that becomes the focal point, rather than the experience itself. It is always best to concentrate on the lesson being taught rather than the vehicle for the lesson.

For example, in many marriages or other close relationships that are apt to produce conflict, it is often tempting to place much of our attention on the person with whom we are having conflict, rather than to ask ourselves, "What am I to learn here? What is this situation forcing me to do? What positive things am I to learn in this situation?" If we cannot come up with the answers at the precise time at which we are posing the questions, we must continue to ask. They will eventually become clear to us as time goes on. Sometimes we have to be patient with ourselves: we are not always ready for the truth.

We will recognize the truth, however, because it will set us free—always. We may have part of the truth in a given situation, but not feel totally at ease because there is still more for us to understand. Once we have faced ourselves in total honesty, we are released from that particular issue, and we go on to learn something else. We are free to move on after we have accepted God's forgiveness and forgiven ourselves for our mistakes.

Spiritual growth has its own rewards. As we near the top of the mountain, our challenges become greater, the energy is finer, and the path narrower. But we know that because we have come this far, our tools are sharpened and one day we will be honed as fine as steel. So let's not be afraid to live our lives. We are not here to be perfect, but we're here to experience all that life has to offer. When we are through, we'll be glad that we came, and we'll thank God we were not afraid to do it all.

So what do we need to take with us on this journey up the mountain? There are certain tools that are available to help us, just as there are obstacles to watch out for on the sometimes perilous path. We will have good days and days we consider "bad," but as we've seen already, there is no such thing as a bad day, only days when learning is more intense, and therefore more difficult. It is also on these days that our light is beginning to shine more brightly deep within our soul. Sooner or later our knowledge and understanding will be made manifest on the physical plane, and we will be attracting others to us who can benefit from our awareness and our strength.

The tools are composed of certain soul qualities that are positive in nature and help make up the personality. They include such characteristics as patience, tolerance, wisdom, and intuition. When we grow spiritually, these qualities become more permanent as we set about to reduce their counterparts. Each quality has an opposite side that we attempt to eliminate; e.g., selfishness, greed, impatience, or intolerance.

Therefore, as we come into greater understanding, our soul is enhanced by the further development of these positive soul qualities. We make our way up the ladder of spiritual growth through their refinement. Through this process, we are better able to serve ourselves and all of mankind as we allow ourselves to learn through our experiences.

These positive attributes, then, become the building blocks—the power base from which we may draw faith, hope, and love to help ourselves and others along our paths. We learn to draw upon our positive qualities; we gain confidence and strength.

However, along this path up the mountain we also encounter obstacles that may, at the same time, be looked upon as blessings in disguise. As we learn to bless the negative conditions within and around us, we can truthfully say that we're beginning to understand what life is all about. We begin to see our life as a series of lessons from which we have much to learn. We can be grateful for the opportunity to advance ourselves.

Our obstacles become stepping stones to understanding and enlightenment. We come to understand spiritual growth as a series of lessons presented to us in love by our Creator. Further, we welcome the opportunities they offer for our growth and advancement. We thank God for all of our experiences as they bring us into greater light and truth.

While building a firm foundation based upon such attributes as faith, trust, patience, and love, we come into greater awareness of our world and ourselves. As we humble ourselves and learn to forgive our mistakes and the mistakes of others, we find ourselves growing into greater light. We accept with love the responsibility for our soul's mission on earth.

ON PATIENCE

As we travel along the spiritual path, we need to develop patience with ourselves. Learning this trait isn't easy: it takes patience. We may stand for what seems to be an eternity at a line at the grocery store when we are in a hurry and need to be somewhere. Then again, perhaps we are in a restaurant and a waitress seems to want to ignore us as we wait and wait for our dinner, which finally arrives. And then, as we gaze hungrily at our plate, we realize she brought the wrong meal: we had ordered something entirely different. These situations test our patience. And as we learn to handle them with greater ease, we stretch ourselves. We test our ability to sit back, be calm, and not lose our temper. We are aware, instead, that we are developing patience, and all is in divine order.

Therefore, when we can see our lessons before us, it makes it much easier to detach ourselves from the situation. We turn our attention from our present predicament for a time, and focus momentarily on what is being learned. "Oh, I guess I need to 'hang loose' here, and just be patient," we say.

If we seem to have a problem in this area, we will go through periods of running into these same situations over and over again until we get the message. The Universe always gives us lots of opportunities to learn our lessons. If we don't grasp them the first time, there will be as many opportunities as are necessary for us to learn.

Learning to be patient and gentle with ourselves is essential for our growth. We need to be patient with ourselves in learning our lessons—forgiving ourselves for our failures and mistakes as we see them. Having patience with who we are helps facilitate our growth process. When we become upset with ourselves and frustrated with what we feel or see as a setback, we take that much longer to move ahead.

Yet it is important always to honor our process. As soon as we accept who we are, including our mistakes and failures, we can achieve balance once again, and progress in spite of what we may see as the worst possible scenario we could have created for ourselves.

All is in divine order, and we need to accept that fact. If we have a particular desire for something, we may send out the thought in the form of a prayer (prayer is strong thought), and wait for the answer. We may say, "I need to know this," or "I would like to have this by next week." If we don't hear anything, it is because it is not for us, or it is not the right time.

We must presume that higher intelligence is neither deaf nor ignorant. The Universe knows what it is doing and can set the time when it is appropriate for us to gain either materially or in knowledge or awareness. Once again, we must be patient. Our Creator doesn't need a hearing aid. Rather, we need to back off when things aren't happening and we're not receiving what we asked for. We need to know there is a reason behind the refusal of our request. And we must understand the answer will come at the proper time. If we don't receive something we are waiting for, it's important, also, to believe that it may not be in our best interest to do so.

We must instead assume that our Creator has a better plan—a better alternative even though we can't see it at the time. It may be that what we think we want may be disastrous for us. It helps to remember to have patience and to let go. It is only in this way that the right conditions can unfold for us.

Having patience with others presents other problems. We must understand that we don't necessarily know what is right for someone else. For example, maybe our son is very bright, and we would like him to go to college, or perhaps law or medical school. Instead, we see the boy not wanting any further education at the moment. He appears to us to be wasting his time in meaningless jobs—one after the other. As parents, we need to be patient here because it might be that the boy is doing exactly what is appropriate for him at the time. Perhaps he is growing up, maturing, and needing the experiences that these jobs and situations can give him.

So we don't always understand God's timing and what is right for another. We all come to earth with a general plan for our lives. Isn't it rather presumptuous to think we know another's plan? We're lucky if we can be in tune with our own. Therefore, we must learn to be patient. We may express how we feel, then we need to let go, trust and take care of ourselves.

We may be surprised at how well others seem to find their way. And even if their situation may not turn out as we had hoped, how do we know what is right? With our limited vision we are unable to see the whole picture. In other words, that which we are witnessing may be just one more step for that person. It may not be the final outcome for them.

Life demands patience. It leads us from one condition to the next. We aren't through until we're through. We continue to grow, to change, and to learn. Nothing is final until we have finished our journey here on earth. And even after our transition we continue to learn and to grow.

Learning to have patience with the process of life is a great blessing and will bring much peace to those who discover the benefit of cultivating this beautiful gift of the soul.

ON FEAR

Fear is contrary to love. When we are loving, we accept ourselves and others around us as well as the conditions in our lives. When we fear, we are doing the opposite. That is, we are resisting something or someone. There are many kinds of fears and many conditions about which we allow ourselves to become fearful. Any way you look at it, this emotion can be totally debilitating. There are times when it is unconscious. We may not even be aware that we are fearful about a given situation until something or someone draws it to our attention. At other times, we are very aware of our fears, and we understand further that in order to feel free and move ahead with our lives we need to deal with these challenges that plague us.

At the same time, there are some positive things about fear. First of all, this emotion lets us know that there is an opportunity for growth awaiting us. It can also make us aware of a very real and present danger from which we need to protect ourselves. At times our fears are rational—at other times, irrational or without apparent cause. Rational fears are generally easier to deal with, while those that are irrational often leave us baffled and confused.

In any case, fear prevents us from moving forward and can be a major stumbling block to our growth. We may have fears and anxieties about our future, our abilities, our talents, or ourselves. We may find ourselves lacking in many areas that seem important to us. We see others as further along, more talented, more "together," or more accomplished. We may look upon ourselves as lagging behind, as slow learners, or without gifts to share with those around us. Of course this is only because we have not yet discovered our true nature. As we do, our fears will vanish. We will allow ourselves to become who we really are. As we begin to use our talents and abilities, and as we learn to express ourselves, we will begin to feel free of the anxieties we once had. We will move forward with confidence and strength.

We may, on the other hand, have fears regarding other people. We may fear that others can hurt us or prevent us from being who we are. We need to know that no one can replace us, no matter how it may sometimes appear. We are all individuals and have different ways of expressing ourselves. Even someone who takes over our job cannot really take our place. No one can duplicate the unique gifts and personality that we bring to a situation.

At other times, we may fear that we are not loved or appreciated. Perhaps we feel we need the approval of someone we look up to. Once again, as we learn to love ourselves and understand that we need only our own approval, we will find ourselves glad to be who we are. We will have learned to be our own best friend. What others think of us will not matter as it once did. We will feel peace within ourselves.

How we deal with our fears is important. If we try to escape from our anxieties, we will find that we dig a deeper hole for ourselves. On the other hand, facing our fears allows us to open our way to freedom as we unlock the doors that keep us from being who we are. Trust is the essential ingredient in living a rewarding life free from fear. As we begin to learn to trust the God within others and ourselves and as we learn to trust the natural and spiritual law that governs our lives—we begin to see that, indeed, all is in divine order. And through this understanding we dare to trust and love who we are and to allow the world around us to be as it is.

No longer will we find the need to control our lives or the lives of others as we discover that giving up control to our Higher Power, or the God of our own understanding, is the answer to our problems. We will come to see that trust can help to bring about love that is, and always has been, the final answer to fear.

So as we come to realize our union with our Creator and as we turn our will and our life over to the God of our understanding, we will find peace. Fear will no longer have a place in our lives. Where there were doubts there will be trust; where there was resistance there will be acceptance; and where there was fear there will be love.

ON LOVE

Love is the most powerful force in the universe. In order to learn to love others, we must first learn to love ourselves. Once again, the lesson begins at home with us. Learning to love oneself isn't always easy.

Many of us tend to be perfectionists. We expect too much of ourselves. We get frustrated and impatient when we don't measure up to the unrealistic standards we set for ourselves. "Rome wasn't built in a day," and neither do we reach perfection in a short time. All growth is a process, and we need to learn to respect that process within ourselves.

How then do we love ourselves? We may begin by accepting who we are as well as the conditions in which we live. Further, we learn to appreciate all aspects of ourselves, including our bodies. We have been given a physical form through which our spirit expresses itself. A body that is handicapped in any way lets us know that the soul is choosing the condition as an obstacle to be overcome. The body itself then becomes an opportunity. Many have overcome great challenges using the physical form as the vehicle for the challenge. It's important, of course, that we learn to respect our bodies and take care of the temple that houses the spirit. Those of us who are able ought to get plenty of exercise, rest, and proper nutrition.

As we take care of ourselves physically, we tend to like ourselves better. The body isn't everything, but it says much about who we are and how much we like ourselves. In other words, it speaks for us in many ways. If one is heavy, that fact may indicate an individual's desire for protection. A sickly body, on the other hand, demonstrates that the individual is choosing subconsciously to overcome challenges of the spirit. These challenges, or opportunities for growth, are always chosen by us at some level of our being, as are all of our experiences.

Nothing happens to us that we have not invited. Therefore, why should we not love ourselves when we know we are in charge? We are responsible for how we look, feel, and appear to others. We have the power to change our patterns if we so choose. This may be accomplished by visualizing ourselves as we would like to be. If we feel we are overweight and wish to shed a few pounds, it helps greatly to start imaging ourselves in our mind's eye as looking as we would like to appear. "Think thin," as they say, "if you wish to be thin." Then affirm to yourself that you are at the weight you wish to be.

Visualization and affirmation are powerful tools that may be used to help transform our very being. If we wish to love ourselves and others more than we do, and to express that love, all we need to do is to visualize and affirm it each and every day. We need to see and feel ourselves loving who we are and giving love to those around us. Before long we will bring our creation into being, and we will, indeed, be transformed. The power of love is great.

Learning to accept our life conditions or circumstances is the next step. We must remember that if we are in a situation that is difficult, it is there for our growth. There is a lesson to be learned. When the learning is complete, it will add to the beauty and strength of our soul. All hardships will eventually bring us a positive return on our investment of time and energy in the problem. Nothing is wasted. If we feel sidetracked by a problem, we can be grateful: it is bringing us eventual benefit that we cannot see at the moment. Gradually, however, we will come to view our problems as challenges and opportunities for growth.

Further, we will view the people and circumstances surrounding our problems as vehicles for our lessons, rather than lessons in themselves. Subsequently, when we are bothered by what someone has said or done, we may ask, "What lesson is this person bringing to me? What soul quality are they helping me to develop? Is this situation requiring me to be patient—to believe in myself? Is this condition demanding that I have more faith and trust in my higher power?"

Working in this way, we learn to love our enemies because we see them bringing us our growth. If, however, we continue to obsess about a person or situation, it means that we still have to discover the truth. After we have learned what we need to learn, we can release the object of our obsession. As the truth is revealed to us, it will set us free.

Love is the greatest gift in the world. We are ready to receive this gift as we learn to love and accept all parts of ourselves at all times. We must accept our bad moods as well as our happier feelings. We would do well to accept and be grateful for the easy, positive circumstances and people that surround us, as well as the difficult and sometimes seemingly impossible aspects of our life situations. In short, accepting ourselves totally and unequivocally is our goal.

After we have looked in the mirror and lovingly accepted ourselves, we may begin the same process with others around us. Remember that what holds true for us applies equally to all. We are all one, and that which we see in others whom we dislike, we are. Similarly, that which we admire in others, we also own. As we give love to those around us, we will receive love in return. What goes around comes around. As we learn to send love, we become free. The love we have given is returned to us without ties or strings attached.

Unconditional love is just that—it has no restrictions. It doesn't say "I will love you if..." or "I'll accept you if you do such and such." Instead, it says, "I love you because I understand that you are part of me. Whatever I do to you will be done to me. However I think of you, I first think the same of me. We are one. And as I send love to you, I send love to myself as well. In so doing, I set myself free to experience all I need in order for my soul to return to the source from whence it came."

ON SURRENDER

What happens if we should fall into a deep hole and see no way out? What is the first thing we do? Would we call for help? Would we look around for something to help get us out? Would we try to climb out on our own?

The answer is that we must surrender before we do anything else. We have to recognize and accept our fate—our present situation— for what it is. The same holds true for all conditions in our lives. Where we feel blocked, we need to say, "This is it —I accept the fact that I am here in this situation and I am powerless to change it on my own. There is no way that I can climb out of this hole on my own. I do not have that kind of power or ability as I am. I surrender!"

This is the first step toward freedom—the first step out of the hole. Without our taking that first step in which we admit powerlessness and defeat, there is nothing on which to build. Would you believe that we receive power from admitting that we have none? Through our admission of powerlessness, we are given the spiritual power we need to accomplish our task.

Dependence on our own human resources may work for us until we run into trouble and find ourselves in a situation that we, as mortal beings, cannot handle alone. It is then that we run into the wall and find ourselves at a loss as to what to do. For those who take pride in being able to "pull themselves up by their bootstraps," this can indeed be a frightening position in which to find themselves. Surrender does not come easily to such individuals. It is nearly impossible for them to say, "I don't know," or, "I can't help you," or, "I can't help myself." Consequently, many people never solve their problems because they cannot admit defeat. In some cases, they can't admit to having a problem. But once the problem is discovered and owned, admission of defeat is the next step.

What happens when we surrender? At first, it feels like the darkest moment in one's life, depending on how severe the problem is. Yet it is often after the darkest moment that we have the brightest flash of truth—the promise of a better tomorrow.

However, this doesn't come until we've been willing to give up everything and admit defeat. If we attempt to jump across an abyss, but still cling to a tree branch, we will not make it to the other side. We must be willing to let go of everything. Great things have happened to people willing to risk all, if it has been done under the appropriate conditions and for the right purpose. However, the old must be cleared away and cleansed in order for the new to fill its place—to take shape and form.

We cannot receive insight into a problem until we are ready to look at all angles of it. Surrendering to the truth isn't always pleasant. But as we develop the necessary humility to be able to say, "I don't know," or, "Help me," we open ourselves to the truth that waits for us.

Sometimes the truth may bring us further responsibility that we are hesitant to accept. Perhaps we have a gift or ability that we could be using, but are afraid of doing so for some reason, so we attempt to hide from the truth. Then one day, we are challenged to use our ability or talent—and we become increasingly frightened. We become afraid to go forward at the same time that we are afraid not to. We feel trapped. If we accept the challenge, there is always the threat of failure. If we don't take the leap, we will feel stifled and unhappy to some degree because we aren't doing what is appropriate for us.

So what is the answer? Could it be that we might develop our faith in a power outside of ourselves and then jump across the abyss—letting go of all support? What choice do we have if we wish to grow and be comfortable with ourselves in mind, body, spirit, and emotion? If we are stuck and not moving forward as we should, our bodies will let us know by an ache or a pain here and there.

It is only as we surrender and give up, saying, "It's beyond me," or, "I can't do this alone," or, "I am sorry, but I don't know how to help you," that new power can flow in from another Source greater than ourselves. The amount of power we receive will depend on the degree to which we surrender our own.

Be not afraid to let go of the past. What represents an old pattern can leave us feeling fearful, lacking in confidence and courage. Further, we become tired as we expend energy hanging on to what has gone before. As we open to a new awareness that there is something better for us, there can be progress, contentment and peace. We surrender our will to a power greater than ourselves that will show us the way—leading us out of the darkness into the light. There we will attain a greater truth about ourselves and our relationship to our Creator.

ON JOY

Joy comes from within. It is a feeling deep down within us that bubbles to the surface telling us that we're happy to be alive, that all is right with the world—our world. For it is possible to learn to be joyful no matter what is going on around us.

Joy can be a permanent state when we understand that it is part of our true nature. When we learn to separate the mundane or worldly part of ourselves from the divine, we see that our varying moods of happiness or unhappiness are indeed transitory. We can be discouraged one moment, ecstatic the next.

In other words, our moods are affected by what's happening

in the world. We react to various conditions in our lives—situations that come and go like the tide, bringing us pleasure one moment and pain the next. We seem to be at the mercy of our karma—both positively and negatively. When one has discovered a wellspring of joy coming from within and representing our natural state—our divine heritage—there comes an understanding that a true gift has been uncovered.

How, then, do we access this joy? And how do we remain in this constant state of bliss and happy reunion with this wonderful quality of the soul? The process of discovering and maintaining the ability to be joyful will be different with each individual. First of all, let's think for a moment of what would make us happy at this very second. When we know what it is, let us reflect on it—getting into the feel of it, exaggerating the sensations as they come over us. Then, let's consider the fact that this feeling is a by-product of our true nature and a gift for us to keep for ourselves as well as to share with others. The state of being joyful can be everyone's goal. There is no law against being happy, even when there isn't much to be happy about.

When we have discovered the ability to be joyful in spite of what is going on around us, we have truly accessed the divine within ourselves. We have found the secret we have been searching for since first embarking on this journey.

We do have to work at the art of being joyful, and it doesn't come overnight. We have to be our own scientist—discovering what works for us. It isn't magic. Like any gift from the Source, it has to be sought. The road will be different for everyone, and discovering what makes us happy and recreating that happiness within our own being will be a part of the process. Then we must trust our own higher power so that we may become a co-creator in discovering and maintaining joy in our lives.

What happens when we've created our joyful state and the bad times come? Perhaps we receive a phone call with disappointing news that we didn't get the job, or we failed the exam. Does our joy disappear? Perhaps momentarily it does.

However, deep within us, we see and feel the transitory nature of our misfortune. We understand that this is simply a life event that has little to do with who we are on the spiritual level. For our true being is eternal and unaffected by the momentary ups and downs of our lives. If we can take a few moments and "do our thing" by finding that place within us—using whatever means we choose to bring us back to remembering how it feels to be who we really are—then our disappointing news doesn't have a permanent hold on us. We see the situation in the proper spiritual perspective, we are able to return to our true nature.

Yet we understand that there will be many more disappointments, just as there will be "good things" happening to us. The ups and downs of life will always be there, but the ability to be joyful will always be present as well. It is up to each one of us to decide if we wish to tap into this wellspring of happy energy. Or, do we choose to just go along, being moved by the events of our lives? The choice is ours.

One way to access joy is to visualize ourselves as we would like to be, seeing ourselves as joyful and experiencing the feelings that accompany that visualization. Another mode of access is simply to state, "I wish to be joyful. Joy is a part of who I am." Or we may use affirmations to claim joy, always remembering to put feeling into our positive statements: "I'm happy!" We become what we think, to what we give energy.

So there are many ways to access this wonderful feeling. The point is to understand that joy is a force, like love, which is always present and can be tapped into if one is willing to take the time to do it. Joy need not be fleeting, but may be a lasting part of our expression of who we are to the world. Wouldn't it be wonderful to be happy, no matter what is going on—to have that ability to stand back and look objectively at life, seeing all things in the proper perspective?

Accessing joy can help us do that. For as we return to our true nature, which is indeed a joyful one, we come to see that all of these seemingly negative life events are like parts to a large and beautiful puzzle. When properly placed, they fit precisely into the whole, creating a pattern that not only makes sense but creates great beauty as well.

Therefore, all of the positive and the negative events of our lives are both necessary and appropriate as we reflect on the whole picture, and to be joyful while the pieces are coming together is a true gift available to all who choose to access it.

ON WISDOM

Wisdom—what is it? Wisdom is knowledge accumulated over time. We all have it. It's a matter of whether we choose to use it or not. Do we wish to tap into that deep well within us, or would we rather just "Go from the top of our head or emotions" in answer to a situation or condition in our lives? Wisdom always proves to be the safer choice. It has been tried and proven over the centuries and never lets us down.

Wisdom comes in many disguises. It may come as humor—a joke made at the appropriate time, bringing lightness to a situation. It may come as counsel or advice to someone seeking guidance. It may come through a song, a bird in flight, or a babbling brook. Wisdom can tap us on the shoulder when we least expect it. It may come through a voice we hear deep within us, or through a poem we read. It may come through a child's voice or through the stroke of a pen or a paintbrush on canvas. It may come through a picture, a photograph, or an instrument playing beautiful music. Wisdom speaks in many ways. Always it is there if we are open. We see wisdom in the stars at night and the clouds by day. Have the stars spoken to you as they twinkle in the heavens? And as the dark clouds gather before a storm, can you not feel the power of their beauty and hear their message of warning they bring? Wisdom is there. It's simple truth, uncomplicated by complex thought and emotion.

Wisdom doesn't analyze or preach. It simply is. We can recognize wisdom because it will ring true when we hear it. We will say, "Ah, yes, that sounds right," and we will know that it's right because we will feel its harmony within our whole being.

Wisdom speaks of many things. It may tell us when to get up in the morning and when to eat at night. It may tell us not to cross the street, even though the light is green. It senses a car speeding out of control. It may tell us not to take our medicine, even though our doctor has prescribed it for us—perhaps we were misdiagnosed. Wisdom wakes us up in the morning and speaks to us in our bed at night.

Wisdom "fits," and generally feels good if we're ready for the truth. If not, wisdom can feel like a threat. "Don't eat the chocolate cake," can be a threatening message to the person who can't wait another minute to taste that luscious dessert. Or, "You don't need that cigarette," can sound ominous to someone battling to quit smoking.

Wisdom can be welcome or unwelcome, depending on whether or not we wish to accept it. Wisdom can save lives, mend marriages, and raise healthy, happy children to become mature adults. And wisdom can transform all those who are open to the messages it pours out to all of us each day.

Where does wisdom come from? Wisdom may come from Spirit speaking to us through people, through nature, animals, and birds. In other words, it may reach us by any means the universe finds appropriate. Again, it may come from within the subconscious mind—that great storehouse of memory deep within us that we have created and built upon over the ages. Our past is never lost to us, and no experiences are ever wasted. All we have ever thought and done is recorded in the subconscious mind. And from this vast container of knowledge we may draw upon our experiences as we need to and as it is appropriate for us. This we very often do unconsciously.

As we draw upon our experiences, a selection process takes place, telling us what is appropriate and positive for us, and what is better left alone. This all happens instantaneously. As we seek for guidance and understanding, we may gain from the wisdom of our past experiences and thus become our own teachers. We draw from the pool of our own accumulated learning.

From what other sources does wisdom come? Wisdom may also come from the Higher Self—that divine part of us that knows all about us, is ever loving, and watches out for our best interests. The Higher Self always knows what is best for us and talks to us often, giving us insight into ourselves and our life situations. Without the Higher Self we would be truly lost. Wisdom may also come from our guides and angels in the spirit realm who are assigned to assist us. It is good to begin each day by calling on divine light and asking for only that which is our highest good. Our spirit guides and other forces that work with us understand our personalities and life plan. Their wisdom can be essential in guiding and leading us forward on our path. They point out obstacles and dangers and encourage our positive efforts, thus allowing us to know that we are on the right path.

Naturally, the Christ force is always there to help us, as are the other great masters who have proved their helpfulness through the ages by sending us their wisdom and energy. Wisdom can also come from spiritual teachers on the physical plane. Those souls may be ministers, priests, rabbis, and others, including, perhaps, our grandmothers or the stranger on the street corner. They all come to help light our path, bringing wisdom to guide, direct, and lead us forward to greater truth.

There is room for all religions to exist together in harmony. Which path we take depends upon many factors. They all lead to the discovery of the Source within ourselves—the Christ consciousness which is the goal of all seekers.

Therefore, as we seek for wisdom throughout our day, let's ask to be awake to the ways in which it speaks to us. Let us be mindful of the many forms it takes and the beauty and harmony its messages bring to our spirits, lifting us up, pointing the way simply, purely, and concisely. As we seek to purify ourselves, we may become clear channels of this great gift to others.

BOOK TWO

ON DISCIPLINE

Discipline is an important key to spiritual growth. We need mental and spiritual discipline to keep us in tow. Otherwise, we may find ourselves off our path, not knowing how to get back on track.

Where does this discipline come from? The wise student of spiritual philosophy will claim that his discipline comes from his Creator. We are tempted, at times, to try to discipline ourselves, but it is much more effective to call on divine power to be our disciplinarian. If we do, we will not be wasting a lot of energy to no avail. At times, it is true, self-discipline may work, but at other times we don't have that kind of willpower. Sooner or later we will let ourselves down. The discipline must come from a power greater than ourselves.

There are those who say that we ought to be able to help ourselves or that it is weak to turn to a higher power for help, but does it not take great humility and courage to admit that we cannot manage on our own? Therefore, turning to Spirit, or the God within, to ask for help and strength builds character as well. We become "God-dependent" rather than independent. This is where we open ourselves to a never-ending supply of God energy that can be used for any purpose, but which will always be in our own best interests. This source is available to us upon request; the energy will be at our disposal at all times.

Naturally, we have to have faith in the help that we request. If we do not demonstrate our faith, the flow will be cut off. In other words, we will block the assistance that we are seeking. If we think about buying a loaf of bread, but in our mind and heart we don't really believe that the kind of bread we want is available at the store, we will not receive it. We deny its existence, and therefore "miss the boat" completely. We don't even inquire because we are certain that what we are looking for will not be there. The same situation exists when we are dealing with assistance from beyond. If we deny its availability or our worthiness to receive it, we deny ourselves the opportunity to be lifted up, to be saved from disaster, to perhaps shed a few pounds or to have help in making a very difficult decision.

We must constantly ask for help if we are attempting to live a spiritual life. We open ourselves to this continual flow, keeping a running dialogue open between our Creator and ourselves. We ask for what we need and for what is in our best interest.

At the same time, we must remember to listen. We must listen to the messages that are being brought to us. If we see a counselor or therapist because we need help, it's important that we talk about our feelings, problems, and desires. However, we've paid our money for therapy—may it not also be wise to listen to what the therapist has to say? After all, he or she is the one who has had the training and is prepared to receive us and our problems, just as our Higher Power is. No situation is ever too big or too insignificant for our Creator. The Divine Source is there to serve us, and we will benefit by listening for the wisdom that comes to us in so many ways. We must be alert to all that is around us as we ask for help. There are so many ways in which the assistance we need may be manifested.

We must allow ourselves to be disciplined by the Spirit. Remembering to ask for help is essential. As we do, we grow in humility and in strength. Further, as we receive from the Universe, we must remember to give thanks. This helps to remind us that we alone are not the source of our blessings. Gratitude expressed makes room for more blessings to come our way. Then we must remind ourselves to listen intently to what comes from within. This takes practice, but as we ask for help, our process is facilitated and we may progress more rapidly.

We must always have faith in ourselves. Many have faith in God, but need to develop more faith in themselves. It's important to be positive, affirming our abilities and talents. We need to speak of our goals and our assurance of attaining all that we wish to achieve. Then we must go forth, setting about to do as we planned—putting one foot in front of the other—not pausing to look back, but moving forward into life. There is no need for fear, because we know that help is always available to us. We need only believe, accept, and listen to what is being given and then follow through as we are directed.

Allowing ourselves to be disciplined by the Source is the key to success. As we learn to trust and listen for the guidance that comes to us in so many ways, we will gain in understanding of what is best for us. We will know our boundaries and become aware of the limits imposed upon us by our Creator. We will know when it's okay to "go off the track" momentarily, and when it's best to stay right on our chosen path. We will learn to forgive ourselves as we occasionally make mistakes. For without allowing ourselves to err from time to time, we can't appreciate the help and guidance we receive on a daily basis.

Occasionally we need to experience the feelings that come from doing the wrong thing so that we can enjoy those that result from doing the right thing. Allowing God to be the source of our discipline ensures that we may reach our goals. For without this additional help from Spirit, however it chooses to manifest itself, we will become stuck somewhere along our path. Let us be grateful for the help that's available to us, giving continual thanks as we allow ourselves to be guided by our Creator, who loves us and understands our true nature.

ON PERFECTION

Striving for perfection is one thing, while expecting ourselves to be perfect is quite another. It's healthy to strive for perfection, but it's not to our benefit to expect perfection of ourselves at all times and under all circumstances. And yet it's good, and even advisable, to visualize perfection in our lives. This can be a very valuable tool in our achievement of our goals.

For example, if we have an interview or presentation to give, it is a good idea to visualize it taking place exactly as we would like it to be. We need to put energy and feeling into the visualization to solidify it. This is a tool used by spiritual students who are interested in improving their lives and learning to work with energy—God's energy—as it is given to us each day. This would be considered working to attain perfection—working in accordance with the laws of the universe. This is a good practice to get into as one makes positive changes in one's life.

However, expecting ourselves to be perfect at all times or expecting perfection from others is neither positive nor healthy. It can be detrimental to one's progress to be compulsive regarding the pursuit of perfection. We tend to backslide if we find we don't measure up to the standards we've set for others or ourselves. Learning to be gentle and patient with oneself is a great and valuable lesson to learn. If we allow room for error, growth and improvement, then we are not so disappointed when things don't turn out exactly as we had planned. However, visualizing and affirming the light in the events and happenings in our lives is part of our growth, just as striving for improvement may be looked upon as worthy and intelligent planning for anyone interested in spiritual development.

What happens when we expect perfection from other people? Naturally, we are apt to be disappointed. And not only will we be disappointed, we will be frustrated and set ourselves up to be angry and hurt as well. We can't control another's behavior, but we certainly can complicate our lives as we attempt to "run the show" for others. In the process, we cause those around us to become resentful toward us as they realize they are being manipulated to fit neatly into someone else's "play."

Often others will not accept the role they have been secretly assigned and in many cases they are not ready or willing to be the perfect actor or actress in someone else's performance. Furthermore, most people feel the pressure, the control, and the conditions that have been laid out for them and they rebel. Sometimes these feelings aren't even on a conscious level. At times neither the director nor the actor are aware that they are playing out these roles. However, unconsciously, the performance goes on—each participant acting out his or her part and thus learning the lesson each has to learn. Eventually, the only outcome is the director's learning he cannot direct unless the actor accepts the designated role. The other outcome is the actor's learning that he doesn't need to be in anyone's play unless he chooses to participate.

This is a hard lesson for many to learn. There are those who think that being a perfectionist is somehow a blessing, when in fact it is a detriment. Setting high standards for oneself is, in itself, admirable—as long as we continue to accept and love ourselves and others in the process. If we dislike ourselves because of our so-called failures, we are missing the mark.

Nothing that we do should call for us to berate ourselves or others. We must learn to be our own best friend, which means being gentle with ourselves, forgiving our mistakes, and being willing to grow while allowing others the same freedom. To love means to accept, as well as to allow another to live and to learn by their mistakes. If we are not allowed to make mistakes, not much learning goes on.

We did not come to earth to be perfect. We came here to experience life in all its many aspects with everything it has to offer. So let's be grateful for each experience that brings its lessons to be filed away in our subconscious.

Imagine expecting a baby or small child to be perfect. We would expect them to walk, talk, and use the toilet at a very early age, with no mistakes or accidents. How would life be for such a child? Essentially, this is what we are expecting of ourselves and others as we set unrealistic standards for achievement. We demand the impossible, causing possible damage to ourselves and those around us. True, the setbacks may be minor. But whether large or small, the problems arising from our perfectionist nature are unnecessary.

Let us, therefore, be kind to ourselves, allowing ourselves to grow in a nurturing, caring environment, as we do for others. Let us focus our attention on progress rather than perfection as we learn to accept the imperfections of ourselves and others. And let's be grateful for the freedom to grow and to be who we are as we each learn to express our divine nature in the world.

ON DENIAL

One of the stumbling blocks we may encounter along our path is denial, or the inability to see ourselves as we really are. Perhaps we're in a situation in which, because of our emotional involvement, we are unable to be objective. We may be in some kind of danger or simply in a situation that is not in our best interest. In other words, we've taken a wrong turn in the road and are not aware of it or willing to admit that we've made a mistake. We feel we have chosen well and we remain entirely unmindful of the pitfalls that lie ahead.

Denial tends to be confusing because it is always accompanied by a feeling of being right. The reason we have to be in denial is usually because we are unable to face the truth about ourselves or someone we care about. Family members, co-workers, friends and others all may be included in our denial system. There are times when whole families are in denial. For instance, this is often the case when there is alcoholism in the family.

When, for example, there is a man with a drinking problem who is well known in the community or who has been distinguished in some area, there is a tendency on the part of the family to deny his illness. Or when a person is very accomplished, talented or gifted, we tend to overlook the fact that the individual is ill and needs help.

There are other reasons for denial. Oftentimes family members or people close to the one afflicted with the problem, whatever it may be, might have to look at themselves. This can be very painful and threatening to many who have been living their lives a certain way, or reacting to the afflicted person with certain behavior patterns. Suddenly, the one who has been sick or behaving inappropriately begins to get well, changing his behavior and ways of relating to people whom he has known for a long time. This too can be very confusing and can even anger those who are close to the one who is changing his ways.

For the person who is coming out of denial and learning to face himself honestly, this can be as exciting a time as it is frightening. It takes courage to become honest with oneself and others and it is usually an unsettling process, although it is healthy and beneficial for all concerned.

There are times when a crisis within a family seemingly affecting only one person will affect the entire family in a very profound way. It is similar to a row of dominoes: when one is pushed over, the others fall in their turn.

Denial can be dangerous business, especially if we are dealing with life and death issues. Our health, for example, is an issue about which people tend not to like to look at themselves honestly. Individuals who may be grossly overweight, or those who smoke or drink too much, are playing deadly games with their health. Often, however, they don't think so. In fact, it is amazing how unconcerned people often are about their unhealthy habits, which appear very obvious to and worry those who care about them. They have created such a protective system of denial that they truly believe they are immune from danger or trouble ahead.

Yet sometimes after such an individual has "seen the light" and given up the unhealthy habit, they often become highly intolerant of others doing the same thing.

They realize their error and find it very difficult to watch others make the same mistake. However, in this regard, we must honor our process. Even addictions have their purpose and timing in our lives. It behooves us not to judge ourselves or others.

Further, sometimes our denial also serves a purpose. There are times when the truth is so painful that we aren't ready for it. We're not ready for the growth that the particular truth will reveal. Therefore, we need to hide from ourselves for awhile, until we are ready. We may get pieces of the truth, but the subconscious will give us the whole truth only when we can handle it. This process is guided always by the Higher Self. The spiritual side of our nature knows how much awareness we can handle.

At other times we may hear the truth, but the protective mechanism within ourselves allows us to feel only a portion of it. This is why we hear people say, "I just can't believe it," or "It can't be true," or "I refuse to believe it." Again, the protective mechanism is switched on and we save ourselves from the terrible pain that accompanies shocking news. So it may be said that there is healthy denial as well as denial which is inappropriate and deleterious to spiritual growth.

Therefore, in order for us to become enlightened, we need first of all to get honest with ourselves, and remain as honest as possible about who we are. It's important to be honest with others, but it is even more important to become self-honest. To deceive oneself is the greatest deception of all. Rarely do we fool the folks "out there" because most people know what we're up to. We all act as mirrors for each other. If we are doing something we aren't especially proud of or that is "out of line," someone is sure to pick up on it as they see themselves in our behavior.

Once we've learned to get honest with ourselves, we find how pleasant it can be to be real and genuine. Others then appreciate us for who we are. The need for dishonesty or "covering up" just isn't there.

Becoming honest and crawling out of our denial can be the most rewarding aspect of beginning to live a spiritual life. The benefits gained from thorough self-scrutiny cannot be overestimated if it is done with love.

As we "clean house" and get to know ourselves in greater truth, we gain a deeper understanding of our true nature. We tend to be more open and honest with others. Thus, our relationships improve, bringing us the courage to be who we really are. As we continue to seek for truth within our own beings, we will be blessed as long as we are gentle and patient with the changes we wish to make within ourselves. Self-acceptance precedes change, and loving ourselves throughout our transformation brings peace.

ON PROCRASTINATION

There are times along our journey when we find ourselves putting off that next step. Sometimes it is difficult to admit that we are, indeed, procrastinating. Often, we want to tell ourselves, "It isn't time yet," or "I've been so busy." We don't realize that we are postponing our duties or responsibilities because we are subconsciously fearful of moving forward at the pace we might be. What are we afraid of?

Fear of failure is a problem for many, even though we seldom see our efforts go unrewarded. There are still unspoken questions: "What if I won't be successful?" "What will people think of me?" or, worse yet, "What will I think of myself?" The thought of failure is intolerable to most people, especially those who have high standards that either they have set for themselves or had set for them. The fear of failure oftentimes is so strong that we can neither admit its presence to ourselves, nor bear to begin our project or plan, whatever it may be.

Procrastination can be an unfortunate thing. The longer we put something off, the more difficult it becomes to begin. Our fear or laziness overwhelms us until one day we decide to give up our plan entirely.

We all have goals that we have set for ourselves before coming to earth. They may be modified to some degree during our years here, but we still have certain things we wish to accomplish. We don't always know for certain what these plans are. This is why it is important to get in tune with our intuition, learn to follow our heart, and get in touch with what these goals might be.

We need also to get a sense of timing concerning our plans, so that we may begin and end our projects at appropriate times, again honoring the process, however long it takes.

When we are flowing with the Universe, things go smoothly for us. This is another reason why it is inadvisable for us to procrastinate. There are certain times when it is propitious to initiate something and times when it is best not to begin new plans. Following the natural flow of our feelings is the best indicator. However, when we are lazy or fearful, even on a subconscious level, we block ourselves from making the progress we desire. The human part of us gets in the way, slowing us down, preventing us from becoming all we were meant to be.

Procrastination can take many forms. Perhaps we need to balance our checkbook. Subconsciously or consciously we fear it is not going to come out right, so we put off doing it. We get up to get a glass of water, or decide to make a phone call, or we go to the refrigerator to get something to eat. Again, perhaps we've decided to write a play or compose a song. We think we very much want to do this, but find the months going by and nothing is accomplished. Often we tell ourselves that we are waiting for a more definite sign to begin. The problem is that we may fear our project more than we realize. Consequently, we aren't feeling the desire to begin as strongly as we would if we did not doubt ourselves and our abilities. Our fear is getting in the way, preventing us from getting started.

What usually happens then is that we're given a "kick in the pants," one way or another, to let us know that "Yes, this is the time—now get going!" If we ask to be on schedule with our plans, the Universe won't let us down. But we do need to ask. A great deal of creativity is lost because people don't follow through with their dreams. All great inventions and works of art begin in the mind with a thought, a flash, an idea that comes—fleeting though it may be. The thought is either picked up or ignored. If it is acknowledged, it may then be expanded upon.

Let's say we get a thought to take a class in poetry. The thought feels good to us. Then we think to ourselves, "Well, I'm really very busy," or "I can't write poetry," or "Would I have to read my poetry to the class?" The negatives start overwhelming us. We have talked ourselves out of taking the course.

Yet we never know what may result from following through with what comes to us from Spirit. We may think an idea sounds foolish, impossible, or out of our reach. But if we pursue what is given to us, and trust in the outcome, we may be completely surprised and pleased with the results.

However, if we say we'll do something and then change our mind midstream or put it off to a later time, we deny ourselves the joy of realizing what was intended to be our creation. We are left empty-handed, wondering why we aren't "gifted" as others appear to be. The individuals who seem to have been given all the gifts and talent are those who have followed their hearts, used their abilities, and striven to follow their ideals. They have not allowed themselves to procrastinate due to fear of failure or simple laziness. They exemplify the fact that the stronger the desire to succeed, the less likelihood there is of failure.

If we wish to succeed and accomplish all we were meant to in this life, we need to pray to be shown the way. So let's ask what our next step is to be. We need to ask, as well, that we be free of fear and willing to take that next step. We must, of course, understand that we will be given the correct indication as to proper timing and any other direction concerning our plans. Thus, our goals may be realized, and we may be proud as well as humbled by our own accomplishments.

ON HONESTY

Why is honesty so important? What part does it play in our lives? We are taught, most of us, as little children, to be honest. Our parents and teachers have told us that we must tell the truth, even if we think it may get us into trouble.

Being honest with ourselves is often the most difficult thing we are called upon to do. Yet when we are aware of being on a spiritual path, honesty is imperative. For as we delude ourselves, overlooking our shortcomings and making excuses for our mistakes and wrongdoing, we set ourselves back. Of course, as we accept God's forgiveness and forgive ourselves, we can move forward again.

Yet only when we have the courage to look at ourselves objectively, admitting our faults and failings as well as our assets, talents, and abilities, will we be able to advance rapidly in our spirituality. The ability to scrutinize oneself honestly, without fear, is an excellent way to prepare oneself for the long journey ahead. If we skip over this important step, we aren't properly warned of possible pitfalls along the way. Everyone encounters challenges on the path.

There are also specific ways in which we, as individualized personalities, tend to deceive ourselves. In other words, we have personal tendencies to make more mistakes in certain areas than in others. In so doing, we differ from one another. One person may be very prone to procrastination, for example, while another may tend to be impulsive—acting too quickly, without thinking, or allowing intuition to direct his or her behavior. We each have our own difficulties and shortcomings. We all make many errors over the course of our lives in many different ways, but it helps to take stock of ourselves to see where we ourselves have the most difficulty. We can then ask our Higher Power for help in these areas.

Self-awareness or self-knowledge is invaluable in helping us to grow spiritually. The more we know and understand about ourselves, without judgment, the better off we are. Have you ever done or said something and been totally surprised at yourself? You think you couldn't have said or done such a thing. "Impossible," you think. We are often surprised at ourselves and what we are capable of, both in a positive and negative sense. Sometimes we are pleased with ourselves and other times we are horrified. "Could I have said that?" We want to sometimes put the blame on someone else, or the situation, or some other condition present at the time. However, we need, in time, to "come clean" and admit who we are, even if that outburst or remark we made seems to be out of character for us.

We are all highly complex, and this condition makes life interesting. If we were totally predictable, we would be monotonous. Variety is the spice of life, but we would do well to examine the sub-personalities that comprise our being. Sometimes one or the other of them may get out of hand, attempting to take over and dominate us. Balance is healthy. Hearing a little from each of the voices within us is normal and helpful, though it can be confusing at times. We may wish to understand the truth about a given situation, but all the various voices seem to want to give us an opinion. There is the nun inside who advises us to "Pray about it." There is the bully who tells us to "Give that guy a piece of your mind." There is the procrastinator who says, "Let's just wait and see what happens." There is the pacifist who says, "Love can conquer all." So what do we do? Our Higher Self will let us know the real truth when we can handle it. Though we can ask for it, we won't receive the full truth until we're ready.

Being honest with who we are allows us to change what we don't like in a loving, healthy way. If we can't admit who we are or that we have shortcomings, or if we aren't aware of our behavior, there's little chance for improvement. If we wish to change ourselves, we need to know what needs improvement.

Is it important that we change for someone else? People who change for others are being dishonest in their efforts. Living to please others is not a worthy goal for people on a spiritual path. In fact, it is one of the more destructive ways one can be dishonest, because we end up deceiving not only ourselves, but others as well. We're calling other people to be actors in our dishonest performance. Thus, we are creating a false image of ourselves for which we will eventually have to pay.

It is good, always, to attempt to be true to ourselves. We're not here to please mom, dad, or our friends. We're here to become all that we can be with our God-given talents and abilities. We're here to co-create with the God of our own understanding. Only in that way can we be truly honest and only then can we express who we really are.

ON NEGATIVITY

What do we mean by negative thinking? Where do we get our negativity? And what happens when we're negative? Often we don't stop to think about these things until we've come to a fork in the road and it's time to decide which way to go with our lives.

Negative people tend to attract negative situations because that's the way Universal Law operates. By the "law," we mean that that which we send out, either positively or negatively, in thought or in deed, is returned to us. We set up conditions in our lives that are either positive or negative. If we send out positive thoughts, particularly if they are accompanied by images that are also positive, we will create conditions that are affirming in nature. In other words, when we send out or create a positive situation in our minds, visualizing it and energizing our "picture" positively, the chances are we will be blessed with an outcome that we desire.

What happens when we do the same in the negative? When we create a negative scene, visualizing it and at the same time putting negative energy into it, we will obviously end up with a negative situation. What happens when we worry about some future event? We first create the feared scene in our minds. Then we visualize it, usually in minute detail, adding our fear and anxiety to the picture, thus creating for ourselves a potential disaster. The more we picture the same scene over and over again, the more we give it life until one day it will be manifested in physical reality.

Therefore, it behooves us to be careful with our thoughts. We must remember our thoughts are "things" and what is true in our mind will one day, under the proper conditions, be true in reality as we know it. We ought to heed what goes on in our minds. Do we think negatively or positively? Is our cup half empty or half full? How do we approach life, and how do we view ourselves?

Our self-image is extremely important: we will be treated accordingly. Therefore, if we think highly of ourselves and respect who we are, we will be treated well. Again, that which we send out comes back to us one way or another. We are all working through our karma to learn our own lessons, and certain situations represent "heavier baggage" for us than they do for others.

It's easy to be positive when we feel favorably toward ourselves and our life conditions. It is much more difficult to stay positive when dealing with heavy situations that are painful and reminiscent of old karma and past situations that have not yet been resolved.

We are all healing on many levels, whether we are aware of it or not, and many times we pass through conditions which we don't always understand but which are painful, or at best uncomfortable for us. Often we are balancing situations and relationships from the past: that fact can contribute at times to things seeming unfair, one-sided or confusing.

Many times people get into trouble one way or another because they are confused by life. This is particularly true of sincere seekers of truth who have a need to understand life in all its complexity. It is often the one who is most sensitive to the varied energies, both positive and negative, that surround him or her, who finds life particularly challenging.

Because of our inability to cope with various conditions, we may become negative and as a result begin a downhill plunge that tends to have a snowball effect. The negativity increases with each unhappy experience we attract to ourselves. We often feel confused and don't know why we are in this dilemma: we feel that basically we are kind, caring people.

It isn't until someone comes along or some experience wakes us up in some way that we know that we are okay and that there is a better way to live. Once taken by the hand and led step by step out into a new day, we see that which was once confusing become clear. We begin to see ourselves and the world in a more positive light. New patterns emerge within the personality and the soul responds by drawing more and more positive situations for the personality to experience.

Once we see that we can experience life in a more positive way, we become enthusiastic about such a possibility. We begin to create more and more images of a positive nature in which we visualize ourselves as succeeding rather than failing. Having experienced success, we then regain our confidence that had been lost along the way. With this newly found strength, we progress to the point at which we expect to succeed. This is where success starts to become almost automatic, because there is no anticipation of failure. The negative images we once used to create are no longer a part of our makeup. We are truly learning to be positive in our thinking by creating the appropriate pictures in our mind, adding our own positive energy to the visualization we have created. In the process, we are learning a valuable lesson in Universal Law.

Working with God's energy as it is given to us each day is a challenge to all of us. How we use this Life Force is up to us. This is part of what free will is about. We may use this gift to build up or destroy. The choice is ours. Learning to work in harmony with the Laws of Nature and Spirit ensures that we will be positive about who we are and our relationships to each other and to the world.

Further, learning to create what we want in our life ensures that we may accomplish our goals. We may ask our Higher Power to assist us in all of our endeavors, keeping our dreams alive and guiding us through our journey. Then, as the positive images we have created within us become our reality, we may give thanks to our Creator.

ON KNOWLEDGE

Knowledge can be a helpful tool on the spiritual path. As we acquire knowledge of the Laws of the Universe, for example, we have a greater understanding of how things work in God's world. It is true that knowledge isn't everything, and it is also true that love is more important than knowledge. However, having some awareness of why things happen as they do can help us deal better with our lives. Just as a chemist needs to understand the laws of science and chemistry in order to perform his experiments, we are better able to function in the world if we have knowledge of God's laws or the Laws of the Universe.

That premise doesn't mean that we have to have an intellectual understanding of all of the universal laws that exist, because that would take years of study. However, having even a limited understanding of a few of the basic laws of God can give us a start in life. From there a student wishing to do so can explore further into the area through reading as well as through meditation, or a combination of both. It is best when reading spiritual or religious literature to allow ourselves to ponder what is being said through the written word. We are free to allow our own intuition to help interpret what the words are saying. People will come up with various interpretations based upon their own background, experience, and intuition. This is as it should be. We are not all in the same place spiritually. True, we are all Children of God, but we are at different levels of spiritual evolution. There will be groups composed of individuals who think and believe in a similar fashion, and this is appropriate.

There are those who may say that their belief, or their way, or their interpretation, is the only one—the only way to be "saved." It is important to remember that God is our Creator. Does a father not love his children equally? Perhaps one chooses to go to one school and another selects a different place to learn. Does it make a difference? God loves us equally, under all circumstances. Could it be that one school would be helpful at a particular time in a child's life, while the same school would not benefit his brother or sister?

We are all individuals, even though we may be in the same family. We have different needs and different perspectives as well as different approaches to life. A certain course of study may be important to one child's overall development, and another for a second child, and perhaps yet another for the third.

We all learn from each other. And one of the important lessons we learn is tolerance. Tolerance is a prelude to love. And learning to love is the bottom line for all religions and denominations. Each course of study, each religion, one way or another, claims enlightenment as the goal. When we reach that point in our spiritual growth, we will have learned to love. In particular, love of self will generate goodwill and love for those around us. Therefore, we need to be tolerant of others, understanding that whatever they may be learning or doing may be entirely appropriate for them.

Who are we to judge another's experience? If we are to learn love, we can begin by loving ourselves. This will open the door to acceptance of all God's Children, allowing each the freedom to choose.

Freedom of choice is a great gift. Our free will, which God has given us, allows us to experience much. Through our experience, we acquire a great deal of knowledge. Each time we stumble and fall, another lesson is learned and we take another step up the spiritual ladder. Our learning is slow at times, to ensure that our lessons are absorbed by the soul.

We are aware, at times, of the fact that we repeat the same learning situation over and over again. For example, let's say we have a troublesome or difficult experience that we feel we handled poorly. Maybe we "blew our top" or became overtly jealous and felt we made a fool of ourselves. The situation becomes resolved one way or another and we're grateful that it's over. We feel we've learned a valuable lesson and vow never to repeat the same behavior again. Several weeks or months go by and a similar situation occurs again, seemingly right out of the blue. We are constantly testing ourselves by inviting these same situations to recur in our lives until we "get it right." Nothing comes to us that we don't invite from a higher level of our being, and we are forever challenging ourselves to new heights and new awareness. How else could we grow? God loves us and allows us to make mistakes, but is always there to help us pick up the pieces.

Knowledge comes to us through many channels, including the written word, our intuition, through meditation and through our own experiences. How else can we gain knowledge? In the experiences of others we have a rich source. We can learn a great deal by what happens to other people. As a result, we may sometimes avoid the pitfalls in life that others encounter. Similarly, we may take positive steps in imitation of those for whom we have high regard. This person may be a Master we read about, possibly the Christ himself, or maybe a neighbor down the block. We learn from each other in many ways.

Learning to live in love and harmony with God, with ourselves, and with our fellow persons is a final lesson and a final test. Can we learn to love ourselves enough to give it all we can? Can we learn to be tolerant and nonjudgmental of our fellow travelers and allow each to experience as his own soul dictates? Do we dare ask to be guided and directed on our own path, regardless of where it may lead? Can we "Let go and let God" in spite of our fears? Do we dare to seek for knowledge that may come from within? Do we dare follow the inner voice though it takes us away from the mainstream? Do we dare be open to the voice of Spirit in a flower or in the song of a bird? Can we admit the miracles we see each day and do we dare ask God for what we want for ourselves?

Knowledge of God's laws, including man's experience, gives us the chance to grow and enrich our lives. Being open to the opportunities to learn helps us to advance along our path, while gratitude for the knowledge we've gained helps ensure that more will be forthcoming.

BOOK THREE

ON DISCOURAGEMENT

One of the problems we face on the spiritual path is our tendency to become discouraged from time to time. However, discouragement and even despair are acknowledged aspects of the human condition. Therefore, we can look upon our unhappy circumstances as merely temporary setbacks along our journey.

Further, we can begin to learn to observe ourselves, blessing the negative conditions that surround us, painful though they may be. We may learn to develop a more detached view of the unhappy conditions in our lives as we come to understand that our emotions do not represent our true nature.

A problem lies in the fact that we don't always understand what is happening. We become frightened, feeling that our despair will never leave us and that we're doomed to be unhappy forever. Then even suicide can become an option for those seeking a way out. Yet if we would only have patience and ask for help in our meditations and prayers, we could make it through these periods.

However, we must have faith. Even the tiniest grain of faith can help us let go enough to get us through the difficult times.

It isn't always easy to have faith when we are feeling great unhappiness and despair. Perhaps we are alone, or have had some experience that has left us devastated. Or perhaps we've lost our family, our home, our health, or our confidence in ourselves. Maybe we feel helpless, lost, and afraid. Perhaps we feel we have no one to whom we can turn to give us the understanding we need. Again, perhaps we don't even understand the reason for our depression. We often hear someone say, "I shouldn't be depressed, I have everything anyone could hope for." But there they are, in the depths of despair with no reason in particular to blame for their negative feelings.

Furthermore, to make matters worse, others are telling them they shouldn't feel that way. "You have no right to feel sorry for yourself. After all, you have more than most people to be grateful for." So feelings of guilt begin to compound the problem.

Then again, maybe we have just begun our spiritual journey from a conscious point of view, and we're hopeful and anxious to improve our lives by taking steps to rediscover who we are. Then suddenly we find ourselves feeling negative and discouraged. Perhaps we've succumbed to an old behavior pattern and felt ourselves slide backwards, hurting another in the process. And instead of seeking God's forgiveness, forgiving ourselves, and vowing to move forward again, we choose to be depressed.

It is sometimes easier to be down on ourselves than it is to forgive our mistakes. This is, after all, an old and familiar pattern for many of us. Often, in the past, we have received some kind of benefit or rewarded ourselves in some way when finding ourselves in this dilemma. For the addictive person, it may mean that because we feel depressed we may indulge excessively in certain foods, for example, which we later regret. For the person who likes material things, it may mean an excuse to go shopping and spend more money on themselves than they ought to. For the compulsive cleaner, it may mean a time to start scrubbing. Whatever the reaction, the behavior is still inappropriate to the situation and doesn't allow the person to advance. It only sets them back because they then have to deal with the new problems that have been created by their refusal to face the issue at hand.

How can we move forward following a setback? The only way to progress is to learn to forgive and accept ourselves where we are. If we are not sorry for our thoughts and actions, we will continue to attract the same negative situations again and again until we do respond with love and acceptance. We need to realize that when we feel unforgiven, we are really unable to forgive ourselves. Once we have truly forgiven self, we must be willing to move forward again.

It is at this point that people frequently balk. We want to return to the past when life seemed easier and more comfortable. We may even revert to some old behaviors and addictions that help us feel secure, even though that behavior seems inappropriate for our present growth. Further, sometimes we become overly concerned with what others are doing or thinking about us, and we allow worry to cloud our vision, conveniently preventing us from continuing on our path.

The only way to progress at this point is to put one foot in front of the other while asking for the willingness to carry on. In this way we can allow the letting go process to unfold. It is often very difficult to take that first step, but in the long run it's even more painful if we choose not to.

We discover that when we hesitate to advance along our path we may develop physical problems. These indicate to us that we have energy within us that is being blocked. As we let go of our fear and begin to proceed in an appropriate manner, the aches and pains subside. Our bodies are great communicators, giving us valuable information about our progress on our journey. While there are times when we find ourselves working too hard, there may be other times when we need a push. However, we must be careful not to busy ourselves in an attempt to avoid that next step or project which may be the key to our growth and advancement.

How, then, do we know what we are supposed to be doing? One way we can know is by asking in meditation for confirmation of our decisions. We may also request that roadblocks be placed in our way if we're heading in the wrong direction. This practice can be helpful to anyone who is confused about what direction to take.

We must remember that to become depressed is normal from time to time. How can we have compassion for others if we have never experienced moments of despair ourselves? We give to others, generally, because we feel sympathetic. We understand how they feel, and we have a genuine desire to give help and encouragement where it is needed. This is part of what learning to love is all about. We would not advance very far if we did not have love and compassion for our fellow travelers. And the only way we truly understand another is through having similar experiences ourselves.

So let's look upon all of our moods—our ups and downs—as blessings. We understand that our feelings do not represent the true self, the spiritual self. They are instead temporary indicators of where we are on our journey. Our feelings often challenge us as they point the way to spiritual growth by letting us know where our weaknesses lie. Without our emotions, we would understand little about ourselves.

When we become discouraged, let's remember that the energy will shift in time: nothing stays the same forever. Change is the one constant in the universe of which we may be certain. Therefore, let's go with the flow, assured of God's forgiveness for all wrongdoing as we forgive ourselves and move forward along our path.

It is only resistance that causes pain as we advance toward our goals. We must move ahead with courage and confidence, knowing that we are all under the loving care of our Creator. Further, let's understand that discouragement is a part of life that is ever changing, bringing us new feelings of hope and joy.

ON SELF-CONFIDENCE

The ability to believe in oneself is an essential tool on the spiritual path. We need to have faith that what we are doing is appropriate and well timed. We need to have confidence in our abilities so that we may accomplish all we came here to do.

God gave us special talents in order to help us become all

we were meant to be. Given this fact, we can see how necessary it is to believe in ourselves and to have faith that we can complete our path here on earth. Thus, we may advance ourselves materially and spiritually in preparation for the next phase of life, whether it is here in the physical body or in the spirit world.

Perhaps we have completed our earthly assignment and it's time to go home. How will we feel as we review our life? Will we be pleased with ourselves? Will we be glad that we dared to risk all in order to complete our work here? Or will we look back in dismay at how little we were able to accomplish?

Our goals may not require that we do great things that make us famous. We do not need to be noticed by others in order to have advanced significantly in our lifetime. Much of our learning doesn't require this kind of public display. An individual may have completed a great deal and yet hardly be noticed by others.

Then again, being famous or becoming a celebrity of sorts can be a lesson in itself. Often that kind of opportunity is there to see how well someone handles it. Famous people have the added burden of being in the public eye. Their personal lives are exposed and their behavior scrutinized by all those who regard them as interesting and worthy of attention.

Whatever our role is to be in this life, and whatever our lessons and tasks require of us, we need to develop confidence in ourselves to help ourselves move forward.

How do we gain that confidence? And what is it that holds us back? Could it be that we are afraid to succeed because of what may be required of us?

When we are successful, it is generally an indication that we ought to either continue with what we are doing or move on to something else requiring even more of us. In any case, success involves responsibility and work of some kind, and often we are hesitant about taking more on. Some of us tend to be a bit lazy. We like to play, to waste time, and not to challenge ourselves. Even those with exceptional talent and many goals to achieve aren't always willing to expend the energy required or make the sacrifices involved.

Therefore, sometimes we are fearful of moving ahead. This fear can be conscious or subconscious. In any case, it prevents us from having the confidence we need to advance ourselves. Fear of failure or ridicule or change can take hold of us and literally paralyze our being, blocking our ability to succeed. Further, being successful often necessitates change. As our activities and relationships change, we are often called upon to adjust our lifestyle as well. All of this can be frightening. How is it going to work out? Is it going to work? Will my family go along with me? Will my spouse change? Will I be happy? Will she be happy? Do I dare make the move? Do I dare not to?

These are some of the questions we are faced with, particularly in this time of transition as we move from the Age of Pisces to that of Aquarius. Preparation is necessary for what lies ahead for all of us.

Indeed, it is an age in which there is not a lot of time to ponder our lives. We need to get into action as our intuition and our hearts dictate. Sometimes our minds get in the way and feed us "horror stories" that attempt to convince us that it's unwise to do this or that, or make this change, or go in that direction. Our mind can be our enemy, slowing us down. It tells us we aren't good enough, smart enough, or talented enough. It compares us with others. It tells us we should be in a job that pays well—that it doesn't matter whether or not we enjoy our work.

It is wise to follow our heart when we decide on a life's occupation. The rest will fall into place if we do as our heart dictates. We will be doing what our talent and abilities tell us is important and appropriate for us. Honesty is very essential here. Nobody else's opinion should dictate what we choose to do with our lives. If we follow our heart and our intuition and are as honest as possible with ourselves, we are more apt to reach our goals. The intellect alone, or doing what others think we should do, can limit our progress. Sometimes we take a circuitous route. We may get into one job and that job leads us to something else even more appropriate, until we finally reach that for which we are best suited.

So let's be gentle and patient with ourselves as we ask for guidance from within. We need to pay attention to the signposts along the way that guide us to our next step. And let's pray, as well, to have the courage and confidence to follow our dreams. We must remember that we can see only so far. We cannot comprehend the possibilities that lie ahead for us. Further, our minds may be telling us that our dream is just that—a dream and nothing more. Yet God has created miracles from the dreams of his children.

Believe in yourself. Believe in your dreams and allow your true identity to emerge. You are a part of the whole and are needed to play a role as only you can play it. We each must bring our best to the performance, not fearing the responsibility our involvement imposes upon us. As we play our part by creating our own music, we need not look for the approval of others because we know we are playing in tune, in harmony with the whole. We are playing our song with an attitude of love.

Abundance and prosperity are ours as we are creating and living in the flow with all of life. And when the time comes for a new song, we will be ready for the change, knowing we are safe and secure. We have placed our lives in the hands of our director, the God of our own understanding, who guides us safely into a new pattern. We are glad to let go and flow with the new rhythm as it brings us to another awakening—a new tomorrow.

Let's believe in ourselves, in our abilities, our strengths, and our talents, giving thanks to the Creator for the necessary faith in ourselves to go forth into the world and manifest the dreams held in our inner vision. Let's ask for the courage to keep our dreams alive as we go forward in confidence and strength, unafraid of what the future may bring because we have placed our faith and trust in our Creator.

ON DISTRACTION

Another obstacle on the path has to do with our tendency to be distracted from our purpose. We are referring here to distraction in its negative sense. It can, of course, be a welcome and healthy diversion from our work and our problems, but it can also be unfortunate when it prevents us from accomplishing the goals we seek.

Distraction can come in many forms. We can be distracted by television, a good book, new romance in our life, or even a beautiful sunny day, depending on what our intent is. We may also be distracted by what may be termed "glamour," which has to do with the appearance of things. We can become carried away by the "glitter" that entices us to undergo, to buy, or to want just about anything. We become easily impressed by the superficial. We are often easily attracted to what appears to offer promising rewards, but what in reality lacks substance or anything of lasting value. In brief, we get carried away by what seems to be the answer for us, in whatever form that takes. Because of our impatience and excitement we overlook many things. We forget to check our ideals to see if this, indeed, is our answer. Instead, we settle for appearances. It isn't until later that we're sorry we acted impulsively and are stuck with something or some situation that really does not serve us well.

How do we avoid becoming distracted? One way is to formulate an ideal or goal and write it down. Then we must set priorities. For example, if we wish to buy a new television, we write down all of the features we want to have. We bring the list with us when we go shopping. We may walk into a store and see a beautiful full-screen console TV set and want it right away because of its appearance. However, after checking our list, we remember that size is a factor, and we must choose a smaller set. We also remember that we want a TV that rotates, and the large console doesn't have that feature. In this way, having our priorities in mind, we may avoid making a big mistake.

One might be wise to be similarly careful about choosing a mate or best friend. Naturally, caring about a person is different from choosing a television set, but at times people would do well to be as cautious. We often seek qualities in people, whether they are potential mates, friends, or teachers, that impress us so much that we tend to overlook other important qualities they may be missing.

Perhaps we run into someone we think may be the right spiritual teacher for us, for example. Let's say this individual is both talented and knowledgeable. But after awhile we notice that something seems to be lacking, although we can't quite put our finger on it. Later on we discover that this person hasn't yet learned to love himself. Therefore, his gifts of time, energy, and ability lack warmth and seem to come from an empty vessel. Certainly this soul is on a spiritual path as well, and has lessons and experiences and opportunities to learn as anyone else does. However, it is essential to ascertain what is important to us at any given time.

The same principles apply when we are looking for a job or a school or a city in which to live. It's easy to become sidetracked by appearances while overlooking the important issues at stake. Again, we need to take a look at our goals and priorities, keeping in mind what is important to us. What do we value? What endures and what fades away? What "wears well," and what does not?

Having faith in ourselves and our ability to discern is essential to this process. We must believe in ourselves and trust our intuition. We may, for example, hear a speaker about whom others have spoken very favorably, but we find that we are not impressed. It's unwise to think there's something wrong with us because we differ in our opinion of the speaker or of what he or she has to say. We needn't become overly critical or judge others harshly, but we must learn to trust ourselves, our feelings, and the priorities we ourselves carefully determine.

So let's avoid being distracted by being true to ourselves

and our ideals. In this way, we can avoid mistakes that can be costly and unnecessary. Instead, as we stick to our path, looking neither backward nor to the side but straight ahead, we will find ourselves heading, always, in the right direction. Further, as we put one foot in front of the other, not fearing that we may be tempted from our path, we move forward with conviction. We know what we are looking for and that we are being guided each step of the way.

We trust our intuition to tell us what is worthy of us as we endeavor to live up to our ideals and pursue our goals. We give thanks to our Creator for keeping us on track as we experience all that is necessary for the growth of our souls. And we continue to climb the spiritual ladder, looking ever upward as we ascend further into the light—undistracted and determined to reach our goal as we fulfill our purpose on earth.

THE SPIRITUAL PATH

What does it mean to be on the Spiritual Path? After all, we're all on a spiritual path. But it's a matter of consciousness as to whether we're aware of it or not. The most violent criminal capable of the most terrible acts is still on a spiritual path, but most likely has not given it much, if any, thought.

Many of us at some time begin to "wake up." We begin to question our existence. Why are we here? Why is there suffering in the world? Why is my life as it is? Why does she have so many problems? Why is it that he never seems to be affected by anything? These are some of the questions we ask ourselves.

In this waking-up process we are confronted with many problems, issues, and concerns we never thought much about. We have been accustomed to going through our life in a state of reaction. Instead of taking some initiative and demonstrating some degree of creativity in responding to situations, we have been merely reacting, often almost thoughtlessly, to conditions as they have been presented to us. We have in the past failed to see certain situations as opportunities or challenges, but thought of them, instead, as problems that we didn't know how to handle.

Consequently, we kept making the same mistakes over and over again, not knowing how to get off this wheel of repetitive behavior that kept us stuck in our issues. Finally, one day we have that last, painful experience and something clicks within us; we say, "Okay, I've had enough of this. There has to be a better way, a more pleasant way, an easier way. I need not go through the rest of my life like this." Whether we are reacting to someone else's behavior, eating too much, drinking excessively, getting our finances messed up, spending too much money, or waking up negative and gloomy every day, we know when we've had enough. The inner alarm has just gone off to let us know there is indeed another path to take.

This moment marks the beginning of a new adventure. For some, it can be life-changing in a rather dramatic way. For others, it will be more of a quiet alteration in lifestyle: less noticeable changes will be made that make a significant difference in the lives of those involved.

Many people believe we live one continuous life with perhaps many appearances here on earth. The time in between these brief sojourns is used for rest, recreation, work on ourselves and the formulation of plans for the next "performance" or "play" in which we take on a new role.

While making these plans, we decide, with the help of others who are spiritually well-equipped to help us make such decisions, what our next life is to be like. We choose our parents, families, and other significant people who will play out their roles for us in the coming lifetime—many of whom have been with us before in other times. This is why we occasionally get the feeling of having known someone before. It explains as well why we are very comfortable and pleased when we meet some people. At other times the opposite is true, and we feel a definite dislike or even fear as we encounter certain individuals. We can't put our finger on it. We just don't care for them. Naturally, there can be other reasons for this negative response. We may sense something about them that reminds us of something or someone. But often these feelings are due to connections from our past.

In helping to create the lifetime ahead, the needs of the soul must be taken into consideration. Where are our weaknesses? And where have we failed in the past? Do we tend to be jealous? Do we have a problem handling money? Are we excessively judgmental? And what about our assets? What do we like to do? And what do we do well? What is most needed at this time by the soul in order to fulfill itself?

We are constantly creating a state of balance within ourselves. If we've gone too far in one direction, we'll attempt to balance the scales by directing ourselves further in the other direction. This balancing act is done on a continuous basis, even though we are not consciously aware of it.

We are often surprised and confused at finding ourselves in certain situations or dealing with some issues that seem a bit foreign or out of character for us. We're merely balancing a previous "performance." Perhaps we find ourselves really going out on a limb for someone. We don't know why we're doing this. Actually, we'd really rather not get involved, but we feel obliged to help this particular individual who comes to us for all sorts of reasons. We may be lending him money or offering hospitality, and so on. Yet all the while we're puzzled by our own behavior. Why are we doing this? We're busy; we're not that well off financially; still we help in every way we can. The fact is that we're most likely returning a favor. A similar kindness done for us requires the same treatment by us to complete the cycle. The scales are balanced.

There are other ways in which we are continuing patterns that started long ago. Perhaps in ages past we were interested in beautiful stones and collected them in order to make a profit at the local marketplace. Now today we are a jeweler doing the same thing in a more modern setting.

In a similar way, we attract our negative patterns as well. We need to confront our weaknesses if we are to be released from them. Therefore we will draw a situation similar to those we have experienced in our past so that we may finally learn our lesson.

The Spiritual Path, approached consciously, is not for everyone, because it requires much that not all of us are willing and ready to give. What does this mean? It means that if we are to grow consciously, we need first of all to let go. We need to be willing to give our lives over to a higher power that will then guide and direct us. It means giving up our will, knowing that we don't always know what is best for us. It means, further, that we acknowledge the good in others and refrain from making judgments about their lives. It means trusting a God of our own understanding when we don't know where we may be led. It means having the courage to remain on the path when the going gets rough.

It means, too, that we are always working on ourselves, confronting our issues and improving our lives. It means not caring what others think of us: we understand that their approval is not necessary. Further, it means living as honestly as we can with ourselves and others and resisting the temptation to stray from our path. It means living free from fear of responsibilities that sometimes may seem a little overwhelming. Again, it means learning to love ourselves. In so doing, we will learn to love all others, because this is how it works according to the law. It means being grateful every day just to be alive and thanking our Creator for the challenges that come our way—opportunities to learn, grow, and teach others by being the best of whatever we are.

We each have our own mission. We each have a part to play in the whole. If we don't play our part as best we can, the music goes sour. But that's why we're here—to practice, to learn, to grow, and to love. When we're through and have the opportunity to look back on our lives, we'll be glad that we came and that we were not afraid to accept the challenges and take the risks that allowed us to come to this place of deeper understanding.

How high we climb our path is up to us. We may move slowly or rapidly. We may go forward or backward as we choose, but eventually we will graduate from our earthly existence and find new opportunities to learn elsewhere. Having completed this work and gathered all necessary experiences from many realms and spheres, our enlightened soul will make its way back to the Source from whence it came.

ON COMMITMENT

In talking about spiritual growth, a discussion about commitment is essential. What does it mean to commit ourselves to something? Usually we mean giving ourselves wholeheartedly to an undertaking. We don't allow ourselves to think or ponder much about whether we plan to continue the project. We know we are going to complete what we've started because we have promised ourselves, and perhaps others as well, that we will finish what we have begun.

How committed we are determines how ready we are to go to any lengths for the desired goal. Some people go into something only partially committed. As a result, they rarely finish the project or complete the task. Instead, due to any number of reasons, they bow out, claiming all sorts of excuses for not finishing what they promised to complete. Their failure is unfortunate, especially if the goal was a worthy one that would have brought them many positive rewards. Often people don't think things through when they decide to discard a project or leave a condition or situation. They leave on impulse because of some emotional experience that arises. They become suddenly extremely unhappy with something or someone involved, and quickly decide that they are finished.

Not much thought is given to the consequences of such a decision. Unfortunately, people often back out during a crisis, just as an opportunity appears for real growth and possibly a change in their situation—perhaps the change they've been waiting for. "God works in mysterious ways his wonders to perform." It's often just as we are at our wit's end with a condition in our lives that it changes for us.

If a person chooses to turn back just as he is nearing the top of the hill, he doesn't get to see what's on the other side. He can't see how pleasant the way down can be. He can't see how easy the walk is going to become, and he doesn't see the new friends he may meet on the other side. When we stop short of our goals, we shortchange ourselves. We can never know how worthwhile life could have been had we kept going. When we know we're on the appropriate path that will bring us blessings, it pays to stay on it, even though the going may get rough. Creator never gives us more than we can handle. We can always know, too, that if we are in a crisis there is a blessing awaiting us on the other side. We may not know what it is or when it will come, but we can be sure that it's there. The Universe is always working for our benefit if we have committed ourselves to improving our lives. We will never be let down. There may be changes taking place that look frightening to us at first, but if we have the courage to stay with it we will see the pathway being cleared and blessings of which we haven't dreamed coming to us.

We don't always know what is best for us because our vision is limited. We see only what's immediately around us. We don't have the airplane view or bird's eye view that gives us a greater perspective on our lives. If we could truly see what we must accomplish in order to complete our cycle on earth, we would be most eager to get on with our lessons. We would see how the pattern of our life comes together and how each piece plays a part in the whole. Each experience weaves into the pattern, a thread that binds and holds our life together, creating a beautiful design. Each design is unique. Some patterns are brightly colored, containing threads of gold and silver, bringing together many different kinds of materials. Other patterns are conservative and stately, with few colors and neutral in tone. All are different and equally important to the whole.

Each soul is composed of many patterns working together to create the final tapestry. As we commit ourselves to whatever goal or concern we have ahead of us, we are weaving another thread into the pattern to help complete a cycle. We may stop in the middle, if we choose, or continue on to the end. If we continue, there is then no need to pick up the thread at a later time. If, on the other hand, we choose to discontinue our path, the thread will then be picked up by the soul and completed either later in this life or further down the road. Sooner or later, once we initiate something, it needs to be brought to completion.

How important, then, are our commitments? They are only as important as we think they are. Our commitments are really to ourselves, though we may feel we are making commitments to others. Only we are responsible for the promises we make. Others don't have to pick up the thread for us. We are the ones who have to complete our goals.

No one else will have to pay the price if we back out of an agreement or condition that we promised ourselves we would complete. At times, it might seem that others have to pay, but they are learning their own lessons as well. Our relationships with others involve learning on everyone's part. No one escapes the lessons he or she needs for growth, whether they desire those lessons or not. Further, as we commit ourselves to the Spiritual Path, we open a door that invites us to participate in a variety of lessons and experiences.

We may choose to undergo these experiences in a state of enlightenment or of being awake rather than asleep, as in the past. We may decide to respond rather than react to life. We can also learn to act from love rather than from fear. While responding with love, we can watch ourselves grow in a way which brings us many blessings. We can be proud and grateful to have kept our promises to ourselves and humbled, as well, at the progress we've made.

ON WILLINGNESS

How do we become willing? Many times we think we want something, but we later discover that we weren't willing to do what it takes to get what we want. This attitude can be unfortunate: often our goals are worthy and we are capable of achieving them, but we lack the one important thing that will ensure our success.

Willingness doesn't always come easily. Many projects we may wish to complete take a considerable amount of doing—whether it means pursuing a new job, redecorating a house, planning a trip, or taking a course in college. It all takes time, energy, and courage. In other words, we have to be willing to risk failure. It's no wonder it is sometimes difficult to begin.

Often we have to pray for willingness to start, just as we pray that circumstances will develop as we like. If we aren't willing, our heart isn't into it—if, indeed, we do it at all.

We may sign up to be in a chorus or in a play, only to find that we have become increasingly busy. Therefore, what was supposed to be an enjoyable pastime has become a burden we'd rather not have right now. So we go off to the rehearsals as an unwilling participant. We have not succeeded in convincing ourselves that this is a wise undertaking at the present time. We are unwilling to the point that we find it best to drop out, which is probably the best decision under the circumstances.

However, let's say we wish to learn to let go of someone with whom we have been having a relationship. This individual has told us that he or she wishes to end the relationship and is no longer interested in seeing us. Nevertheless, we continue to obsess over this person, wondering about what they're doing and where they are. We find we can't sleep at night because we can't stop thinking about them. Will they come back? Will they find someone else? Maybe they already have a new love. How could they have done this to me? All of these thoughts keep running through our mind, day after day, and night after night.

We know in our heart we need to let go, and we honestly try. We begin by getting very busy, calling friends and making plans to get out and do all sorts of things. But nothing works. Then we remember the phrase, "Let go and let God." What does that really mean? How do we let go? Our next step is to pray about it. In our despair, we ask God to help us to become willing to let go of the relationship.

Soon we find we're not thinking of this person as we once were. Perhaps by now we've even found a new companion to whom we relate well. Our life has changed. Our willingness to let go of the old relationship is now complete. We begin to understand that this person was in our life for a purpose, but the need for them has ended, and both of us are free to go our own ways and have new experiences. What a gift! And it all came about because we had the willingness to let go.

But how did we become willing? Thinking back, we remember that we had to pray for it. It didn't come naturally or easily. It didn't come even when we worked hard at it. It came only as we asked for it. There are times when our human will is not enough. We can't simply make a decision to do something and work ourselves to death to accomplish it. That's not how it works. There are times when we need to humble ourselves in order to get what we want. Our Higher Power then sees to it that we do acquire what we seek. There are people who can seem very self-sufficient and strong-willed. They may even admit that relying on a supernatural power is unnecessary or distasteful to them for some reason. For awhile they may get along this way, but eventually they will come up against a challenge they can't handle alone. They will discover that they must get on their knees and rediscover the Creator they've been trying so hard to avoid.

Actually, this is a blessing and an opportunity for them. But it won't be seen that way for some time. They will first be brought down to size by whatever means is necessary to make them reckon with Creator's power. Later on they will be grateful, and even fascinated, to see how this power works "magically." They will have learned to leave things in God's hands.

We all need to become willing to accomplish much in our lives, and we need to call on a higher power to help us. As we do, that which we must complete becomes a joy. We find we have the desire implanted within us by our Creator to do whatever needs to be done. Further, we rejoice as we begin to ask for willingness for lots of different things: willingness to wake up with joy and gratitude each day; willingness to begin loving ourselves and treating ourselves as we would our best friend; willingness to bless our family, our friends, and our neighbors; and willingness even to pray for the willingness.

There are times when we need to will to become willing. But once we've discovered the power available to us, we can "Let go and let God," and watch as our lives merge with a power that guides our very being. Our emotions, feelings, and attitudes become one with the Creator at that instant. We must move ahead in those situations where it has become necessary to pray for willingness.

ON DISCERNMENT

Why do we need discernment on the spiritual path? What does it mean to be discerning? What can it mean for us should we choose not to exercise discernment when dealing with others in the world?

Discernment gives us security in knowing that what we have chosen is safe for us. It comes most often with experience. There are times when we must make some mistakes before we understand the meaning of the process. Sometimes we have to be hurt or waste time or make a bad move before we understand we have had a lesson in discernment. Generally, it's a lesson we weren't prepared for, and it usually means we have become involved in something that is not in our best interest. Then we find we have to pay the price for our mistakes.

Sometimes we may hurt others through our lack of discernment. There are times we say the wrong thing or are thoughtless in our interactions with others. We have not "discerned" the circumstances in order to know or be aware of what is appropriate behavior.

Discernment is a gift. It comes easily to some and not as easily to others. People who are endowed with this beautiful quality always seem to know the right thing to say and do at the right time. They are able to size up the situation, understand the dynamics of what is going on, and know how to handle not only themselves, but others involved as well. The non-discerning individual will tend to "put his foot in his mouth" or not say anything when something should be said. Or, he or she may leave a situation when help is needed, or stay too long when they ought to leave. The non-discerning person is difficult to have around because they seem to care little for what is going on in their immediate environment. Instead, they are more wrapped up in themselves and their own needs or comfort with little to offer others around them.

There are other ways to use discernment. We use it all the time. If we go to buy peanut butter, we have to make a choice between several different kinds. If we think it should be "all natural," then we read the label to make sure nothing is added that would make it not to our liking. If we want it smooth, we will not get the crunchy kind. Here we are using discernment based upon our preference.

We also make decisions when we go to the movies. We consider which kind of movies we are in the mood to see. If we are depressed, we may not wish to go to a long, sad movie. Again we use discernment in making our selection. In making these kinds of decisions, it is quite easy to be discerning, because generally we know what we like and want.

However, there are other times when it is not as easy. For example, when we don't know which direction to take, or when we aren't even aware that we have a choice, we may find ourselves in a dilemma that we can't solve so easily. Perhaps we are in a strange place and are looking for a restaurant. We've heard of several, and have to make a choice. What do we do? Often we have to ask someone which he or she might recommend. In other words, we have to rely on the judgment of others. In this case we reserve our discernment for the persons we ask. Do they seem as though they know what they're talking about? Are they honest? Are they looking out for our interest or theirs? Can we take what they say at face value? These kinds of thoughts run through our mind as we listen. Then we make up our mind based on our conclusions.

At other times we may be in situations in which we don't realize we have a choice. Maybe we're taking a course in college. We sign up for the course and attend the first class. The professor announces that there is going to be a quiz every Friday, and he expects near-perfect attendance. We also learn many students fail the class every semester. And to top it off, the lectures are very boring. Then someone tells us that there is someone else who teaches the same class and is very popular with the students. Previously, we didn't know we had a choice. However, now we are faced with a decision. Do we wish to remain in the class we're in, or should we switch to the more popular one? This is where the issue of discernment comes in.

What does this have to do with being on the spiritual path? In making the decision to transform one's life, many such decisions are made daily. More and more, discernment becomes an issue. It is vitally important to be discerning: there are issues that become increasingly significant as we embark on this journey. Lack of discernment can put one in potentially dangerous situations as one delves into spiritual matters. In other words, the potential for problems increases, just as the potential for joy and fulfillment becomes a reality.

Many decisions must be made along this path of spiritual discovery. People will look in different places according to their needs. We are all in different stages of our evolution as souls here on earth, and we will choose to be where we are the most comfortable. Therefore, that which is right for one will not necessarily be right for another. We are all individuals. Some will, for a period of time, seek solitude, while others will look for groups for companionship. Some will find a teacher to help them get started, while others will seek within themselves for their answers. Some will look to traditional religion, finding comfort in the doctrines found there, while others will seek for truth in other ways that give them peace and fulfillment.

All religions and spiritual philosophies teach love. If we find that that which we are pursuing does not include love in its philosophy, we are looking in the wrong place. Love in this sense refers to the nonjudgmental caring about others. It is a love that does not control, but allows individuals to experience the lessons they need in order to grow. It is helpful and considerate, yet understands what detachment is all about. It understands that to love another we must first love ourselves. For without first accepting ourselves and the conditions of our lives, we find it impossible to appreciate others around us. Thus, once again, the importance of discernment is underscored.

We must continue to ask for help and guidance each day as we leave ourselves and others in God's hands. Further, we must accept with gratitude the choices that are made for us.

BOOK FOUR

ON COMPULSION/ADDICTION

Why is it necessary or appropriate to discuss compulsive or addictive behavior in connection with spiritual growth? The reason is simple. There are many on the spiritual path who have experienced their conscious awakening as a direct result of their problem with addiction.

Usually we awaken to the need of something truly spiritual in our lives only after we have known what it feels like to be disconnected from the spiritual. When we are fearful, we will attempt to control our lives or the lives of others so that we can "be comfortable" with the situation or condition that is causing our problems. This need to control causes us to act in a manner that becomes habit-forming and, indeed, obsessive at times. Soon we lose trust in God. Instead, we begin to use our minds over our spirit in a never-ending struggle in which we seek for ways to control our environment. We put God "on the back burner," making the decision, albeit unconsciously, to take our lives into our own hands.

Unfortunately, to our dismay, things don't work out the way we hoped they would, and we wind up making mistakes in our attempt to run the show. If we could only know at this point that we are doing ourselves a great disservice, we would not insist on doing things our own way.

Our situation can be compared to a walk along a highway. We believe we are aware of all that is around us, while in reality we can see only what is immediately in front of and behind us. On the other hand, if we had the perspective of an airplane pilot, we could see for miles around. We would know what was coming from all directions. We would see where it was sunny and where there were dark clouds forming. And we would be able to make a long-range forecast because we would have a greater picture of conditions, past, present, and future. In contrast, when we are walking along the highway, we see little. Yet, we attempt to predict the future without the proper information. Given all this, it is unlikely that we will know how to handle our lives entirely on our own.

How realistic is it to believe that we can understand all the complexities, not only of our lives, but the lives of those around us? How can we think we know what's best for another walking down a nearby road when we lack information concerning their path, as well as their ultimate destination? We can only guess, based upon what we think—and often what we think is colored by our own misperceptions of the situation. We tend to see what we like to see, and though we may feel we are being objective, we may be sadly mistaken.

Therefore, using the mind to control ourselves and solve all of our problems becomes a great burden that can be very tiring at best. Compulsive behavior tries to assure us that we are somewhat still on track and gives us a false sense of security. All the while we are shutting out God, or Spirit—that divine part of ourselves. If we would allow to the spirit to open, it would cause us to feel a great relaxation and peace. We could let go and allow things to flow naturally. Our attempt to control our lives takes too much energy, determination, and reliance on self.

Self-reliance may seem noble, but, sadly, it becomes the downfall of many. Unfortunately, people are often taught self-reliance without any incorporation of the spirit. The spiritual or intuitive side of our nature must be included if self-reliance is to become a worthy goal. Otherwise, we are involving only the mind and emotions, both of which, when used alone, can get us into trouble. However, it is very important not to judge compulsive or addictive behavior: it, too, has a place in our development.

In any case, it is essential to include our connection to the Source if we are to become well-rounded individuals. We must keep balanced, remembering not to go overboard with either the material or spiritual aspects of life. There must be both—a unification of mind and Spirit, a blending of the material and spiritual—if we are to move smoothly along our path in life.

It is appropriate to seek within in solving life's problems. Further, as we allow divine spiritual energy to flow through us and at the same time learn to trust in our Higher Power to help solve our problems, we can learn to let go. As we learn to trust the intuition that God has given us, we find that our lives become much easier. We are no longer trying to handle everything alone.

There is no need to attempt to control the world around us in order to be comfortable, because we've turned that job over to the God of our own understanding. We now trust that the Universe, in its infinite wisdom, knows what we need at any given time. We may be at peace with ourselves, realizing that the way will be made clear to us as we pray for direction and guidance each day. Addiction no longer has a place in our lives, because we are willing to allow God to help take care of all of our needs as we climb the spiritual ladder. And as we take each step, one by one, our addictions leave us. We surrender ourselves to the Source, asking for help with our problems and trusting in God's power to relieve us of our compulsions. We must ask, however. God won't step in unless invited.

Amazing things will start to happen as we patiently allow ourselves to be healed in God's way and in God's time. We may encounter many situations or lessons that we find unpleasant. But having passed our test and seized the opportunities as they come to us, we will grow. Further, as we develop, we will find increasing joy and peace filling our days. We will discover, as well, that we are in greater alignment with the Source of our being, who, if allowed, will render us whole.

ON TRUTH

We must understand that when we talk about spiritual growth, truth becomes a relative term. We are all at various stages of spiritual development. Therefore, that which we know to be true changes with our evolution as spiritual beings. That is not to say that truth itself is altered, but that our perception of the truth changes as we grow. A baby sees the world differently than does an adult. Our perspective shifts as we grow and are able to take in and understand more and more.

What makes this change or growth possible? As we think, feel, and perceive based upon our past experiences, our perception of the world expands and we add new experiences to our lives. A small child has limited experience; therefore, he is capable of understanding only a limited number of facts. If we give him more to learn when he is not ready, he will only become confused.

This is true for all of us as we learn about life. We can absorb only so much learning at a time in order to be comfortable and grow properly. Do we place a small child in the eighth grade in order to give him what we feel is the best education? No, we start him out in kindergarten or nursery school, allowing him to work his way up to the higher levels.

Our Creator does the same for us. We are given bits of truth as we are ready, allowing our spirit to grow step by step into greater awareness of ourselves and the world. Each religion and philosophy teaches us something important, while none can claim to contain all of the truth that exists. Further, it may be said that we're all individuals, and while our journeys eventually bring us all to the same destination, we may get there by different means. Therefore, we must refrain from judging another's path. Whatever they are experiencing may be just what is needed to further their progress.

Lessons may involve various aspects of a particular faith or other experiences one encounters along the path. All the appropriate opportunities will be there to help us learn what we need to know, until we are ready to seek within ourselves for the truth which lies within our own being, awaiting us there in the silence. Our Higher Power comes to us speaking truth every day of our lives in many different ways. As we learn to pay attention and watch for the signs, we may attune ourselves to the truth that is everywhere around us.

Others can tell us what is true and what we should believe, but only we can know it in our own hearts. Someone may tell us we should believe this or that, or that we must do this thing or that thing, but if we can't feel truth, we have not found it. Knowing truth is not experiencing truth. Once truth is experienced, we will never wonder or doubt again, and no one can take our experiences from us.

We all experience truth in our own way. There may be similarities, but basically our paths are our own and unique to each one of us. We don't come to the same place by the same road. There are many pathways that lead to the center of the circle, but always the final expression will be the same. It is defined as love.

Thus, it is the expression of unconditional love as Christ taught and lived that is the reward—the pot of gold at the end of the rainbow. As we seek for truth, through books, through teachers, as well as through our own experiences, let's allow others to learn in their own way as they experience that which they must in order to fulfill the needs of their soul. While growing and allowing others the same opportunity, we make further advancement along our path possible. And what is growth but the soul's gathering experiences in order to further its ability to grasp what is true?

Therefore, once again, truth on the path is a relative term. Though truth does not change, our perspective on that which is true shifts as we grow and change. When we have gathered sufficient experience, knowledge and wisdom, we will know, beyond a doubt, that we have found that for which we have long been searching. We will know it through our feelings of peace, joy, and unconditional love for ourselves and everyone around us. We will no longer need to search outside of ourselves for what we know is found within.

We will, moreover, be able to understand and use the tools that enable us to open doors to further enlightenment within our own being. We will understand the place of traditional religion as well as of all of the spiritual philosophies of the world. In the same way, we will understand the meaning and place for knowledge and discipline in spiritual practice. We will grasp the truth that the journey is unique for each traveler along the road.

Yet what we know as truth and experience as truth we see as two different things. And our experience eventually brings us to the wondrous feeling of love—not as an emotion, but as a state of unconditional acceptance of life, as it is.

ON FAITH

What does it mean to have faith? What can it do for us? And how may we acquire faith? As we ponder these questions, let's also imagine what it would be like to live without faith. What would such a life be like, as compared to a life built around total faith? Would there be a difference? Would we be affected differently by our experience of both these conditions? Of course we would. We know it from our own experience.

For example, do we worry that the sun may not come up tomorrow? Are we afraid that evening may not come and so we will not have the opportunity to look forward to the passage of another day? And do we worry that the cut on our finger won't heal, even though we have covered it with a bandage? Of course we don't harbor such foolish fears.

It is true that we have faith in the regularity of these conditions that occur in nature, because we've seen them over and over again. We know that there is a Supreme Being or Universal Intelligence that puts it all together, making everything work. Why then can't we have as much faith in other aspects of our lives?

The reason may be that our mind tends to get in the way. We begin to think, "Maybe I don't deserve that job," or "Maybe I'm not supposed to have much money," or "Maybe I'm not good enough." The fact is, we are all meant to share in God's blessings as we understand and live by the Laws of the Universe.

As we think, so we are. We need to have faith in the Law of Attraction. Consequently, if we think negative thoughts about ourselves and our lives, we will attract negative experiences. Similarly, if we think in terms of success, we will draw opportunities to become successful. In other words, God will give us that which we desire as we deem ourselves worthy from the soul's point of view. However, from our limited perspective, we cannot always see what is best for us.

For example, we may want a particular job, but we may not see the problems or hazards that surround that particular position. Perhaps the work environment, though it may appear to be pleasant enough, is fraught with tension and disharmony. Therefore, unless we need to be in such a condition for our growth experience, it may be in our best interest to find a more suitable place to work. There is much we don't see, but if we ask our Higher Power for the best job or work opportunity for us, we are in a better position to get what is most appropriate for us.

In other words, we need to let go and depend on the Source to provide what we need. When we hold on to our problems, worries and fears, we prevent the occurrence of the very things that we would like to see come about. Therefore, the only way in which to see the results of our faith is to let go and trust in our Higher Power.

This is part of the lesson that faith teaches. We can understand that faith is necessary to bring about that which is best for us. We may think we are exercising this quality just because we understand it, but it isn't until we practice faith by surrendering our will that we actually are demonstrating it in our lives.

Letting go is the key. And in order to let go we have to believe there is something we can count on to help us. How can we leave our child in the hands of a babysitter who we feel is unreliable? We wouldn't do such a thing. Nor do we let go of our lives, placing ourselves in the hands of a greater power unless we are certain of our caretaker. Until we have established a sense of trust in the infinite, we continue to hold on.

Once that trust is established, little by little, we begin to release each worrisome situation and negative condition that we encounter. Further, as we let go, we start seeing the most wondrous things take place, not always as we predicted or planned, but as God has determined is best for us. We find, eventually, that we can be grateful as we see how things turn out for us. And although we can't fully comprehend until our life is over why things happen as they do, we will then be able to see how the pieces all come together.

Therefore, trust becomes very important. As we learn to trust in one situation after another, we begin to build our faith until one day it becomes almost automatic to us. Instead of becoming fearful or anxious about a given situation, or attempting to control the outcome, we choose instead to let go, because we know the situation is going to be resolved as it is supposed to be. We don't have to ponder it, or wonder about it, or even hope. We know, beyond a shadow of a doubt, that as we leave things in the hands of our Creator, all will turn out well for us.

Therefore, we have to let go of the need to have things our way as we accept God's will for us. As we do, peace begins to flow. We allow God to direct the play in which we become the performer, reading our lines as they are given to us, knowing that the outcome depends on our ability to trust in the Director. We must develop trust in the other actors as well. As they read their lines, we respond in the way that most represents our character. We attempt at all times to be true to ourselves.

We each have a part to play, and it is important that we refrain from taking over the roles of others, or becoming too involved in how they should perform. We leave that to the Director as we continue to pay attention to our own role. The best performance occurs when all the actors are playing their parts to the best of their abilities. Any corrections or suggestions can be left up to the Director. Thus, we may continue to act out our role, supporting each other and refusing to become jealous of those who appear to have larger roles. Instead, we accept who we are for this time in the play. Later on, we may have the larger role. Larger, however, does not necessarily mean better: we are all equally important to the theme of the play. At the end of the production, we may all take a bow and congratulate ourselves on our performance. After it is over, we each leave our roles behind and go back to being who we really are in spirit, with another performance behind us and greater wisdom gained from the experience.

ON ANGER/RESENTMENT

How do we cope with anger on the spiritual path? As we encounter it along our journey, let's remember that to become angry from time to time is part of what it means to be human. If we try to suppress our anger, we are not being true to ourselves. Further, our feelings will have to come out sooner or later in other ways, but most likely they will be inappropriate to the situation, and will tend to further complicate the issue at hand.

Therefore, it is best that we express our anger as it occurs in ways that do not harm another person's integrity. As we learn to express ourselves honestly and appropriately, we prevent anger from old wounds from building within us, causing resentment.

Resentment is anger that we have been unable or unwilling to let go. Many people spend much of their lives being resentful about something that happened long ago. Anger that has been held within the body can cause many problems, from ulcers to cancer, as it acts as a poison destroying the very cells that give us life. It is important to let go of our resentments: they can destroy our bodies as well as a chance for a happy life.

Resentments affect our mind, body, and spirit. They immobilize us and prevent us from moving forward along our path, holding us in the darkness of our own being and preventing us from seeing the light that is there. If we desire to transform ourselves and our lives, we must release the resentment that holds us down.

How do we let go of the hurt and anger another has caused? At times it's difficult, if not impossible, to accomplish this on our own. We must turn in prayer to a power greater than ourselves in order to release this potentially dangerous emotion.

After we have asked for the willingness to let go of our resentments, it is wise to visualize ourselves as free of this negative condition. What does it feel like to be at peace, to feel acceptance and even love toward him or her? What does it feel like to experience harmony and peace in our situation?

Visualization is a powerful tool and, when used in combination with the appropriate feeling, helps greatly in our transformation. As we see and feel ourselves in harmony and peace with the person or situation that is troubling us, we begin to feel free. Further, bringing this visualization clearly into our meditation will allow the desired transformation to take place. All of this will take some time, depending on how long one has nurtured the particular resentment.

If it is a very old resentment that we have allowed to remain with us over a long period of time, it has to be treated accordingly. It is much like treating an old wound that has been allowed to fester. Such wounds can be stubborn and require persistence and patience on the part of the healer.

As we continue to look at our part in the situation, asking for the willingness to let go while at the same time visualizing the situation in the light, we can begin to heal ourselves. Further, as we do, new power flows in to uplift us, bringing us out of the darkness and into the light. Our Higher Power has accomplished the task that we, as human beings, were unable to do alone.

While trusting in the God of our understanding to help show us the way, we will discover the freedom we have been seeking as we search within ourselves. We have learned that our troubles are not outside of ourselves but lie instead within our own being. We no longer blame exterior conditions for our unhappiness, but look instead at that which is within and seek to heal what lies in the shadows deep in our own heart.

While becoming honest with what we find there, and willing to make the adjustments that we must make within ourselves, we will begin to see the changes that we desire take place in all of our relationships. And when we become even momentarily angry, let's ask ourselves, "What is it all about? Is it anger from the past, or does it reflect a current situation?"

Perhaps we need to forgive someone who has been rude, thoughtless, or hurtful. Perhaps we are angry at ourselves for not being perfect or for not living up to all we feel we should be. Perhaps we've made a mistake or hurt someone. Whatever the case may be, anger—past or present—needs to be dealt with if we are to grow along the spiritual path. While taking care to keep ourselves clear of negativity, we make way for new energies to transform and uplift us.

Therefore, let's recognize our feelings as they come to us, speaking up when we must, forgiving when it is appropriate, and letting go when that becomes possible. All of this requires the help of our Higher Power in order to be accomplished properly. As we learn to trust in that strength, we'll find greater peace and harmony in our relationship with God, ourselves, and all with whom we come in contact.

ON GUILT

What is guilt and why do we experience it? In reality, guilt is a useless emotion that doesn't bring us any benefit unless we use its uncomfortable feeling to initiate beneficial changes within ourselves. Otherwise, it can be a harmful emotion that blocks our growth and prevents us from moving forward on our path.

Many people spend much time feeling guilty about real or imagined mistakes that occurred long ago. Consequently, they are often unaware of the source of their guilt, which comes often as a feeling of unworthiness. When we feel guilty we block our good—our ability to receive. We often feel we don't deserve that which is positive. Therefore, we deny ourselves the possibility of becoming as prosperous and productive as we would like to be.

We often use guilt as a means of punishing ourselves for what we perceive as our wrongdoing. Thus, for as long as we choose to punish ourselves, we block our ability to move forward. Holding on to our guilt in this manner may create an excuse for our not taking responsibility for our lives. We choose instead to wallow in our feelings of unworthiness.

However, as soon as we decide we're through being remorseful, we begin to make the necessary changes that help bring us into alignment with who we are and where we are going from a spiritual perspective. In other words, we begin to align ourselves with our purpose once more. We've released the guilt that is within us and allowed ourselves to enjoy life in its fullness.

On the other hand, feelings of guilt may be of help, as they indicate to us where we have made mistakes that need correcting. For example, guilt may indicate to us that we need to apologize to someone. Perhaps we have hurt another, or perhaps it is to ourselves that we need to make amends. Often we tend to be hard on ourselves and unforgiving of even the smallest mistakes.

We need to learn to be gentle with self, so that we may be forgiving of others as well. For as we punish ourselves and hold unforgiving thoughts toward ourselves and our mistakes, we tend to do the same to others. While learning to forgive and accept who we are with all of our shortcomings, we can, in turn, accept others with their weaknesses as well. We thus relieve ourselves of the guilt that comes from making negative judgments about ourselves and others. We leave all in God's hands.

As we allow our Higher Power to be the judge, giving us the experiences we need as well as the feelings to indicate where we may have gone astray, we are able to let go. Further, as we do let go, we are guided into the right thought or action that is appropriate for us under the circumstances.

It is important to recognize that nothing that we have done in our past can prevent us from being worthy today. If we are humble and sorry for the mistakes that we have made, we are then in a place to accept God's forgiveness—as we must if we are to grow as spiritual beings. Holding on to the old feelings of guilt and remorse over events of the past leaves us drained and unable to function fully and freely in the present. When we are nursing old wounds and always looking backwards at what has gone on before, we are not in a position to accept all that our Creator has in store for us. Therefore, we need to forgive ourselves and move on.

There are those who mistakenly believe that they must feel guilt in order to be worthy of God's love. Many feel that guilt is somehow a noble emotion related to our degree of spirituality. However, we must remember that we are always worthy, no matter what we may have done or not done. Our Creator will love us in spite of our mistakes. Therefore, we must set aside the notion that we are required to feel guilty in order to be worthy of His love. God is love and does not need anything from us. Instead, we need to give love to ourselves and others.

As we continue along our journey, it is wise to begin to observe our thoughts and feelings, making sure that we aren't harboring any negativity from the past. While at the same time, as we study the laws of the universe and the ways in which we can work with God's energy, we learn how to transform this energy into something positive and useful. We may view our negative feelings as pieces of the puzzle and see how they may be looked upon as opportunities—the beginning of a new pattern for us.

This conclusion doesn't mean we should never feel negative emotions. It simply means we can more productively allow our feelings to transform us—to lift us into greater awareness about ourselves and our world, bringing understanding and clarity into our lives. These attitudes help us to accept ourselves.

ON SECURITY

What does it mean to feel secure and why is the need for security so prevalent today? People search for security in many forms—financial, emotional, physical—as well as the spiritual security that, though something may happen to the physical body, the spirit lives on after death.

More and more, as we come into this time of extreme turmoil in the world, there is a need for many to believe in the survival of the spirit. We need to believe in the immortality of the soul as we see so many leave the earth plane through death. We need to believe, understand and take consolation in the fact of survival of the soul following the separation from the body. This makes it somewhat easier for us to accept the loss of loved ones and even those whom we don't know.

Security is also necessary if we are to feel balance in our lives. It's not easy to remain steady and calm when all around us there is chaos, confusion, sadness, anger, and fear. It's wise to find ways to steady ourselves and remain peaceful in spite of all that is going on. And how do we do this? How do we remain in the eye of the hurricane? How do we seek and maintain a feeling of security in spite of great obstacles? Once we have established our security on certain basic principles, we discover that we are indeed blessed, and we remain calm.

If we can acquire a deeper understanding of life that tells us that all is well no matter what is happening, we are indeed fortunate. If we can see beauty and order in chaos and find value and meaning in pain and loss, we have gained much. If we can gather strength from our misfortunes and learn to rise above our difficulties, we are progressing well on our journey in life.

But how do we get to the point where we can feel such security? In order to feel secure, we must develop faith. And faith often comes through knowing that we've made it through past occurrences or unpleasant events, and we can make it again. It also comes through knowing that our Creator doesn't give us more than we can handle. Faith also comes in knowing that God will give us what we need as we need it.

For example, certainly a woman doesn't ordinarily have the strength to lift a huge truck off the ground. Yet such strength has been given when it was needed to free a child pinned underneath. Obviously, the child was meant to be saved and the mother was given the strength to rescue the child. So though we may not now be prepared for what lies ahead, we can ask to be prepared as the time approaches for us to handle whatever comes our way. In this way, we can let go of our fear of the future and know that we will be given whatever we need to meet all challenges awaiting us.

Further, we may feel secure because we know nobody can take that awareness from us. Others can leave us, hurt us and attempt to destroy us. Yet no one can prevent us from believing in ourselves in time of trouble. Finally, no one can prevent us from being true to ourselves, even when others turn against us. Thus it is with faith and trust that we leave ourselves in God's hands, knowing that whatever challenges may come our way, we will be taken care of.

BOOK FIVE

ON VISUALIZATION

One of the more valuable tools on the spiritual path is a technique called visualization. When used properly, it can help bring about positive conditions in our lives.

We can use visualization for many different purposes. Always it should be used in accordance with the natural and spiritual laws if we wish to create positive conditions. It must be remembered that whatever we put out into the universe comes back to us. Therefore, if we visualize the conditions we want and add feeling and energy to our images, we can help bring them about. In this way we are capable of creating our reality.

Conversely, if we put out a negative thought along with a visualization of what we don't want to happen, we will also help the condition to manifest itself. Often we do this when we fear something. If we are afraid, for example, that we will make some mistake in our work and we dwell on that thought, adding energy to it, we are very likely to make the mistake that we fear. Visualization can work for or against us, depending on use.

If we visualize a negative thing occurring for someone else we must be careful! Remember, by the law of Karma (i.e., that which we send out, either positively or negatively, in thought, word, or deed, will be returned to us), we will be, in turn, setting up a negative situation in our own lives. This is spiritual law, and whether we believe in it, subscribe to it, understand it or not, it is in effect, just as the law of gravity is relevant in the physical world. The fact that a person does not understand the law of gravity, or has not yet learned about it, doesn't mean it isn't in operation. So we must be careful with what we give out: it will be returned to us. At the same time, when we create positive pictures in our minds involving ourselves and others, that which we create will manifest itself positively.

There are many creative ways in which visualization may be used. In fact, it is being used more and more in all aspects of life because it is being discovered to be so very effective. One use has to do with healing. Its been found that visualization can help greatly in healing the physical body, even when recovery was thought impossible. For example, it has been demonstrated that children who make a game of visualizing white blood cells attacking and destroying diseased cells have overcome serious physical conditions.

We may also visualize ourselves and others healing emotionally. Let's say we desire to feel better about ourselves and have more self-confidence. All we need is to see ourselves as happy and confident, knowing that as we visualize ourselves and add feeling along with the image of how we want to look and be, we can change not only our self-image, but our appearance to others as well.

Further, visualization is being used in all kinds of sports. Basketball teams, for example, are using this technique as they visualize themselves playing in cooperation, making baskets and then winning the game. Business is another area which utilizes this technique, (We have to be careful here of our motives, and remember that, as always, the Creator is still the director, and that which we help to create in our lives will be overseen and monitored by our Higher Power.)

Nothing goes forth that is not known by God. If we have a lesson to learn, we can be sure it will be there waiting for us. We don't get by without answering for all we create. If we choose to send out beautiful, loving thoughts and create lovely positive pictures that include ourselves and others, we will draw to us experiences that match what we have created. If we choose, on the other hand, to create thoughts of fear, reinforcing them with powerful visualizations confirming the worst, we can expect to bring fearful experiences into our lives to challenge us.

By understanding how we can replace the negative images in our minds with positive ones, we can change ourselves dramatically. Further, through learning and applying that knowledge, we are taking responsibility for creating our own reality.

Similarly, if we fear something, we may also dispel the fear by refusing to give power to that particular thought. Instead, we may decide to change the thought or picture to a more positive one. In other words, we vow not to create the negative pattern which will one day manifest itself if it is given sufficient energy. As an alternative, we may create a new feeling, affirming what we desire and bringing positive feeling into the picture. In this way, we learn much about responsibility and our exciting ability to take part in creating what we want in our lives.

ON MEDITATION

The art of meditation is well worth pursuing for anyone serious about spiritual growth and enlightenment. All of our answers can be ultimately found by going within. We can search in many other places for knowledge, truth, peace, comfort, and personal guidance. But if we are to grow spiritually, we must eventually learn to rely on ourselves.

If we are new, at least consciously, to the spiritual path, we may have been looking elsewhere for peace and comfort. Perhaps we sought out a friend to talk to, or used chemicals in one form or another to calm our nerves. Maybe we went to the movies, discovering that this type of distraction took us away from our problems, even if only for a short time. In any case, we found something that helped us to settle down for a bit while we "pulled ourselves together."

What does one do in order to find the answers to the problems in one's life? We may pray, asking that things work out for the best for us. We may seek guidance from a trusted advisor. We can go to another friend who may or may not have the best advice for us. Then again, we may go ahead impulsively with a major decision, without much thought of the consequences, hoping that we've made the right choice. On the other hand, we may think hard about our problem, taking care to look at all the options open to us. There are many different ways we can hope to solve our dilemmas.

And what do we do when we find we are in a crisis? Do we panic? Do we tear our hair out? Do we yell for help? Do we get in our car and drive aimlessly for several hours with the radio blaring? Again, many reactions are possible.

What do we do when we wish to seek for knowledge about something that no one can really know with any certainty because it involves a future event—something that hasn't yet happened? What do we do when we feel lonely on a Saturday night and we can find no one around, even on the phone, to keep us company? Perhaps we've had a loss and are looking for comfort, but no one seems to be there who can fill that empty space within us. What can we do? And what do we do when we wish to know the truth about something? Maybe we need to make a decision on whom to hire for a particular job, or who would be the most appropriate couple to invite to a party when we have room for only two more people. These decisions are hard to make when things seem fairly equal. Nevertheless, we have to make a choice. We want to make the best choice based on all the possible variables. So what can we do? How can we possibly know all the factors involved?

All of these situations mentioned can be resolved through the art of meditation. In other words, it is possible to find our questions answered, our fears calmed, our loneliness assuaged, our moods changed as we gain inner peace while seeking within.

Meditation is an art, in that it is highly individual and we each experience it differently as we grow. There are many and varied ways to meditate, as well as numerous books out on the subject. And while a person may choose to begin with a particular method or posture, this practice may change as one grows spiritually.

It is suggested, perhaps, that we begin by sitting comfortably in a chair with our feet on the floor, our back straight but not rigid, and our hands in our lap. We may wish to visualize a rose or candle or a peaceful scene to keep our mind off our material concerns. Before beginning, it is essential to ask for divine protection from our Higher Power or God as we place a white light—or a clear light, if we prefer—around us. At the same time, we ask that only the highest forces appropriate for us be allowed to enter our midst. This protection is very important as a safety factor, but it enhances our meditation as well. The practice of meditation can give us many wonderful gifts, but we must also be aware of the responsibilities involved—one of them being to ensure that we invite only the highest energies to mingle with our own.

Then we can begin our meditation by learning to relax the physical body. It is very important to be gentle with ourselves when learning to meditate: it takes much patience and diligence. We must stay with it, meditating each day for short periods. Perhaps even ten minutes is enough at the beginning. Then, if we wish to increase our time, we may. Very long meditation periods are not recommended. We usually don't require lengthy sessions, and we need to remember that we have to balance the material and spiritual life. We must exercise caution in not getting carried away by meditating too much or too often.

We can, however, accomplish a great deal in a single meditation period. We ought to relax and allow ourselves to be in God's care for a short period of time. We need to come to our Higher Power in a mood of humble expectancy. Further, meditation is listening. Therefore, we can expect to be passive, rather than actively talking to our Creator. When we wish to talk to God, we refer to that as prayer, and as we sit quietly each day, we may do a little of both prayer and meditation. However, be aware that we haven't meditated if we haven't learned to be still and listen to the voice within us.

There is also what is known as active meditation, in which we may interact with others. Communication with others in meditation can be a very effective way to deal with situations that are awkward, uncomfortable or impossible to confront physically. For example, if we've had a misunderstanding with someone and feel it's not appropriate or timely to call them up and discuss the situation openly, we may talk to them by calling on their spirit. How does one go about doing this?

In order to speak to someone on the spiritual level, we may simply visualize the individual, telling him or her we would like to talk. The individual will then appear to us as we close our eyes. At this time we may open a conversation, saying anything we wish to say, being as honest as we can without becoming hurtful. We must never dump negative energy onto anyone, but we may tell someone we are angry or hurt or whatever we need to say to convey our true feelings. Everything we send out comes back to us, so we must be careful how we talk to others on the spiritual level.

Then we may wait for answer. Often people will answer us. We have only to trust and believe in our ability to receive such messages from spirit. But we must also remember to ask for divine protection before doing any spiritual work.

There are times we may need to reach someone and a phone call is impractical or impossible. We may tell them spiritually what we have to say. Perhaps we can't make our appointment with them on time. This is an opportunity to let them know without actually reaching them on the physical level. We may also wish to encourage someone or tell him or her we care and wish them well. Perhaps we wish to send love—which we can do by visualizing a pink light of love going from our heart to another's—or apologize to someone for something. All this is possible and encouraged. And those who receive our messages, if those messages are properly sent, will receive them either consciously or unconsciously.

If the person we send to meditates regularly and has developed his psychic abilities to some degree, he may indeed receive our message just as though we had picked up the phone and talked to them. Others will receive it on an unconscious level. Nevertheless, it is still an effective way to communicate.

When we are having a difficult time in a relationship, this tool is an excellent way to communicate. It is important to remember that those people who give us trouble are our teachers and we should acknowledge that fact as we talk to them.

If we wish to heal a relationship, we may follow these steps: 1) Ask for divine protection. 2) Visualize the person. 3) Tell him or her how we are feeling honestly without dumping negative energy. 4) Indicate that we recognize that he is our teacher, but remind him that we are also his teacher, so we need to be honest with him. 5) Tell him we are doing our best to forgive him as God forgives, even though it may be very difficult. We may let him know how hard it is. This is the time for honesty. 6) Ask that healing be sent to the relationship. The other person may not accept this healing yet, and that's OK. We are doing our part. 7) Wait for a response if we choose to.

This is a very helpful exercise. When we "take care of business" on the spiritual level, we free ourselves from carrying around a lot of extra baggage that can end up as tension or disease within the physical body.

We may also help ourselves by sending love and protection to ourselves and others. Love is the most powerful force in the universe and may be sent to anyone at any time. Those who receive it can feel love. It can be both personal and universal. Personal love will be received as coming from the sender, while universal love is impersonal but enables the receiver to feel more loving. We may wish, for instance, to send love to our child if we've had a misunderstanding and fear we may have been hurtful without meaning to.

We may also send divine protection to ourselves and those we care about. Protection can be physical or non-physical. We may place protection around anything or anyone simply by asking God that it be there. We may wish to request God's protection around our husband, our child, our house, or our car. If something should happen to something or someone around whom we've asked that protection be placed, it simply means that higher laws have overridden the protective force. If it is our time to leave the earthly plane, our asking for protection will not prevent the car accident that was meant to take us out of the physical body. It was simply our time.

We need to remember that accidents and illness have their place in life and can act as teachers for us. When we become ill, it slows us down, does it not? Perhaps we need to be slowed down. Maybe there is something we need to deal with—something we're pushing aside that requires our attention. In any case, divine protection can save us from disaster or small mishaps, but higher laws will ensure that we get the lesson we need for our growth. All is indeed in divine order. There are no mistakes in God's world. What happens, happens for a reason.

Another way in which divine protection can help us has to do with the protection of the spiritual body. Let's say we are recovering alcoholics and need to go into a bar for some reason. Asking for spiritual protection from our Creator will help protect us from temptation or discomfort if we fear we may be uneasy there.

We may also ask for protection from being drained psychically by others. There are times when people unknowingly drain our energy. We can merely be in their presence sometimes and we go home feeling exhausted. We may be protected from this phenomenon if we ask. We can also ask for protection, for example, when we go to the mall, or when we're in a crowd. Here is a situation in which we may be bombarded by the thoughts and feelings of others; again, we go home drained. At times the news on television is so depressing it tends to wear us down. We can ask for protection from this as well. It's good to be able to listen to the information without becoming depressed by it. Much can be written about the use of protection, which, incidentally, can be sent to anyone at any time without fear of intruding on that person's space.

We can also ask that healing be sent to others. However, here we must remember that not everyone is ready for a healing. We may ask that a person accept our healing energy as that person desires it. We don't force healing onto people. The person's higher self will monitor the healing sent, giving it when and where it is needed.

We may also ask that direction be sent to ourselves and others. This is fairly self-explanatory. It simply means that we have asked to be guided during our day so that we will know which step to take next.

Indeed, there is so much we may gain from meditation. We may heal ourselves through listening to the inner voice that helps us become aware of who we are. We are able to gain knowledge, strength, and enlightenment as we open our psychic centers using that divine spiritual self that is separate from the physical or material body. We may also gain comfort as we sense that wondrous communion with spirit that lets us know that we are not alone. We can learn, as well, to love, as we send love out to ourselves and to others. Remembering that everything we give comes back to us reminds us of our responsibilities to ourselves and those around us. Time spent in meditation when we learn to share ourselves spiritually with others as a pure unselfish act of love teaches us much about who we are as children of God and what we are capable of becoming.

ON DOUBT

As we seek within, we occasionally run into doubt. It can be troublesome. Our fears and hesitations, whether they are about ourselves, our abilities, or our spiritual philosophy, can be either easily overcome—or downright paralyzing.

Our doubts can cause us problems that can hold us back on our path. However, as we work through them, we discover many things about ourselves that can be rewarding. It's better to look upon our doubts as stepping stones or opportunities to discover more about ourselves as we journey forward.

Our confusion, if regarded properly, can bring us fresh knowledge that can lay the groundwork for a new and solid belief in oneself and one's abilities. Actually, our doubts, however subtle, and whether they have to do with our abilities or our faith, can be looked upon as blessings. Once they are confronted and overcome, we become stronger and clearer than ever before. They allow us to explore more deeply ourselves, our processes, and our purpose. We may come to see more clearly how best to use our talents and abilities and where it is most appropriate to use our gifts at any given time.

It's great, for example, to be able to do many things, but at the same time it isn't wise to scatter oneself trying to do too much: important projects are in danger of being pushed aside. It is helpful to be focused if we plan to accomplish something worthwhile in our lives. We need to be able to say, "I will focus on this now. It is important, and perhaps these other things I wish to do as well will have to take a back seat for awhile." If we try to do too much, our doubts about our abilities in all areas are apt to increase. In other words, we are treading on thin ice if we try to do too much. We are in danger of not doing justice to anything.

Again, however, our doubts can actually cause us to grow, for as we hesitate, we examine ourselves and our issues more clearly. A doubt in one's abilities can be looked upon as a handicap that causes us to slow down, almost compelling us to study in depth the world through which we move so carefully.

Most of our doubts, particularly about ourselves and our abilities, may be temporary. But as we delve into their cause, wonderful things can be discovered that help to bring us even further along our path. That which we discover can lead to greater self-awareness. That, in turn, can open doors to other aspects of ourselves and to opportunities that we never knew existed.

It's important, therefore, to see our doubts as stepping stones to greater self-awareness and greater opportunities to become even stronger in our beliefs and our abilities than ever before. Our misgivings actually help to strengthen us. They give us further confidence and understanding of ourselves. Further, they help to make us aware of our responsibility to ourselves and our world by ultimately forcing us to use our talents and abilities to confront the confusion within us.

If we continue to grow along the path, each of our doubts will give way to greater strength and clarity as we pause to examine its cause. As we seek God's help in understanding the reasons for our hesitations, we can overcome our dilemmas.

We all want to move forward, but at times we are confronted by fears which may even be subconscious. Their cause seems to be hidden far back in our past. Our fear may be due to an experience that was unpleasant. Some individuals believe we bring with us, buried deep within our subconscious, memories of past lives that affect how we react to circumstances today. Therefore, often when it appears that something should be easy for us and a natural opportunity to get ahead, we find ourselves nearly incapacitated and unable to discover the cause of our dilemma. The next step requires that we pray about it, asking for help and guidance in being able to remove whatever obstacle is in our way.

We needn't always know, and may never know consciously, what has been holding us back, but if we are willing to ask for help and then let go, leaving the problem in God's hands, things can work out for us. Once the cause of our fears is removed we will be clearer than ever and moving forward will be easy for us.

There are also times in our lives when we may doubt our spiritual philosophy. In other words, our faith becomes shaken or we find ourselves wondering if it is all really true. Do we really believe that the laws of the universe work as we've been taught? "Can I really be prosperous? Can I really bring love into my life by simply sending out love to others? Do I really have a purpose in life, and am I really that important to the whole? Can I actually become better at what I do by visualizing and affirming my own success?"

We doubt these things at times because we doubt the divine power that we are. We forget that we are co-creators with God. We forget that we are "Gods in the making," as Scripture states. We forget our divine heritage. We forget that we need not look outside of ourselves to find strength, peace, confidence, and faith in ourselves. We forget that our Higher Power is not outside of us, but within us. We don't have to run here and there seeking affirmation and approval.

All we need is within us. That divine spark which is part of God is still a part of us. Becoming aware of this, and accepting who we are and the responsibilities that come with being willing to express ourselves, we will find ourselves growing. Being willing to confront our doubts, which are really opportunities for further self-awareness and greater clarity, we will find great joy as we begin fulfilling the pattern of our soul. And in doing so, we allow ourselves to complete our mission which was started as we entered life.

Therefore, as our doubts beset us, let's not be dismayed by them, but let's instead be grateful for the opportunity to learn greater truth as a veil of doubt is lifted from us.

ON INSPIRATION

How may we be inspired? Inspiration strikes us in many different ways. One is through people. By watching what others do and accomplish, we may be encouraged to continue on our path, or perhaps move in a new direction. Seeing what others have created motivates us to use our own gifts.

On the other hand, we may be influenced by what others seem to be lacking. As we are aware of people's wasting their talents and abilities, we may wish to remind ourselves not to make the same mistake. Thus we follow the example of others, both in the positive and negative sense, and are impressed one way or another by their behavior.

Often, too, as we look back upon our lives, especially to the successes we've enjoyed, there has been someone who has served as an inspiration to us by helping to set us on the right path through example or encouragement.

How else may we be inspired? It is well known that music of all kinds is a source of inspiration. Different kinds of music can inspire us in various ways. Perhaps we have trouble getting going in the morning, so we turn on lively music to wake us up. Perhaps we like to unwind at a certain time during the day and find that classical or other soft music can relax us.

Music can put us into all kinds of moods and inspire and motivate us in very powerful ways. It can affect the heart by helping us to feel more loving and open to ourselves and others. It can also give us a feeling of hope. It can lift us out of our depression, as well as help us complete a chore by encouraging us to stick to the task at hand. Music can open creative channels, allowing us to discover more about ourselves, as well as to heal our wounds of the past. Finally, certain kinds of music can encourage us to move forward with courage and confidence. In other words, as we are attuned to the vibrations of different kinds of music, we can be inspired on many levels.

Another way we may be inspired is through nature. We are all aware of this when we sit by a lake and gaze at the water, allowing feelings of peace to come over us. And we have all experienced the serenity of a meadow or the calming effects of a stream or the security of the grass beneath our feet. We have felt the strength we gather from being in the shade of a giant tree. The magnificent force of the tree seems to tell us that beneath these branches lie strength and protection. In the same way, the ocean sends a message of timelessness and reminds us of Creator's power.

Nature can indeed heal us. As we are rejuvenated, we feel inspired to move ahead on our path without fear. We are encouraged as we think about taking that next step because we have allowed nature to inspire us, giving us a feeling of confidence and a broader perspective on our lives.

Nature has also been known to build us up when we require encouragement. This helps bring us peace. We discover our place in the universe. We know who we are and where we are going. Having this perspective can lift us to greater heights: our lives are in balance and our hearts are at one with our Creator.

Becoming aware of spiritual truth can also be inspiring to us. As we hear truth, we can become relaxed because there is no fear connected with truth. We let out a sigh of relief when we hear a message of truth. Truth allows us to say, "I am OK," or, "I will be all right," or, "All is well." Truth informs us that there is, in fact, nothing to worry about.

If we hear a message of truth and become upset and fearful, we have not heard the truth. Truth is often misinterpreted, not only by the people who hear it, but also by those who supposedly are speaking truth. Truth properly spoken and received will always bring peace. Sometimes, too, we hear only a portion of the truth and, as a result, it may sound negative to us. Again, only messages of truth delivered in their entirety will bring real peace and comfort.

Similarly, the beauty we find in art—in painting, sculpture, or another medium—can be inspirational. A tall building or beautiful cathedral clearly speaks to us. Even an effort to make something out of cloth that takes much creative ability, time, and diligence can be inspiring by reminding us of our vast capabilities for creative endeavor. We may be awed by our power to create as we survey the world around us. This thought can inspire us to better ourselves so that we may enjoy and appreciate all that we have been given. Thus, inspiration comes in many ways, providing us with opportunities to co-create with the Source.

ON TOLERANCE

Making our journey along the spiritual path, we discover our need to become tolerant. There will be those who may oppose our efforts to improve ourselves or who may disagree with our methods or our philosophy. They may wish to warn us that we're going down a forbidden road or opening ourselves to danger as we discover the need to seek within for our answers. As we hear their protests, we need to be tolerant —even though we do not accept it as our own.

There are many who fear seeking within their own being, fearing what they may find there. Consequently, they prefer to believe, experience, and read about only what others tell them is safe for them. They may prefer an outside source to outline what is right for them and what is not. Their belief is legitimate and indeed appropriate in their present stage of evolution. For this soul to press further at this time may indeed not be timely.

We must experience truth as our soul dictates. We will draw situations, conditions, and experiences from which to learn. And if we are at a stage where meditation would be advantageous to us and if we are willing to pursue our development, we will attract a teacher in the form either of a person or perhaps a book to help us get started.

Often people change course somewhere along the path, and this can also be a part of the soul's plan: it needs certain experiences to fulfill itself. Sometimes people appear to make drastic changes in their spiritual outlook. These changes may seem sudden, but actually the process of change may have been occurring over a long period of time. It has only the appearance of being a recent development. Therefore, although we may feel our way to be the only way, we must take care to recognize the rights of others to choose their own path.

If one is sincere about his faith, he will be following the prompting of his soul. He will be drawn to the situation that can give him the most benefit at a given time. We are not all alike, nor do we grow in the same way. Instead, we are each unique and have our own timetable. Some persons may seem to be working very rapidly on improving their lives, while others appear to be taking their time.

However, we must be careful not to judge. Appearances can be deceiving. Furthermore, we can't really know where a person is spiritually. Sometimes an individual may appear to be quite lacking in spiritual values. Yet what we are witnessing is the personality playing out its role in this lifetime. The actual soul may be far more developed and evolved than we imagine.

Certainly we realize that people can behave poorly and need to be reprimanded by the law. Yet these persons may be gathering experience or playing their part, while the "real" person or spiritual being behind the mask may be quite different. Naturally, we have to respond to what we see, yet it helps us be more tolerant to understand that the entire soul isn't represented.

The person who is behaving badly may be showing only a small fraction of his real identity. This person may be likened to a large tapestry that appears at a glance to be very beautiful. Looking at the whole, we are hardly able to discern the flaw. We have to search in order to find it.

Therefore, let's refrain from criticism as we look at others. When we judge, we bring judgment upon ourselves. The process becomes a circle, as does everything that we send out into the universe. If we become intolerant, we invite intolerance. We can ignore this law, but it won't ignore us. We can doubt it, even disobey it. Yet it doesn't matter: it's still the law.

As we become more open to others—accepting their ways and points of view while still holding to our own as it feels right for us—we discover that a whole new world awaits us. We let go of our fear of differences and move into a consciousness that brings us freedom. We breathe easier. Our heart is more open. As we allow others to think, feel, and believe, we allow ourselves the same feeling of freedom. We are then able to open up and experience all that has been awaiting us.

Our thoughts and attitudes can make or break our way to experiencing the freedom we desire. Therefore, as we allow others to grow, we will open up the way to freedom within our own being. Conversely, if we are judgmental, critical, or intolerant of others, we will be locking ourselves in. We will be preventing ourselves from experiencing fully the beauty of life.

This is not an easy process, but awareness is the first step. Once we are aware that we are responsible for our own ability to feel and express freely, we can take steps to eliminate the errors of judgment in our thinking that keep us like a bird in a cage, unable to experience fully the joy of living.

In time we will learn to be tolerant of others who may be in a different stage of development and who may be expressing themselves differently than we do through their beliefs, attitudes, and awareness. As our tolerance increases, we will become aware that we have indeed learned to love, which is the highest expression of who we really are. Our true nature as spiritual beings dictates that there is no real difference between us.

Therefore, as I look at you, I see myself. I can't hurt you without hurting myself, and I can't love you without first loving myself. We are indeed One. And as we are One, there is no need for tolerance because there is no difference between us. What we are seeing is an illusion that needs to be fostered on earth in order to get beyond it. Love can only be created out of fear that has been overcome.

ON REINCARNATION

Have we lived before? Many think we have; others deny it. If so, what could be the purpose of making many appearances on the earth plane? Why would we need to keep coming back to experience the same emotional drama over and over?

We might ask ourselves why basketball games are played over and over. Do we learn something different each time we play? Do we help ourselves become better players? Do we understand more things about ourselves each time we play? Do we learn about our limitations as well? And each time we practice, do we attempt to refine the skills we have, so that our game will improve and we'll be able to better assist our fellow players, as well as make a mark for ourselves? Obviously, we make progress through practice in all of these areas.

However, even the best players need time on the bench and a chance to rest. We need time to reassess where we might have gone wrong. We need time off the court to look at ourselves and study, with the help of our coach, how we may improve our next performance. Without some time out, we would not allow ourselves the proper time to assess our mistakes, as well as our progress. With the help of our coach and perhaps a videotaped review of our last game, we may pick up many pointers that assist us in avoiding similar mistakes in the future. And even though it is a new game with different players, perhaps even in a different town, the rules of the game haven't changed and the basic principles stay the same.

Coming back into a new earthly life for those who accept the view of reincarnation is much the same. We have had a rest—time off in which to sort things out and plan, with the help of other wise souls, our next experience living in human form on earth. Had we not had this break we would become "tired" and would be endlessly repeating the same mistakes.

According to those who adhere to the theory of rebirth, we learn a great deal from repetition. Therefore, as we attempt to learn our lessons—which we must do if we are going to evolve as spiritual beings—many lifetimes are necessary in order to gain sufficient experience to merit our return to the Source.

However, experience, they say, is not enough. We require opportunities of the kind that instruct and encourage us to become all we can be. Further, our experiences help to make us aware of who we are and where we are going, and in order that this can be accomplished, we must be drawn into situations that help us to grow. Therefore, we will return often with the same souls we have known before. Some of them may have challenged us in past times and some may have been our friends.

Those who believe in reincarnation claim that this why we often have a vague sense of recognition about people whom we meet. We may be very comfortable with them, or we may feel uneasy in their presence. Whatever the case may be, we generally form friendships in groups, according to feelings of mutual attraction based on our past experience.

Oftentimes, groups, such as hunting clubs or civic organizations that come together for a specific purpose, have their origin in the past. The group "agenda" may also parallel its previous content. Furthermore, the people we meet may often have "business" with us. They may be here to support us or bring us opportunity and challenge in order that we may grow.

All of life is continually attempting to maintain balance, as are we in our relationship to God, to ourselves, and to those around us. Where the scales have been tipped, there needs to be a shift in the opposite direction so the balance may be restored. This process often involves painful lessons.

Many who hold to the theory of reincarnation claim that their belief is based upon an intuitive thought or feeling. It is something they know deep within themselves, while others feel it is not a fact at all, but an excuse which people use to explain their lives and perhaps excuse their behavior.

We would be wise to consider both points of view, remembering to be tolerant of any differences. We still have lessons and opportunities in either case. Nothing changes that. Whether we believe in reincarnation or not should affect us little. If we are consciously on a spiritual path, we're doing the best we can to improve our lives. Thus, our learning and growth continue whether we have further appearances on earth or choose to continue growth in the spirit world.

Perfection is our goal. As we align our purpose with our Creator's will, we will reach that goal when we have gained sufficient knowledge and experience that teaches us to love.

BOOK SIX

ON EMPOWERMENT

What does it mean to be empowered? Where does the power come from? To be empowered spiritually means to accept and use God's energy as it is given to us each day. It means that we must let go of the material mind and align ourselves with the God of our own understanding, trusting in that divine spark within us.

It means letting go of our will, turning it over to the will of the Creator who directs our lives and shows us the way to freedom. And how do we become free? We become free by allowing Spirit to work through us. For as we do, we allow ourselves to be led. We find that we are in the right place at the right time, doing that which is appropriate for us.

We are free because we are not putting limits on ourselves. We are not allowing the material mind or the will to stand in the way of our success. Instead, we are trusting that our Higher Power will show us the way. Therefore, our success is ensured. In other words, we don't allow fear to curtail our ability to progress. We are limitless. The spiritual body knows no bounds, so with divine power anything and everything is possible.

However, as we are learning to trust in this power, we make mistakes. Consequently, when we err, we must pay the price. That is the universal and unchanging law. Though we don't often intentionally set out to break the law, we must learn our lessons. Thus, it is often through experiencing the feelings that accompany our doing the wrong thing that we learn to do the right thing. For example, if we eat something that disagrees with us, we will experience indigestion. Further, it makes no difference whether we are aware of our sensitivity or not. In other words, we pay the price whether or not we have knowledge of our mistakes.

For example, God doesn't say, "I won't make you suffer for eating this food because you didn't know of your sensitivity to it;" instead we simply experience the sick feeling that comes from ingesting the wrong foods. In this way, we learn to stay away from whatever is not good for us. God will allow us to suffer as long as we must in order to learn what we need to learn. We are not punished for our behavior. We are only allowed to feel the consequences of our actions. God does not judge. He loves us as His children. As a loving Energy, God allows us to have our experiences so that we may grow and be more like Him/Her.

Therefore, we have choices to make, lessons to learn, and abilities to develop all in regard to God's energy. How we handle that assignment will indicate how far we advance in this lifetime. We can dilly dally, waste time, make mistakes, and learn our lessons as slowly and reluctantly as we wish, or we can take charge of our lives in a mature, efficient manner.

We may assume a readiness to learn at a rate which is suitable for us so that we may accomplish all that we were meant to—and more, if we choose—in this life. All we must do is send out that very thought and then let go. The most amazing things can result. Many of us must be prepared to undergo some dramatic changes in our lives as we redirect our own energy and begin to discover who we are.

Aligning ourselves with our purpose can be as exciting as it is demanding. The rewards always outweigh the hardships as we take control of our lives. Contradictory as it may seem, we are essentially turning over that control to our Higher Power. We are allowing our director to direct the show while we go along for the ride. At times the ride is smooth. At other times it's a rocky road. Regardless of what the journey entails, we begin to see the changes in our lives take place.

Subsequently, we are amazed as we see relationships heal and lives transformed when we place ourselves in God's hands. We learn to trust that each step we take will bring us farther down the path as we learn to let go and have faith in the Divine Power that leads us. We still make mistakes, but we may take satisfaction in the learning that comes from our increased awareness. We can be grateful for the understanding we gain from each experience we have along our path.

ON SELF-PITY

All of us have times when we're apt to feel a bit sorry for ourselves. We struggle along sometimes, feeling alone and without exact knowledge of where we're going or how we're going to get there.

Sometimes we feel discouraged, believing no one cares or understands us. Then there are times when we wonder whether the struggle is worth it. We have our doubts about whether or not we're ever going to be happy or feel successful in our lives. We wonder whether we'll have the material things we desire. We become even more discouraged when we see other people appearing to be well adjusted, active, and busy. The conditions in their lives seem ordered and harmonious, and even if they're not, others somehow seem to be handling their problems better than we are. We feel at a loss and can't seem to see a way out. There are times we wish we could just disappear. We're sure no one would miss us a great deal. It seems all we do is work hard and never seem to get anywhere. Everyone else seems to be getting along so much better than we are. They seem to have things to look forward to and things they enjoy doing.

Often when we're feeling sorry for ourselves we can't even think of what we would like to do. Usually the things we come up with are fairly out of our reach or really not appropriate for us anyway. Furthermore, if we could do those things, we wouldn't really enjoy them because they're not for us.

So what can we do? How do we cope with the indecision, low self-esteem and boredom that come with feeling sorry for ourselves? How do we get over the loneliness and despair? How do we stop struggling and start living? How can we begin to change these self-destructive patterns? For it's true that if we want to change, we will have to work at it.

People who feel sorry for themselves generally have a history of this self-destructive tendency. Therefore, they continually attract situations in their lives that will bear out their feelings of low self-worth. If we send out the thought to the universe that we feel sorry for ourselves and that life has been unkind to us, we will continue to attract what we claim to be. The universe will never fail to respond.

If we happen, on the other hand, to be very positive, secure persons, our world will reflect these traits. We will surround ourselves with positive, affirming people. We'll have a job, if we work, which will be satisfying because we have created it. Further, we will look forward to the future because we are secure. We know it will be bright and that we will be able to handle any potential crisis that comes along. In short, we will be at peace with ourselves.

However, if we tend to feel sorry for ourselves, the scenario is different. Because we are fearful and negative, we will draw situations that hold this kind of challenge. We will draw situations we feel we can't handle because of our insecurities. We will also attract conditions in our life that affirm our dislike of ourselves and our criticism of others.

Our self-pity continues because we find we don't cope well with the normal challenges of everyday life. This is understandable. It's difficult to battle negative forces day after day. Negativity will be coming from both within and without. The negative energies within us can drain us, while that which we attract on account of our attitude will increase our uncomfortable feeling with life in general. No wonder we get tired.

We can also become bored because we've allowed ourselves to get into a terrible rut. Our repetitive pattern of negativity becomes a burden that even we can't carry, let alone those around us. People begin to notice our sour mood and may comment, even if lightheartedly, on our attitude.

Finally, one day we are openly confronted with our behavior. Someone says something to us that wakes us up, or perhaps the occasion is even more dramatic. Maybe our spouse says he or she is tired of our grumpy, negative behavior and threatens to leave. Something happens that snaps us out of our lethargy. Finally we're a bit scared. We have been "found out." It's time to change and we know it. The clock has run out. What can we do? Now that we're finally willing to make an effort, how do we do it? All we know is that we're frightened.

How do we change? It seems as though it will take such effort. "What's on the other side for me? Is it worth it? How can I pretend to be happy when I'm not? How do I become more content with my lot in life? After all, what is the meaning of it all? Why are we here? What is it all about? Is there any purpose to it all? What do I do next?"

These are some of the questions that occur to us as we're about to take that first step toward liberating ourselves. Becoming willing is the first step. Then we must admit that we can't do it on our own. We need help. This help may come from a therapist or a good friend. Maybe we call on our Creator right away, eliminating the "middle man." Whatever the case may be, we are looking for help from a power greater than ourselves. God often speaks through others, so if we've picked someone who is "tuned in" to their own source of help and is able to blend harmoniously with us, we will have found a worthwhile friend in whom we can confide.

Finding a suitable confidant is very important. The wrong person can lead us astray, sometimes getting us into deeper trouble than we were in. A positive person who listens carefully and allows us our feelings is important. After all, isn't that what our Creator does? We don't need a judge. We need a friend who can objectively assess our situation and offer help or suggestions as we ask for them.

Once we have clarified our situation in our mind, we can ask ourselves how we want to be, how we want to look, feel, and act. Sure, we may have to keep our present job for the moment. But what other things do we want to add to our lives?

Have we always wanted to paint, but never got into it? Here's our chance. Do we really like to ice skate because it makes us feel good? Or would we like to take a course in upholstering furniture? Now is the time. Maybe we would like to attend a workshop on how to become prosperous. Whatever it takes, we should look at the things we would like to do naturally, without effort, and get into them. Then we can visualize ourselves—our body image. How do we wear our hair? Would it be appropriate to change our hairdo? Are we satisfied with our figure and how we feel? We must begin to see where we'd like to make changes and set about doing it.

It's very beneficial to create visions of ourselves in quiet moments alone, seeing ourselves exactly how we would like to be, feeling how we want to feel. This adds energy to our visualization. We affirm to ourselves, out loud, anything we wish to become. "I am beautiful. I like myself. I believe in my abilities. I am kind and gentle."

As we affirm who we are, we will start believing it. We will no longer feel sorry for ourselves. How can we, when we are so busy doing the things we always wanted to do? How can we be unhappy when we have affirmed and created a new identity—one that has much self-love and inner beauty? How can we wish we were someone else when we are happy to be ourselves?

The only way to go is up now. There is no turning back. The person that was is gone, never to return, and the real self is emerging. This is the person who was always meant to be. That other person was only a part of the whole, only a small flaw in the tapestry of our existence—one sour note in the symphony. So we can forgive ourselves and continue playing. This time we're on key.

Jill Downs

ON HUMILITY

What does it mean to be humble? People sometimes confuse humility with putting themselves down. They confuse having humility with low self-esteem—something entirely different. Humility is a desirable condition; feeling poorly about oneself is not. When we are humble, we are grateful. When we have low self-esteem, gratitude escapes us: we don't feel there is much about which we can be grateful. Humility bears fruit, but when we put ourselves down we gain nothing worthwhile in the process.

To be humble ensures that we are "in the right place." We are seeing ourselves in the proper perspective in relationship to the whole of life. We don't feel "better than" or "worse than" the rest of created beings, and we are grateful for who we are and what we have.

There are times when to be humble offers a challenge to us, particularly when we are in a position in which we are more knowledgeable, more capable, more talented, better looking, more prosperous or have more opportunities than those around us. This perception may be ours alone or others may share it. In other words, it may be a true assessment of oneself based on fact, or it may not be. It really doesn't matter: it is what we do with it that counts.

Everything is relative. We may be rich or considered wealthy in our neighborhood or town, but seen as middle class somewhere else. We may be regarded as smart in the school we attended in our earlier years, but be an average student somewhere else. We may be a very talented musician but appear to be lacking in talent at a school for musicians only. In other words, life is a matter of perspective.

Similarly, we may feel that we are better than others are, or more talented, or better able to do a job. However, our perspective may not reveal the truth. In any case, it's the attitude we carry about ourselves that reflects whether our spiritual perspective is correct or not. We may be an artist or we may be mediocre, but if we acknowledge within our heart and mind that our talent is a gift from God, then we are demonstrating an accurate spiritual perspective. Whether our material assessment of our worth is accurate or inaccurate is not important. It is how we see ourselves in relation to the whole of life that indicates our spiritual maturity.

As we grow spiritually, our lives become better in all ways. We learn to work with the universal laws. In other words, as we learn to work in harmony with ourselves, with others, with our environment and the world, we become spiritually richer. Because of this personal advancement, however, there is a temptation at times to think that we have done this. We wish to take credit for our newly found success, forgetting that we have had a partner.

We didn't get here by ourselves. We didn't come alone to this new understanding of life that has brought us such peace and fulfillment. No. We were led. Sometimes we were even carried. At other times we were dragged, kicking and screaming, along the path. In fact, our resistance at times has been so strong that we've wanted to stop, turn around, and go back. However, we momentarily forget all this. And when someone says "Your life seems to be going so well. How have you come so far?" secretly, even if only for a moment, we want to take full credit for all the wonderful things that have been happening to us. We think for a moment that it was all our intelligent thinking and planning that brought about such change. Or perhaps we want to attribute our success to our ability to "stick to it." Some of this type of reasoning may be true: we are co-creators. But very little of the credit is actually ours.

During our lifetime there are moments when we have great help of which we are completely unaware. We have been protected from potential accidents that would otherwise have killed us. We've been saved from intruders and protected from disasters that we did not even realize existed. We have been steered away from people, situations, and conditions that could have made things difficult for us.

There are some things we need to experience, of course, because they are on our path in life. We cannot be protected from all the situations that we don't like. However, upon later scrutiny we find we still benefited from such experiences and conclude they must have been there for us to learn from. How cherished we are. We are watched over carefully. Our every move is known, and nothing escapes our Creator's watchful eye. If we truly knew all that could have happened if our protective forces had not been with us, we would find being humble an easier path. From our present perspective we feel we are "running the show" to a much greater extent than we are. Many times we would be better off doing nothing and letting spirit take charge. We find at times that we are running around aimlessly, plotting and planning, spending much time in grandiose attempts to manipulate our lives or the lives of others—to no avail. We are going around in circles, blind to the futility of our own actions and wasting our energy. We fail to see that what we want to happen is not, for some reason, meant to happen. Nothing we can ever do can make things come out "our way" in some circumstances. Our salvation lies in our surrender.

Humility comes with learning to let go. When we admit defeat, we allow new energy to rush in. The universe takes over, and knowledge that feels risky to us is really our salvation. Once we let go and make that leap across the abyss, we have found safety and security in a new place, and all is well.

Where do we learn humility? Nature teaches us to be humble as we watch its beauty as well as its destructive power. We are humbled by the wisdom of children. We are humbled as we watch the lives of others turn into disaster by an earthquake or war. We are humbled as we see an airplane full of hundreds of people crash in an instant, killing all on board. We are humbled when we see a butterfly dance on the porch screen. We are humbled as we watch the sunset and see the dawn of a new day.

We are humbled by all of these things that we encounter each day we are alive. It's a wonder we think we do anything alone. When we recognize the power that's available to us, who would want to?

ON GRATITUDE

Why is gratitude important for spiritual growth? Being grateful for what we have creates an opportunity for more to be given. We must have an attitude of gratitude if we expect to keep on receiving. Being grateful means that we're being humble—that we've accepted our rightful place in God's kingdom. Gratitude says that we know we aren't running the show and are willing to acknowledge our Higher Power.

Acknowledging God's power is essential if one is on a spiritual path. The more we recognize the presence of this power, the more we get in touch with what it can do for us. Further, as we work in harmony and cooperation with the forces that aid and protect us, the more we find we can accomplish. And as we do, we must thank God for helping us complete our path, whatever it may be.

For what are we grateful? We can be grateful just to be here. We can be grateful for the opportunity to experience our lifetime here on earth. It's important to remember that we chose this opportunity. We chose, as well, some of the people with whom we would share our dream, as well as the circumstances of our lives.

In other words, we have to set the stage for the play in which we are the major performers. We called in the other actors and helped to assign the roles each would take. We played a part in deciding who would be most appropriate to star in the other leading roles with us. We helped in setting the scene, the time period, the background, as well as choosing the crew who would help backstage. However, although we assisted in creating our play, we remained well aware that we were not directing it.

As spiritual beings on the earthly plane, we are here to grow. We don't grow unless we have something or someone motivating us. We need an impetus to grow—a challenge. Otherwise, we would sit idly by not doing much of anything except, perhaps, getting ourselves into trouble. Therefore, as we picked our cast of characters we set about to choose a villain or two to challenge us and help us to grow. These difficult people or circumstances in our lives act as teachers because they offer us knowledge about life and ourselves. Actually, they are blessings in disguise, because without them we would not be able to move forward as we hoped to.

In order to progress on the spiritual path we have to pass certain requirements. As we pass the tests in any given path of life, we move forward in that area. Conversely, when we fail a test we stay "stuck" and keep repeating the same experience until we get it right. There is no failure, as we might think of failure. There is only the inability to move forward—to go into the next grade. Eventually, however, we will succeed. It is, moreover, only a matter of time until we graduate completely from our earth experience and move on to a new existence elsewhere. It is the difficult teachers in our lives who provide us with this opportunity for growth. They deserve our gratitude.

Perhaps the villain was our father. Maybe he caused us to feel inferior much of our life. Perhaps he put us down, telling us we'd never amount to anything and we believed him. Now we are adults and realize that we must overcome the effect his behavior had on us. We realize how silly it is to believe that we should be unworthy for any reason. Yet we still have to overcome the emotional scars with which he left us. Our challenge is to learn to love and accept ourselves under all conditions and believe in ourselves and our abilities. It's only in this way that we will benefit from the opportunity this teacher has brought to us. Through playing his role perfectly, he has assisted us in our growth and actually done us a great favor.

We can also say, "Thank you" for other circumstances in our

lives. We have been born rich, poor, or middle class. We may have several brothers and sisters or we may be an only child. We may have a very harmonious family in which there is lots of love and acceptance. We may, on the other hand, live in a family in which there is discord, much quarreling and tension.

There may be some family members with whom we get along well—but there may be one who really gets us down. We all have a challenge somewhere.

We will have some positive, as well as negative, aspects in our lives as well. Perhaps we're very talented or intelligent—talents which give us an opportunity to create something worthwhile for ourselves. Or perhaps we are fortunate materially, which means we need not focus on that part of our lives while we need to be taking care to improve in other areas. (However, extreme wealth can bring its own lessons with which we have to deal.) Maybe we're blessed with good health, so that being sick is not an issue we have to confront on a daily basis.

Often, that which we have, we have earned. We must earn the opportunities to be healthy, wealthy, or wise. These gifts don't just come to us. They are usually the result of working diligently on ourselves over a period of time. However, this fact doesn't mean that if we see someone who is relatively poor, he hasn't earned the right to be prosperous. It may mean that he is choosing that condition to learn something else. Perhaps by not having many material goods, he is developing humility. Whatever the case may be, we can't judge another's situation: we don't have all the information. We know only what we see. That which is apparent to us may not represent the truth.

Our circumstances, therefore, are designed specifically by us and for us. We can be grateful for the people as well as the conditions that help us grow. Both the positive and the negative circumstances in our lives are important to us. We need both. And as we progress, we can thank God for the opportunity to serve others as well. For it is as we help to heal others that we ourselves are healed.

In brief, as we deal with the challenges, teachers, and circumstances in our lives, let's be grateful, remembering that one day our life will be over. We'll be able to look back and thank all who were in our play. We'll be grateful to our director, as well as to ourselves, for the opportunity to experience a fine performance. Lastly, as we review our life with the wise souls who help counsel us, we can be grateful for the greater knowledge and understanding our earth experience has brought us.

ON INTUITION

What does it mean to follow one's intuition? Is it safe to follow the inner voice? Does it lead us along the right path? How accurate is it? Can we dispense with using our mind and our logic and go with the thoughts and impressions that come from another source—our intuition? People have been laughed at for following the inner voice. And yet those who had the courage to follow the wisdom spoken to them through their intuition have accomplished great things.

Usually this inner wisdom defies logical thought and reveals facts and offers suggestions on a course of action that often seems inappropriate, illogical and sometimes even irresponsible. It takes great courage to follow one's inner voice, especially where others are involved and are aware of the source of this information. Many prefer a more logical approach. They want to see proof, much as a scientist needs to measure the validity of his experiments. Yet there is no proof regarding intuition.

Perhaps we intuit that we should drive home from work in a different direction. Later on, we discover that there had been a terrible car accident that tied up traffic for hours where we were originally going.

Again, perhaps we feel that it's unwise to fly home on a certain day, so we cancel our plane ticket, only to discover later that the plane had crashed. Following the inner voice can, indeed, save our lives if we choose to listen to the wisdom it brings to us. Then again, perhaps we feel directed to go into a store that we normally wouldn't enter, but when we do, we find a particular item marked way down. This happened to be something we've been wanting, but have waited to shop for because of the expense involved.

These kinds of things happen to people every day. It is not an unusual occurrence for any of us. As we ask for guidance in our daily lives, we are constantly dealing with the opportunities our intuition presents us when we set aside our logical mind.

The problem is that very often we are unwilling to change our routine or alter our plans to follow our intuition. We say to ourselves, "What if I'm wrong? What will they think? Maybe I'll waste the whole day if I do this. Maybe this really isn't a good idea;" or, "I can't allow myself to take off and go along and enjoy myself. It's not like me to behave irresponsibly like this. Maybe it isn't right!" Yet, in a deeper sense, maybe it is.

Furthermore, it may be just the thing we need, and the timing of this mini-vacation may be just perfect where our employer is concerned. Perhaps he's in a very good mood now and just happens to be thinking we need a vacation. Perhaps later on, when our mind and powers of logic tell us it's time, our employer won't be ready to give us the time we feel we deserve. And we may not be as ready as we are now for a break.

Following intuition often demands that we change our routine. For those of us who like order and discipline, this is sometimes hard. On the other hand, those who think they are living intuitively may instead be avoiding getting their lives together and buckling down to what they need to be doing. They're procrastinating rather than following their intuition. It can be difficult at times to tell the difference.

There are situations in which our fear will prevent us from moving forward with something. We may be waiting for a strong intuitive feeling to go ahead in a new direction with some particular plan. We discover, as time goes on, that we aren't receiving this "bolt of lightning" to tell us when to start. Therefore, we take that as a sign that it's not yet time to take action.

However, it may be that, either consciously or subconsciously, we're afraid to begin for fear of failure, and we block any strong prompting from within. We may feel a vague sense that it's okay to move forward, but to actually take the steps necessary to begin becomes another matter.

We become stuck and unable to move ahead because our fear is blocking us. So how do we know what to do? The best thing to do is ask for continued roadblocks if it is, indeed, not time to move; and a push forward if it is actually time to go ahead. In this way, we will get the impetus we need.

Following our intuition often takes courage. But as we learn to go with it, we find that our life changes and becomes much more exciting as we discover the help we get. Our spirit forces that work with us are more than happy to show us the way. Further, as we are open to the guidance and direction from the Highest Light, which will be available to us, we are safe and in good hands. It's always wise to call on divine light to surround, help, guide, and direct us each day. It is also valuable to get to know the spirit forces that work with us so that we may feel familiar with the energy they impart. Then, as something unfamiliar enters our space, we may be alert to any changes as we attempt to discern the purpose of its presence and its value to us. As we grow spiritually, the energies we attract to us will change. As we move up the spiritual ladder, new guides and angels come in to guide us. These forces will always be appropriate to our progress.

Sometimes, as people move up the spiritual ladder, they feel comfortable and secure and thus become complacent. It is wise to keep up the practice of affirming divine light in our lives—always asking for the Highest Light to be with us and around us, and giving thanks to our Creator—for it will help make room for more blessings to come to us. Furthermore, we will come to trust our making wise choices based upon our own intuition.

BOOK SEVEN

ON HUMOR

Why is humor important as we make our spiritual journey up the mountain? How can humor help us to maintain a sense of balance?

First of all, humor helps by giving us a perspective on our life. We know how it feels when we're tense and anxious about ourselves and all that is going on around us, and suddenly someone tells a funny joke. Everything changes for that instant, and nothing seems so important that we can't laugh. As we do, the energy changes and for that moment our whole life takes on a new perspective. This process is healthy: we tend to be too serious at times, and as we do, we shift out of balance.

Our ability to play and enjoy life no matter what is going on is essential if we're going to accomplish our goals and complete our path. Joy is one of the qualities we all seek in life; it is the mark of a person who is spiritually fit. In other words, we may be undergoing all kinds of difficulties in out material life—problems with children, parents, or other family members. We can have problems at work or with health or with finances. Yet we are able to smile and laugh if we see our problems in the proper light. We understand that we may be learning from our particular situation, and it need not take our joy from us. Instead, we are able to detach ourselves from the worry and tension and see the positive side of every situation. We prefer to live in the light rather than dwell in darkness.

As a result, we can go through our lessons, viewing them not as stumbling blocks or punishment for past failures, but as opportunities for growth. We understand the rewards that come as we pass each test and focus on our progress as we climb each step of the ladder. We do not look down in fear at where we could fall should we fail, but instead keep looking upwards toward success, understanding that it is only a matter of time until we reach our goals.

If we knew, always, that success would be ours, how could we not laugh all the way to receive our reward? Why not enjoy life along the way?

Humor allows us the freedom to be who we are. Because we can laugh at ourselves, we can open the door to proper perspective and balance. We tend to see ourselves in the light, ensuring more accuracy in our assessment of our life conditions and situations involving others. Our relationships improve as we take ourselves a bit less seriously. We are more apt to admit our mistakes, and less apt to be rigid in our evaluations of others and ourselves.

When we judge ourselves too harshly and make judgments where others are concerned, we usually create unnecessary entanglements that prove to be negative. At the same time, we create additional problems for ourselves as we allow rigid opinions to dominate our thinking. It is best to leave judgments out of our thinking and instead allow others and ourselves the benefit of the doubt.

Having humor means we accept ourselves as we are and allow others to be themselves as well. We all have a right to be here and to express our thoughts. If others seem to get in the way, not being or expressing themselves as we would like, or interfering with the smoothness of our life, may they not be there to teach us something?

Often people who enter our lives, interfering with our security or serenity, are there to strengthen us in some way. And once we've gone through the opportunity to experience what they have to teach us, we can be grateful for the lesson. Perhaps there will be a similar situation that we must experience later in our journey. We will need whatever it is this person or this present set of circumstances can teach us in order to be strong enough to pass the next test.

Each experience strengthens us for the next one. In that way, we learn to handle all that we need in order to complete our journey. Having humor in the form of acceptance of life as it is, and taking things as lightly as possible while still acting responsibly, we prepare ourselves for the challenges ahead.

If we are devoid of a sense of humor, we take life too seriously, missing all opportunities for enjoyment. Being, to a large degree, caught up in ourselves and what we are doing, we become closed to new creative thought that could uplift and inspire us. We tend, instead, to be very rigid in our thinking, as well as judgmental of others and ourselves. As we become enmeshed in negativity about our lives and ourselves, we transmit that negativity to others around us. Subsequently, according to the universal law, it doubles back to re-enter our own life—thus creating a never-ending cycle.

Why not create positively instead—bringing love, acceptance and the ability to view one's lessons as opportunities for growth? In this way, we leave ourselves open to the joyful things around us. Learning while living in the light becomes the only alternative if we are determined to retain the enjoyment of life that we know is possible. Being able to laugh at ourselves and life, even if only for a moment, deepens our understanding that we're merely in a play which we may take as seriously as we choose.

We gain valuable perspective in our lives when we realize that we have only to perform our role as best as we can while still being aware that the play will one day end and we'll return home to take on our true identity. We are reminded that we can lighten up and be who we are. Having humor reminds us that it's all right to be caught off guard' to be ourselves, to be God's children.

ON GUIDANCE

As we open to spirit and commit ourselves to following that which we receive in the silence, we attract many teachers to assist us in our growth. Such a teacher of truth can come in the form of a book that we are led to read, or perhaps a person who helps to guide us in the right direction, or a group that inspires and instructs us. Again, maybe it comes in the form of an experience that is necessary in order that we may take that next step up the mountain path. Then again, perhaps it is nature that becomes our teacher as it offers its wisdom to us in so many ways. Learning may come through animals, birds, and other non-human spiritual energies that tell us so much about life. Further, our guidance may come through a song we hear or a sign on a billboard we see along the highway. Then again, it may come from the Higher Self—that part of us which is divine and eternal and knows all about us: our goals, our aspirations, our weaknesses, and our desires.

The Higher Self knows our strengths and our shortcomings and is there to help us discover the truth that lies within. Our goal is to become in tune with that divine part of us and live and function from its perspective. We are able to operate more fully from that aspect of ourselves as we transcend the lower levels of our being, working through our lessons, discarding old patterns while creating new, more appropriate responses to our life conditions. In that way, we act in harmony with that part of us that continually works for the enhancement of our soul.

Then again, we have our own personal guides from the spirit realm who are specifically there for the purpose of leading us forward on our journey through life. Their purpose is to help us accomplish the goals we have set out to achieve. These loving beings help to keep us from straying too far from our ideals, while at the same time they are careful not to interfere with our free will as we make our choices in life.

For a long time we may choose to go our own way until we see the wisdom in listening intuitively to that which is within. It must be understood that all spiritual guidance that is for our edification and growth comes from God. In other words, there is only one Source. If our deceased grandmother claims to be acting as a guide for us, and her wisdom feels appropriate, very likely she is receiving her information from a Higher Source.

In other words, if we are on a spiritual path and are asking for the Highest Light and guidance each day from God, then the voices which speak to us in silence, regardless of their source, are always consistent in working together for our soul's progress. We may at times hear a different slant or perspective on a particular issue, but basically that which we receive from spirit should be based on love and should serve our highest interests.

As we go forward, our teachers in spirit also progress. That is, as we pay attention on the spiritual path to the information that is being given to us and regard it as work to improve our lot, we help our guides in spirit at the same time. As we move forward, we attract new helpers, both on earth and in spirit, who are better able to assist us.

Similarly, spiritual progression is going on in the spirit realms. Evolution continues even after death. Although we may spend time in rest and recreation upon our arrival in the spirit world following our sojourn on earth, we will continue to work on ourselves in the afterlife. Perhaps we will even act as a guide to someone on the physical plane, until that time when we will merge with the Source of all life.

Therefore, as we attract the necessary and appropriate guides and teachers, we grow through each experience we encounter. Each condition we pass through, whether it is here on earth or from the world of spirit, teaches us something about ourselves; accordingly, we ought to see all of life as a blessing. Some of our experiences will come as positive encounters, while others may seem negative. But as we learn to bless all conditions, we will find our fear dissolving when we see everything as One.

In this way, all aspects of our lives will be seen as positive, because we know that the outcome of all our experiences teaches us to be more accepting of others and ourselves. Thus, we learn to love in all situations. That is what life and learning is all about.

ON ACCEPTANCE

Acceptance doesn't come easily to most of us. The problem is that we think we know how life is supposed to be. We set about to control situations in order to fulfill our preconceptions. Unfortunately, we haven't taken into account our limited vision. Only God is able to see the whole picture

When we are up in an airplane, our perspective is quite different than it is from the highway below, where our vision is limited. On the ground, we are able to view only what is directly surrounding us, and most often find it difficult to interpret accurately what we see.

In other words, we may look up and see a dark sky. We conclude that we're about to have a storm. We are, however, unaware that the wind is about to pick up and move the clouds away, leaving a beautiful day full of sunshine and warmth. We waste time and energy preparing for a storm that never comes.

At other times, we don't know what is best for us and we resist the experiences that we need for our growth. In our aversion to pain and discomfort, we fail to see the rocks in our path as stepping stones to greater wisdom.

For example, when we are sick we go to the doctor. He asks us how we feel, and from a description of our symptoms he writes a prescription. Because he understands our condition, he prescribes what he feels is best for us. We, on the other hand, may not like the taste of the medicine, but we take it in the belief that the doctor knows more than we do about our illness.

Our healing in many life situations is often like that. It calls for us to listen to the spirit within us, to follow our intuitions as best we can, to take what life gives us and be patient. Most often, there are no easy cures, but if we have faith in the universe and in ourselves, we may ride out the storms and learn from each experience we encounter. As we pass each test, we take one more step in the journey to further awareness of our world and ourselves.

All experiences have a purpose. When we feel like rebelling and are forced to follow a path not chosen by us (we think), let's look for the signposts along the way. They point to what makes that part of the journey a blessing in disguise. Sometimes the things we think we want in our lives could turn out to be disastrous for us. If we were able to look ahead, we would never take the course we think we want.

Therefore, to be patient and know that we are loved, protected, guided and directed can help us overcome our disappointment with what may look like God's mistake. Sooner or later, we'll be able to look back and see the purpose behind our challenges and we'll be glad for what we've gained. Granted, it won't be until our life is over that we put together all the necessary pieces of the puzzle.

In the meantime, as we learn to trust the universal intelligence and God's love for us, we come to understand that it all has a purpose. As we learn to discern our will from His, and accept His will for us without complaint, we will add great joy to our lives. Resistance causes pain.

Further, it's important to remember that on another level we have chosen all of our experiences as we work with that higher part of us which knows what is best. Therefore, it may be said that nothing comes to us as a total surprise. However, on a conscious level we are most often unaware of these plans. If we knew everything ahead of time, how could we grow? If we knew how our life was going to go each step of the way, there would be no need to develop faith in God or in ourselves.

Acceptance allows us freedom to enjoy what is there for us. When we focus on what we don't have, we have little time or energy to appreciate what we do have. Acceptance helps to make life interesting as we look for the rainbow in the storm and the sun that follows. Little blessings come and go each day, often accompanying supposedly negative experiences in our lives.

Acceptance also precedes change. For as we learn to accept

a person or condition with which we are unhappy, we will see the situation transformed before our eyes. Further, acceptance is the signal that a lesson has been learned and has become a part of us. The challenge is not there for us any longer. We are released from one negative situation after another as we learn to accept the unacceptable.

While we are learning what we need to accept, we also come to understand what we can change. We are not always meant to take passively everything that comes to us. We may be required to speak up or to take action. We come to learn that peace is the acceptance of life as it is, while wisdom is our understanding of what we can change about ourselves.

ON PURPOSE IN LIFE

Is there a purpose to our lives? Why are we here? How do we know what our purpose is?

Before coming to earth, we make some tentative plans. Imagine sitting down with some other "people" or spirits who act as counselors for us and help us to plan our next life. It might be similar to an academic process. We need to be aware of what courses we need to take in order to graduate. Maybe we're lacking in languages, so we add a language to our schedule. Perhaps science is difficult for us, but we wish to get it out of the way; we put in a biology class. Then perhaps we love music and know we can do well by being in the band, so we include that as an easy course we know we will enjoy.

Imagine that the process is much the same in planning life. We choose some challenge that we know we need in order to fulfill our soul's ultimate purpose. These challenges may come in the form of people or situations in our life. Then, for diversity, we may choose to add some people or conditions that will be pleasant and easy for us.

For example, we may have a loving family, but our financial

poverty may offer a real challenge. It's our lack of material goods, including money, a nice house, a nice neighborhood and all the other things that go with being prosperous, that brings us the growth that we seek. There are many ways to learn lessons, and being poor is one of them. Similarly, being extremely wealthy can also be a challenge. Other kinds of lessons are learned under these conditions, of course. These are just two examples. Another may lie in our being handicapped. This condition may be chosen as a method whereby one may learn many soul qualities very quickly—qualities that perhaps would not be learned without major physical problems.

Similarly, many of us have chosen to have in our lives some people who represent difficult challenges for us. Maybe a family member, a mother or father, has problems that are inflicted upon us, causing us to take a good look at who we are. Perhaps our self-esteem is challenged as we feel put down by one or both parents, albeit unknowingly. Often people who do this are unaware of their tendency to hurt others in this fashion. They're probably doing what was done to them. Nevertheless—aware or not—they are responsible for their actions.

However, the child, as he becomes an adult, has the opportunity to look at what he had to endure as a blessing. It has taught him a valuable lesson in learning to believe in himself, to stand tall and not allow himself to be misused.

Therefore, we ought to be grateful for our challenges as well as the gifts in our lives. They all serve a purpose. An example of a gift may be a person who is very loving, fun to be with, and accepting of us. Then again, it may be an asset or talent that we have developed in the past; it has become a part of us and therefore comes easily. This gift will bring us only positive things or conditions, and thus will bring pleasure to our lives. There is, as such, no real challenge involved. We don't necessarily grow with the gifts as we do the challenges, but we may be required to be grateful and share a gift or talent when that is appropriate.

How, then, do we find our purpose in life? If we feel confused about the reasons why we are here, we would do well to take a look at our challenges in life, as well as our assets. Our challenges will indicate to us what we came here to learn. If we have a major challenge, it may be teaching us many things. For example, if we have become paralyzed due to a car accident, we are learning much. Because of our suffering, we are being given an opportunity to learn many lessons that would take the average person without our challenges a long time to absorb. In this example of becoming paralyzed, we would be learning patience, tolerance and faith in ourselves and in God, as well as in other people who care for us. We may be developing courage, hope, perseverance, and diligence with the therapy our condition requires. We may be developing a greater understanding of life as we are forced to seek within for the answers to our dilemma. We may discover a greater meaning and purpose in our own condition as we search for answers. Consequently, perhaps we can help others come to term with their challenges when they come to the rehabilitation center with problems similar to ours.

Perhaps we may use our gifts to teach and counsel these people: we might not even realize that we possess these gifts until we choose to use them. Our challenge also requires that we learn acceptance and a sense of humor if we are to meet the challenge gracefully.

Imagine that with the help of the wise souls who counsel us, we decide that we wish to speed up our spiritual journey to a considerable degree. Perhaps we could again employ the academic process as an analogy and assume that we are in school, deciding to go to summer school. This decision means we will take several courses in a short period of time. Or again, perhaps we've elected to take accelerated courses. In any case, we've agreed to accept a challenge in order to move ahead quickly.

The following procedure will help us to discover our purpose in life. We simply take a sheet of paper and write out the challenges we face. Then we ask ourselves, "What is this teaching me? What soul qualities am I developing? Is it patience, acceptance, belief in self? What are the assets that I must use and share with others?"

After taking this kind of inventory, we ask to be made aware of our purpose to the extent to which it is appropriate. It isn't always necessary or even advisable to know too much at the present moment. There are situations in which truths require time to unfold. If we know all that may be required of us for the future, we may become overwhelmed or discouraged.

We must learn to live in the moment; however, moments spent in meditation can give us clues and feelings as to what our life may bring to us at a later time. On a higher level, of course, we have all this information. Sometimes we catch glimpses of this as we seek within and ask for guidance so that we may be prepared for what comes. Often we would not believe the wonderful things that can happen to us as a result of staying on our path and forging ahead, day by day, doing what is before us to do. Further, as we develop this kind of patience and trust that being on the path requires, we will one day find ourselves in a totally different setting, doing things we wouldn't have thought possible.

It is those who give up their faith in themselves and God or become impatient on the path who do not realize their goals. They stop somewhere along the road and build a house, thinking that it's better to be safe and secure rather than to reach for the stars by completing the journey. How can we ever know what's at the top if we don't finish?

If we simply send out the thought that we wish to accomplish the goals we set for ourselves, we need not become wrapped up in what they are. It is enough to know that our request will be answered. Then, as others stop by the wayside, we pass them. We move determinedly onward and upward, not looking back or sideways, but only forward. As we progress, we will see our purpose reveal itself. One by one, our lessons are learned as we climb the mountain.

When times get rough, we need only remind ourselves to turn within, checking for peace and guidance. We may ask, as well, to be replenished in order that we may continue on, keeping our vision of success ever before us as we seek to complete the earthly mission of our soul.

When we reach the peak of the mountain, we'll look back in the knowledge that our purpose has been fulfilled. We will say to ourselves, "I'm glad that I came and was not afraid to do it all." As we watch others struggle up the path, we will go back to assist them in order that they might discover that they, too, have a purpose as well as the courage to follow their dreams.

ON PRAYER

What is prayer, and how can it help us with our daily life? Any strong thought in the form of a desire that something occur either for ourselves or someone else may be considered prayer, though we don't usually think of prayer in that way.

When we are kneeling beside our bed or before an altar at church, we are well aware that we are there for the purpose of praying. It becomes an intentional act of sending out a message to God. Usually this is in the form of a request of some kind. The child asks for a new toy for his birthday or a sunny day for the picnic. As adults, we make many requests to our Creator, concerning various aspects of our lives and the lives of others we know. We also pray for those we don't know. We ask for help for those at war or for those who are suffering around the world or close to home. We may send out prayers for healing for those in nursing homes and hospitals, for the poor and others who have special needs of all kinds.

When we ask for help for ourselves, we may ask for material things, or we may beseech God for a new boyfriend or love in our life. We may ask for relief from loneliness, fear, pain or doubt. We may ask for courage, strength, hope and faith. We may even ask for the willingness to have faith renewed, if ours has been lost because of the disappointments that life has brought us. These are some of the requests which are sent out into the ethers as we each seek what we feel is our rightful heritage as the children of God.

Some feel their prayers will be answered; others don't. Some have great faith and as they seek, the doors are opened for them; others remain in doubt. Why do those who are doubtful continue at times to pray? One reason may be that they've tried everything else and nothing seems to work. Another reason may be that they see, read and hear about other people's prayers being answered. Still another reason may be that intuitively they know, deep down, that they're attempting to build their faith. And what better way to do that than to see if one's prayers will be answered?

Learning to work with prayer is an interesting as well as rewarding process. We have to be careful what we pray for, as the saying goes, because we might get it. In other words, we must be ready to accept what may come to us through prayer. Is it something that is good and appropriate for us? Is it a worthy goal? Will it bring us the happiness we seek, or will what we ask for bring us pain instead? Again, this issue goes back to the understanding that we don't always know what is best for us.

Occasionally people say, "Visualize what you want, and it will be yours." This may be true, but do we really want what we visualize? Let's say we visualize a new home we think we desire. We see it as being large, out in the country, with a swimming pool in the yard.

Then one day, we get our dream house. However, after a couple of years of living there we realize that being far out of town was a mistake. We also have to deal with the fact that our children are older and not interested in being at home making use of the beautiful swimming pool which, incidentally, demands a great deal of work and attention. Being large, the house is difficult to clean and keep up. We had not foreseen these circumstances when we sent out our prayer. We need to be careful in phrasing our prayers.

It's good to limit our requests so that they represent our best interests. If we think we want a large house in the country with a swimming pool, we can say, "I want this or something better that is in my best interest." In this way, we are allowing our own spirit forces help us create what would be the very best situation for us. This is true of all for which we pray, whether it concerns our health, prosperity, job, relationships or whatever we seek in our lives.

We also must pray to have faith in ourselves. What good is it to obtain a job when we don't have the self-confidence to do what the job requires? At other times we need to pray for patience. We cannot always achieve what we desire overnight. Our work with God, in which we are co-creators, takes time and preparation. Therefore, we need to be ready in all respects for what comes to us. Sometimes what we ask for requires others to be ready as well. The universe takes all into account as plans are made and conditions are set down.

All must come together in perfection and at the right time for everyone and everything concerned. If we are praying for new employment, the employer has to be in the right place to give us the job, just as we have to be ready to take it. Things don't always move along as we would like. We need to trust in God to bring things to fruition at the right time for all concerned.

When we pray, we must always thank God for what has been given. It is only in this way that we may continue to receive. As we pray for ourselves, let us not forget to send out positive thoughts for others as well—always asking that God's will be done. In this way, we will help bring about the best conditions for all. As we pray for others, we also make way for more blessings to flow to us. "As you give, so shall you also receive." This is the law.

We will learn to be aware, as we keep working with prayer and spiritual growth, when we are out of balance. We will know, for example, when we feel unloved that it is time to send out love. We will know when we need healing that it's time to send healing thoughts to others. And we will know when we are feeling lonely and rejected that it's time to reach out to others who may feel the same. In this way, we live in constant prayer: we are communicating with the higher part of ourselves, with God, with spirit and with others. Sending out our best in thought, word and deed is our way of praying for the very best to come back to us. As we continue that process, we will see wonderful and amazing things take place in our lives until one day we will find ourselves totally transformed.

We will have learned how to work in harmony with our Creator as He gently and patiently shows us how to work with His energy. Then, as we cooperate with this energy that comes through us, we can indeed know our prayers have been answered and we are at one with the Creator. We are learning to manifest in our lives and to see in the lives of others that which is best for all.

This is how we create a new and better world and learn to be responsible for and proud of our part in creation. It is through our prayers that we continue to maintain the peace and harmony that have made us co-creators with the God of our own understanding.

BOOK EIGHT

ON RESPONSIBILITY

If there is one thing we need to become on the spiritual path, it is responsible. As we journey forth on our path to self-awareness, we need to begin to take responsibility for who we are, what we stand for and where we are going.

It's always easy to blame someone else for our disappointments in life. That is a pattern common to many before consciously embarking on a spiritual path. However, after only a brief time into our journey up the mountain, we discover that we are no longer able to blame others. Whatever school of learning to which we happen to adhere to in our development, it will not allow us to blame anymore, no matter how traumatic our abuse from others may have been. We are told that instead we must look upon our misfortune as a blessing, learn from it, and get on with our lives.

This sounds easy enough, but to accomplish it isn't always that simple. It helps to understand that perhaps we attracted and even asked for our unfortunate upbringing so that we may learn to believe in ourselves a little more. In order for us to develop a particular soul quality within ourselves, the issue has to be forced upon us. If we had been born into a loving family, there would be no need to work on our self-esteem. Family members would always be loving and supportive. Often it's only when our backs are against the wall that we make an effort to change.

Our soul is perfect, but within us we carry the potential for imperfection. In other words, we have areas that are somewhat weak and need further healing for our perfection to be made manifest. When we see a small baby, we think of it as being perfect. But this soul—this child of God—also has the opportunity to gain for itself from earth experience.

Let us imagine that we carry our history with us. Within us is a record of all we have ever said, thought or done. This record within us acts like a computer that relays messages to the universe, telling it to send us whatever is required for our growth.

That which comes back to us may come in the form of experiences of all different kinds. Whether they seem positive or negative to us doesn't really matter: it is all considered learning. There is no judgment involved. The computer doesn't say, "Naughty boy! Now you need a bad experience." It simply gives us what we need to balance the scales and keep us steadily on our path. If we stray from our path, it will occasionally give us another experience to bring us back to the middle of the road that leads us up the mountain.

We tend to view God sometimes as a person on a high throne, passing out judgments and punishments. God consists, however, of loving energy. God doesn't punish us. Instead, our soul draws to itself the experiences it needs, whether they appear positive or negative to us. In other words, the soul, acting as the computer, sends out the appropriate message and the universe responds. God, on the other hand, is always there to pick up the pieces should we fall down. This is the energy that loves us all the while, allowing us to make mistakes.

Our first responsibility on the path, then, is to understand our relationship to God, to other people and to the events in our lives—so that we may stop blaming something outside of ourselves for our troubles. Actually, it can be a great relief when we discover we can stop looking everywhere for someone or something to blame. It can be a relief to know we need only look in the mirror to find the source of our troubles. But at the same time, we can congratulate ourselves on our courage to confront ourselves. And as we begin to uncover our issues one by one, and as we begin to heal, we come to see how much easier it is not to have to look far for our answers.

Then, when we have an experience that puzzles or dismays us, we can ask ourselves how we may have drawn that particular circumstance to us. Maybe we have a problem with self-confidence on which we have been working for some time. Our boss constantly cuts us to ribbons in front of everyone with whom we work. It's not hard to see why this happens to us. Most likely we were testing ourselves to see how far we've progressed with the confidence issue.

Even when we think we've entirely healed something and we have completely changed, we will still draw an experience on occasion just to see if we've really overcome our problem or weakness.

Our responsibility here becomes two-fold. Our first task is to look to ourselves for the cause of our difficulty. The second is to begin to look at our experiences in life and see if we can start to understand their meaning for us; i.e., to be consciously on the spiritual path.

As we start looking at life in this new way, it can be seen almost as a game. We stop looking from a judgmental point of view at others and ourselves and start looking more with interest at the events and experiences in our lives as we attempt to ascertain what they are intended to teach us. Now we are, indeed, becoming responsible and taking our growth seriously.

Another way we need to become responsible is in the area of relationships. This is a whole area of concern on which one could write an entire book. But for the time, let's say only that our greatest responsibility in relationships is owed to ourselves. We need to be as honest with ourselves as we can. To the extent to which we are honest with ourselves, we can practice being honest with others. This is the bottom line for open communication between two or more people in a relationship of any kind.

Once we have established honesty as the foundation, we can learn to trust. Trust comes from experiencing the honesty of another. There can be no trust if there has not been some history of honesty in the relationship. We first need to get honest with self; then we can both extend our honesty to others and expect honesty from them.

This is not the kind of honesty that hurts people's feelings by telling them we don't like their dress when they haven't asked our opinion. This is honesty based upon being who we are. It speaks well for us, allowing us to be our best selves and allowing others to be who they are—without granting anyone license to offend another intentionally.

We all need our space to experience and to grow spiritually without hurting others in the process. And when we offend, we need to make amends. In this way, we will be on the road to establishing an honest rapport with those around us.

We also need to forgive others who wish to ask our forgiveness. We must include in this category even those who don't really need forgiveness; our willingness to be inclusive helps our own soul to embody forgiving attitudes. Refusing to forgive means we ourselves are as yet unforgiven and, as a result, will continue to draw unpleasant experiences to ourselves. As we forgive others, we are forgiven, and our "house becomes clean."

Responsibility in relationships is important if we want any measure of peace and harmony in our lives. We're here to learn to have loving relationships in which we can share ourselves with others in honesty and in acceptance of who we are: spiritual beings, each trying to make our way up the mountain. We each carry our own load, and, though we may help another, we can't walk another's path. We each must go it alone, being responsible for ourselves and the load we carry.

If someone we love chooses to sit by the mountainside or go swimming in the nearby stream while we wish to keep climbing, we have a choice to make. Do we forge ahead, or lag behind? The choice is ours to make. How can we best be true to ourselves? Though we love this person, can we be happy staying behind? Where does our responsibility lie? Does it lie with us, or with the one we love? Responsibility involves making choices that aren't always easy. However, as we leave our problems in God's hands, they are solved for us.

Our responsibility to the God of our understanding implies that we trust in the infinite wisdom He provides. The universe will never let us down as we acknowledge our rightful place in it. Our realization that we are co-creators means that we must ask for help: our perspective may not offer us a clear picture. Therefore, we have a responsibility to know our place in relation to God as we accept with gratitude all that is given to us each day.

ON MORALITY

What are morals? Who decides what is moral and what is not? Do morals change? When we think about morals, we may get the image of the Victorian era when women wore upswept hairdos and long-sleeved blouses buttoned high up on the neck. We may think of the military and moral codes of honor. We also speak of the moral squad and moral ethics. Where does it all come from? Who makes the rules? Who decides what is moral and what isn't?

Morals are man-made. They are rules or codes of proper living and behavior set down by individuals or groups of people. Their purpose is to help keep people "decent," and within some kind of established code of behavior so that society can feel comfortable with itself. Without morals there would be chaos in human behavior. Just as children need rules when playing games, we all need morals to help tell us what society regards as right and wrong.

The problem with morals, although we need and value them, is that they are man-made and pertain to groups or the mass of people for whom they were intended. As such, they do not necessarily take the individual into account—nor could they. How could there be morals pertaining to most people, but not to all? (Indeed, sometimes this discrepancy does occur, but not intentionally. We may have laws for some people, but not for others. But what we consider moral behavior usually pertains to all.)

To lose one's sense of morality is considered tragic, undesirable for anyone, no matter to what group he or she may belong.

However, where is the line drawn between moral and immoral behavior? This issue is complicated by the fact that, from a spiritual perspective, that which is generally regarded as immoral behavior may be considered appropriate given the individual soul or souls involved and the circumstances surrounding a given situation. Peoples behavior varies as they are prompted from within for whatever reason. It is not, therefore, for us to say it's good or bad, because we don't really know. We can see only how it appears to us. We may feel that we don't like what someone says or does. Yet we are unable to truly judge its appropriateness without knowing all the facts. We lack the complete spiritual perspective.

It is a good practice to become an observer of human behavior, but from our vantage point, it is difficult, as well as unwise, to make judgments about behavior, whether it be "good" or "bad."

As a society, however, we do make these judgments based on the facts that are presented to us. We then deal with the situation, often in a court of law. This course of action is necessary if society is to function in relative peace. Yet from the spiritual perspective, we do not have information from the point of view of the soul or souls involved in a crime. We are not aware of the challenges, the lessons, or the opportunities for growth surrounding the circumstances. We see from only the earthly perspective. Therefore, once again our vision is limited. Spiritual reality can be quite different from earthly reality.

We would do well to remember that life is constantly balancing itself. As nature needs to maintain balance within itself, so do we as spiritual beings. If we go too far in disobeying God's laws in one direction, we will be brought back to experience what we may have inflicted on others. We're constantly creating balance over and over until one day we start doing consciously what we have been doing unconsciously for a lifetime.

One day we understand the meaning of "creating our reality," and we set about doing so with great care because we know what happens when we create disharmony. We are responsible for all we create. We reap what we sow.

We need not make excuses for our behavior, explaining that our past made us what we are today. On the contrary, we must take responsibility for who we are by attempting to learn from what comes to us as well as creating positively for our future. Morals created by man can keep us in line on the earth, while God's laws, even though they may sometimes conflict with what we see as moral, keep us spiritually intact. They move us as we need to be moved, placing us where we belong whether we're aware of it or not. Just as a river flows downstream, we're carried to our destiny by fulfilling our roles and working out our relationship to God, to ourselves, and to all of life as it unfolds before us.

ON SELF-ESTEEM

Why is it important that we like ourselves? Having the ability to be one's own best friend is, indeed, a great gift as we make our way on the spiritual path.

The issue of self-esteem becomes increasingly important as we deal with the various issues involved in healing ourselves. As we learn to like ourselves, we're better able to cope with the events and experiences we attract when we are confronting other issues in our lives. For example, if we're learning about relationships and how to maintain our identity within a meaningful relationship, we have to learn how to like ourselves: it "goes with the territory."

Self-esteem is also important on the spiritual path as we learn to stand up for our beliefs. If we are indecisive in dealing with ourselves, it's difficult to respect who we are. We're liable to disregard what we know to be true. We say things like, "Oh, maybe I was wrong in believing such-and-such," or, "My friends think that what I believe is wrong, so maybe they are right." Similarly, we're more apt to doubt what our own inner voice is trying to tell us in any specific situation when we have difficulty believing in ourselves in a more general way.

If we have low self-esteem, we tend to put ourselves down. For example, perhaps our inner guide is saying, "Buy that book: it will be interesting," but we tend to doubt. While doubting our intuition, we come up with all sorts of rationalizations like, "I don't need another book now," or "I can't spend money on a book," or "That book is kind of far out." It's true that our rationalization may be correct. At the same time, our guide may be giving us information. We need to learn how to discern what is guidance and what is our own lower mind speaking to us.

As we seek within and develop our own sense of what is coming to us from spirit and what is the mind or intellect, we will then be able to distinguish one from the other. However, this is not always an easy process, and it takes time to develop such discernment. This type of discernment also requires one to believe in oneself. The more we doubt our ability, the less able we are to make the right choice.

The more we believe in ourselves, the more we come to problem solving of any kind with a positive attitude. When we feel vague and indecisive, it's difficult to make up our minds about anything. We vacillate, and in this case find it very difficult, if not impossible, to discern whether we're being guided to buy this book or if our mind alone is talking to us.

It is important that we ourselves decide what is best for us. There are times when others like to choose for us, feeling that for some reason we are incapable of deciding for ourselves. They may feel we are unwilling to take a stand or afraid to make a commitment which would require that we defend our rights. True, it is sometimes easier to sit back and allow others to decide how the game of life should be played. We allow ourselves to be walked on in this process. As we do, our self-esteem is lowered. We constantly try to rationalize our behavior. We say to ourselves, "Well, it's easier just to give in rather than to start a fight," or, "It's easier to keep the peace than to confront the issue." We would rather retreat than stand and fight for our rights. However, in the long run, it's easier to confront the issue for several reasons: first of all, as we confront the issue, we confront ourselves—something we will have to do eventually, sometime, somewhere. If we don't learn this lesson with this person in these circumstances, we'll have to face it somewhere else. We know we can't run forever. We also know that when we do stand up for ourselves, those who would have put us down will treat us better. Often people are treating us not only in the way we've implicitly asked to be treated, but as they themselves have been treated. In other words, people turn and do to someone else what has been done to them. Sometimes our parents may have put us down in certain ways that were characteristic of their parents. Thus, patterns of behavior are carried on one way or another from generation to generation, until we put our foot down and say, "That's enough. This isn't appropriate or healthy." Once the behavior is recognized for what it is, it can then be exposed and healed within both the perpetrator and the "victim," if each is willing. Sometimes, only one is willing to look honestly at the situation. In this case, only the one who is aware can change his or her behavior. We can't change another person—only ourselves. But armed with this knowledge, we can set about to do just that.

A change in our behavior is sometimes difficult for those around us. Suddenly, that which has been a long-time pattern will shift as one person in the relationship changes and a new pattern emerges. There may be a period of adjustment as the new relationship emerges. This is not always an easy time, but worth it for both parties. If only one is willing to accept the new relationship, then that individual may have to go it alone in order to maintain a new identity as a self-respecting human being.

However, time should be allowed for the new relationship to form. Sometimes the resisting party within the relationship will eventually agree to the new patterns. In fact, he or she may be relieved. Or it is possible that one person is there precisely for the growth of the other. Perhaps there has been a pact or agreement before coming to earth that this learning process would take place between the two individuals involved. Most likely, this is the case. Difficult relationships have their purpose. Difficult situations and conditions at the workplace also have their reasons for being.

We must stop and ask ourselves what is going on. If we would take an honest look at how people are treating us and how we feel about that treatment, we would be making a good beginning. We could then go a step further and ask ourselves when we would like to learn this lesson—now or later. Usually "later" means "never." If we say, "Now," we're making it easier on ourselves. If we wait until "later," the lesson becomes more difficult.

Actually, this is true of all of our lessons. If we pass up opportunities to change our ways, we will eventually get new chances. However, the longer we wait, the more challenging they become. If we pay no attention to the knock on our door the first time we hear it, the knock will become louder and louder until we respond. How loud do we wish the knock to become? Answering it at the first knock is to our benefit: at that point it seems hardly an issue at all. But that's what we're here for—to learn and to grow and to complete our mission. How we wish to learn is up to us.

It should be remembered that it is important to be kind and gentle with oneself when learning lessons. Nothing is learned overnight. We must have patience with ourselves. Some lessons take literally years to learn, and this may be entirely appropriate.

Our opportunities tend to come in cycles. And what isn't learned this time around will come again next time. If we have a big lesson to learn, most likely we will learn it slowly. Like the peeling of an onion, it will be learned layer by layer as we are healed from within. The healing process can be slow. If a wound is to heal completely, it needs to heal from the inside. This takes time, diligence, patience and faith.

As we learn to turn these difficult and sometimes seemingly impossible situations over to our Higher Power, we can be amazed at what can happen. It's good to be aware of our issues. That's important. But if we would then ask for help and leave our situations and ourselves in God's hands, miracles can start to happen. Often as we think too hard about our problems, they tend to get worse rather than better. But if we leave them in God's hands, asking that we be guided and directed and trusting that we will be, we are better off. It is the trust and faith that bring the changes we like to see. We are so accustomed to thinking that we have to work, work, work for everything. To think of letting go and letting God is contrary to this work ethic with which we've grown up. Therefore, we need to reverse our thinking and remember to let go of our problems rather than focusing on them. As we let go, things will change for us in a most dramatic way.

While learning to take care of ourselves and believe in ourselves, allowing our Higher Power to direct the show, we are reborn. We become the people we were meant to be and are able to carry out the responsibilities required of us when we recognize our own capabilities. We may ask that our goals be made known to us as we strive to fulfill our mission. Learning to like and respect who we are, we help those around us discover who they are. If we hide dishonestly from others and ourselves, our true spiritual identity cannot reveal itself. Whereas, if we expose our true feelings and speak our piece, we affirm our true nature and declare ourselves as worthy and deserving children of God.

ON BALANCE

What does it mean to be balanced, and why is balance important as we embark upon the spiritual path? To answer these questions, we need to understand that we have three bodies: the physical, the mental and the spiritual. Although the physical body is the only aspect of our being that is visible to us, we must realize that all three bodies need to be functioning properly and in balance if we are to be completely healthy. We may be physically healthy, yes. But it doesn't do us a lot of good if we're emotionally falling apart or if we are spiritually lacking. As we seek to become healthy and happy human beings, we learn to acknowledge all three of these bodies as contributors to our wholeness. When they are out of balance, or too much attention is paid to one and not the other, we pay for this imbalance in some way.

It's important, therefore, to keep balance in our lives. We need to take care of our bodies as well as our minds and our spirits. And how best can we accomplish this?

The most obvious object of our concern is the physical body, which we care for through proper diet, exercise and rest. At times, people go overboard here. Sometimes they concentrate too much on diet without taking care of their exercise. Then again, perhaps they go on all sorts of eating regimens that actually harm the body rather than bring about the desired changes.

Eating a balanced diet and paying attention to our sensitivity to certain foods or elements in the food we eat is wise. As the vibration on the earth is heightened, we are all becoming increasingly sensitive to toxins, which may affect us in many different ways. Often we discover that what we used to eat without problems may now cause indigestion or other sensitive reactions within us. These are not necessarily serious. Nevertheless, we should be mindful of our response and limit our intake of what is bothersome to our system. Eating the same foods over and over is not a good practice: we may set up a sensitivity to those foods. Eating a variety of fruits and vegetables as well as other types of foods in each food group is wise.

Balance and variety are important to remember as one heads to the grocery store. Keeping our sugar intake down keeps our emotions under control and saves our teeth as well. There are times when we crave a particular food because we need something that it contains. More often, however, when we crave certain foods, it is because we are sensitive to them. In other words, we crave what we shouldn't have. (This explains what happens within the alcoholic. The craving he or she experiences is the result of the body's sensitivity.) In brief, then, research on diet indicates that balance is important in the food we eat and that eating a variety of foods will afford the balance we require.

Exercise is also important for the body. It provides the means of developing ourselves physically. As might be expected, variety is very beneficial here as well. Variety in exercise allows for the development of strength, flexibility, tone, and stamina. Our inclusion of a wide menu of exercises in our weekly schedule ensures that we will get what we need. Lifting weights, running or jogging, and practicing yoga all do different things for the body. Swimming is an excellent overall exercise that combines a number of skills. Bicycling also is a beneficial exercise, and can offer us the fresh air we need to lift our spirits, as well.

It's important that we like the exercise. Doing what we enjoy will bring about the best results. Having a variety of types of exercise available to us is great for our minds and spirits, as well as for our bodies. Balance and variety in both exercise and diet help the body restore itself, maintain proper health, and provide protection against accidents and disease.

Rest is also important to our health. We may find that as we grow spiritually we require less sleep. This is also true as we age. In any case, as our sleep patterns change, we may discover that we sleep less, but require more periods of relaxation, or rest periods during which we take just a few minutes to lie down. Sometimes even sitting in a chair in total relaxation and perhaps even meditation can bring great refreshment to the body. The point is, we need to stop what we're doing now and then and "regroup." It's good to pull ourselves away from what's happening in the world, even if only for a few moments. Then, as we "awaken," we feel refreshed and ready to go again.

Sometimes people find it valuable to learn yoga or tai chi, for example, for the purpose of relaxation. Both of these practices are excellent in bringing balance to the mind, body, and spirit. Again, doing a combination of things to relax us is good because each does something helpful in a unique way. Further, as we incorporate several means of relaxation into our schedule, we will increase our chances of becoming a well-rounded and healthy person. It's true that variety is the spice of life, especially as we learn different ways of caring for ourselves.

What about the mind? How do we bring balance to the mind? First of all, we need to take a look at how we are using our mind. We must take care to be in balance here, too. Do we spend most of our day thinking about our work or how we're going to get ahead? If so, we're out of balance. Do we spend our waking hours worrying about a relationship that's going sour on us? Do we spend time obsessing about someone who has hurt our feelings and made us angry? If so, we're putting ourselves out of balance. It's often very difficult or even impossible to control our thinking. It's good, then, to recognize that we simply can't; i.e., to admit defeat and become willing to have our Higher Power direct our thoughts.

As we admit that we can't control our thoughts, we can invite the spirit to take over, monitoring our thought processes so that what goes into our brain will be determined not by us, but by a Higher Source. As a result, when that which we are trying to avoid wants to pop into our mind, it will pop out again.

The only "catch" here, as in all other requests we send out to the universe, is that we must mean what we say. If we ask only half-heartedly, we will get a half-hearted response. Our success will be determined by the amount of faith we have as we ask. If we ask, knowing our prayer will be answered without a doubt, we are fortunate. For we have then at that moment set into motion the necessary impetus to achieve that which we desire. Here again, we must trust in our process. Even obsession can have a place in our growth.

Balance within the mind will come about through patience and diligence, as does balance in the body. Turning our attention to a variety of things during our day keeps us from becoming fixated on a single goal. However, we don't want to overload our minds, either. Trying to accomplish too much can put us in this dilemma. Let's learn not to take on more than is appropriate for us. Further, we can learn not to become overly concerned with the results of what we do. As we ask for guidance and direction each day, we can then do what we must, putting the results in God's hands.

Having a variety of interests and hobbies in our life keeps us from becoming bored as well as boring to others. There is an added blessing that as we enrich our lives with activities that we enjoy, we are less apt to think about our problems. Let us reemphasize the fact that we do not solve these problems by focusing on them, anyway. They are solved only as we ask for help and leave them in God's hands.

Therefore, making ourselves happier by finding activities that we enjoy brings not only balance, but also comfort to us: we eventually see that our problems aren't so big after all. We gain perspective by paying attention to all that is around us and available to us. By focusing on these positive aspects of our lives, we save ourselves from becoming negative.

It's wise to attempt to keep emotional balance as well. If we are to grow spiritually, we need to learn to keep our emotions under control. This doesn't mean that we suppress our feelings. It does mean that we don't allow our emotions to get the better of us. We don't allow our feelings to run our lives. To be truly spiritual, one must learn to recognize feelings, express them when appropriate, and keep as quiet as the situation demands.

How do we keep our emotions in balance? First of all, we can recognize that our emotional selves aren't necessarily our true selves. Our spirit and our emotions are two different things. Our emotions have to do with our personality, which is expressing itself now in the human body. Our spirit is quite different in that it is more knowledgeable and has an understanding both of our lives and of the experiences that are necessary for our growth. Therefore, the spirit does not respond in an emotional way to the situations that confront us each day. This is why, for example, meditation is recommended to calm us. For as we get into that spiritual realm allowing the higher part of us to take over, we leave the emotions behind. We become "spiritual" rather than "emotional."

People often confuse the two states, thinking that if they become very emotional in regard to their faith or their religion, those emotions will bring them closer to God. The fact is, it takes us further away. Having a reverence for the Almighty and His power is one thing, but becoming emotional concerning one's faith or any aspect of spirituality doesn't enhance spiritual awareness.

The same can be true as people attempt to feel their loved ones communicate with them after they have made their transition. As people tend to be emotional, they block what could be a coming together of the two spirits. It is when we are still and at peace with ourselves and the world that such encounters are apt to take place. However, heavenly beings and messengers are also known to come to us in great need. Still, for the most part, as we learn to calm our emotions, our best communications with spirit can occur. Being open to this form of communication can help us greatly on the path to self-awareness. But we must always ask for Divine Light to be placed around us as we purposely seek such communication.

When we become emotional, we attract to us other energies of similar vibration. If we are angry and resentful, we attract similar thoughts and energies from the universe. This can increase our anger and make it difficult to release. The same holds true if we are sad, lonely, or unhappy. The same principle is in operation when we are positive, carefree, and enthusiastic about life. We attract to us that which we are, whether it is from this plane or the spiritual realm. Therefore, it helps to remind ourselves that if we wish to be happy we will get reinforcement from the universe. This is why it's important that we begin our day asking that only that which is for our highest good be allowed to come to us. "Seek and you shall find, knock and the door shall be opened unto you, ask and it shall be given." As we seek and ask for assistance from our Higher Power, in whatever form that may take, we will receive help in maintaining our emotional balance. Sometimes the process takes some time.

We need to experience our feelings, even if they are negative, because they are teaching us something. Without our emotions, we wouldn't know ourselves enough to know what needs to be healed and what doesn't. If we are angry, lonely, hurt, or wallowing in self-pity, we know we have healing to do. It is at this realization that we allow God to take charge of our emotions. We allow our Creator to direct the play.

Perhaps we need to speak in anger occasionally, or maybe cry alone some evening. Perhaps we need to laugh. Laughter releases pent-up energy. It can be the best healer of all. The more we laugh, the better we feel. We can't use laughter to disguise what is going on with us on a regular basis. But it can help us to gain perspective, even if only momentarily. So we ask God to direct our feelings, keep us in balance, and surround us with the Highest Light. Then we seek communion with spirit through moments of stillness in which our emotions are calmed and we return, if only briefly, to our constant, eternal self. When we regain our spiritual perspective, we see our emotions as fleeting and temporal. We see how our emotions indicate where we are in our growth and where we need to heal ourselves. Instead of allowing our feelings to run us, we use them to indicate what needs to be said or done or not said and left alone.

Our emotions teach us to be wise through our mistakes in interpreting their meaning for us. Perhaps we think our anger means "speak up," when maybe it's indicating that we need to be patient. Becoming openly angry with another when patience is indicated will bring further anger upon ourselves. While reflecting on the situation, we'll understand that patience is the preferred route to go. Sometimes it's difficult to know the most appropriate way to handle our feelings. We may learn totally through trial and error, or we could speed up our journey and ask for help. Whichever way we choose, eventually we learn about our emotions and how they can help or hurt us.

Another place in which we seek balance is our spiritual life. Often when we feel a spiritual light has been lacking for us, we tend to overdo. By overdoing, we become too focused on matters pertaining to our spiritual growth, while leaving other areas in our life unattended.

For example, as we see others improving their lives by attending a particular group or spending time in meditation, if we join them in our enthusiasm, we are asked to overdo and neglect other aspects of our life such as family, our health, school, work or our creativity. For a time, under certain conditions, this may be beneficial as one is healing and the primary focus needs to be on the healing process. However, there comes a time when we need to become balanced so that we heal properly.

If we overdo in the spiritual area just as in other areas, we become lopsided. And our newly found spirituality, though it is bringing us many good things, will not be serving us as it could be if our lives were in balance. It's like erecting a great tower. If one of the legs is strong but the other three are weak, the tower isn't going to remain standing very long, if at all. All the strength and sturdiness being put into the one leg will be to no avail as the tower tumbles to the ground.

We must keep all aspects of our lives on an even keel. The physical or material life should be balanced with the spiritual. When we leave the earthly plane and look back upon our lives, we will see how important our material life is to our spiritual growth, for it is through the material that the spirit is expressed. It is through the use of our talents, abilities and personalities that our soul gains expression. If we spend too much time in meditation or in therapy trying to get well, we pass by the opportunities that come to us offering the vehicle to express. It's true that we need these avenues to help us discover who we are, but we then need to take a risk and express this new personality. Without the opportunity to express ourselves, we'd be nowhere.

If we have a gift, talent, or ability, we can be sure, if we are willing, that we'll be given opportunities to use it. The question is, will we take the challenge when it comes? We never know what we can do until we do it. We are often much more capable and talented than we realize. Thus, it is only through following our guidance that we may find out what situation or condition may be suitable and timely for us. We may feel directed to do something that feels totally "off the wall" and inappropriate for us. Further, maybe we feel we aren't talented enough in that area to partake in that particular venture. Yet we may be very surprised as well as pleased to find the opportunity not only enjoyable, but beneficial to our career as well. Limited vision prevents us from seeing all we are able to accomplish. So let's allow God to direct the play, and we'll read our parts as they are given to us.

Being spiritual means being balanced in all that we do. So as we move forward on our path up the mountain, let's stop and smell the roses, taking in their essence. Let's look around us occasionally to see if we're not missing something we may wish to take part in. Let's add zest to our journey by taking side trips now and then in order to create something beautiful or gain some knowledge or unusual experience. Then we may come back to the path in gratitude for what we have gained in further awareness of ourselves and our world.

BOOK NINE

ON ATTITUDE

Our attitude reflects how we feel about ourselves. Generally speaking, if we have a good attitude we feel good about who we are—with the reverse also being true. Poor attitude is a reflection of how we are feeling about who we are. We can have a poor attitude about something, but not have it reflect on who we are. That amounts to an opinion. For example, maybe someone asks us to go to work for him in a new business venture. Our intuition is telling us that this isn't a good idea, and that the business itself may not last. Therefore, in our opinion the idea is negative. However, that opinion doesn't mean that we feel poorly about ourselves.

However, when we're talking in general terms about attitude, we're speaking of a way of looking at life in general. As we change, our attitude changes. We may say we have a negative attitude concerning a war. What we are really saying is that we have a negative opinion about a war. Then again, we can approve of a war and still have a negative attitude about life.

Our attitude toward many things changes as we become more positive. As we aim at improving our lives, we change how we view the world. For example, let's say we used to smoke. As the restrictions on smoking became more evident, we became resentful and our attitude toward those who were attempting to curb our smoking became one of anger and intolerance. Then, as we later gave up the habit, we found that our anger toward that same group who wished to curb our smoking changed. Suddenly, we were with them, agreeing wholeheartedly with what they were saying. We totally changed our tune. Perhaps, in turn, we began becoming intolerant of those who still smoked. In any case, we had a total change of attitude.

On the spiritual path, we find that our attitude changes on

many things as we change. As we grew up we took on the attitudes of our parents in most cases. Then, as we rebelled, some of us, as teenagers, formed our own attitudes according to what our peers thought. Then, as we became adults, we changed our attitudes again, based on where we were emotionally and mentally on many different issues. Further, as we have become consciously aware of being on a spiritual path, our attitude changes once more.

Why all the changes? The changes are necessary as they reflect who we are at the time and where we are coming from. In other words, the source of our information greatly affects our attitude toward the world. When we were children, our information came from our parents. When we became teenagers, our information came from our peers. When we were adults, our information came from whatever source we deemed important and significant at the time. Perhaps it was the neighbors. Maybe it was the newspaper or the television. Maybe it was what our minister or therapist said that became our source reflecting the values to which we wished to adhere. At any rate, we probably chose our value system from a combination of sources. That which resulted became our frame of reference, which, in turn, helped to form our attitude on different issues.

This is why we are all so diverse, and unless we have chosen to adhere to a strict school of dogma, we will all be unique in our attitudes, as well as our opinions on various subjects.

Thus, it is our differences that make life interesting. Can you imagine how boring it would be if we all thought alike? Sometimes we are surprised by the opinions of people whom we think we know well. We think we know how they will respond when asked about something, and we are totally surprised when they respond differently than we had anticipated. The reason they responded as they did was because they chose as their point of reference a different source than we anticipated.

Why is our attitude so important? The answer seems fairly obvious enough, yet we all can have problems with the way in which we approach life. Most of us know the attitudes we carry with us are important because we've been taught that since we've been very young. Often you hear that children who are in trouble have "a bad attitude." "How can we get him to like school? He has such a poor attitude he'll never pass."

Instead of expressing a view common to what they may hear on the news, for example, they chose instead to respond as their minister would have responded. They chose a point of reference different from the one we thought they would choose. That's why people we know well and who are close to us surprise us from time to time. They say things that are unexpected and out of character, as though they are coming from another place or "attitude" that seems uncharacteristic of them.

The point of all this is to show that as we are out and about in the world, we are obliged to take in, decipher, and discern pieces of information all the time. We hear things. We ponder them. Then we decide whether we believe them or not. Then, while making up our mind, we go to the point of reference we feel will best help us decide if what we hear is true. Then we make up our own mind.

As we are all coming from potentially different points of reference, depending upon what we think is important, our opinions on the subject at hand will vary. Also, as our attitude about life changes as we grow, it alters how we feel about things. For example, as we become more spiritual, we tend to be more tolerant of other people. We tend to recognize that because everyone is coming from a different place, depending on where they are in their growth, their attitudes on life, religion, philosophy and the world will vary. Therefore, we can be tolerant of the attitudes of others because we trust in their integrity. We trust that they are coming from the only reference point they find appropriate at the time. If we differ with them, it's okay. But as spiritual beings we need to understand the process.

We like people to think as we do, and sometimes we fear those who don't because they threaten us at times. They threaten us only as we doubt ourselves. The fact is, our truth is our truth, and it is very appropriate for us. It may change next week or tomorrow, but for now this is how we feel and what we think. This is our opinion on a particular subject today. As we learn that our opinions, attitudes and beliefs are valid, we feel right within ourselves. Therefore, as we allow ourselves to be who we are, we have less fear of others. However, when our right to how we feel or what we believe is impinged upon, our feelings about who we are become distorted. We must respect our process and allow ourselves to think and believe in a manner we feel is right and appropriate for us. Further, if we feel we have an obligation to share with others what we know and believe to be true, even though it may change tomorrow, so be it. We all have a place in this world and things to accomplish. In addition, we have viewpoints to share and teach to others.

If someone or something is attempting to interfere with our right to do this under the proper conditions, obviously they are impinging on our freedom. Nowhere in God's laws does it tell us not to share what we think or believe with others as long as we aren't trying to control them. We must allow others to express themselves as they choose, as long as they aren't violating anyone's rights or freedom. As soon as we attempt to control others through fear or any other device, whether it's physical or psychological, we are actually putting shackles on ourselves. Conversely, if in any way we allow others to control us by threatening words or "messages from God," we are again imprisoning ourselves. We cannot take what belongs to another, nor can anyone take what is ours.

As we grow, our attitudes change, and as we allow others to believe and experience what they must for their growth, we come to understand the meaning of love. Love is not telling people they must behave in a certain way. It is not threatening. Love states that there are many ways up the mountain and to follow one's heart will lead us to the path which is for us—not necessarily for everyone else, but for us alone.

ON LEARNING

Learning on the spiritual path can be fascinating because we are aware that we are learning. No longer do we think in terms of punishment or threats or making bargains with God. We've rid ourselves of the need to find excuses, to blame others, or to fear our feelings. No longer do we hide from our challenges, because now we see them as opportunities, and no longer do we run from our enemies, because we now know that they're there to teach us something.

We've come to understand that everything has a purpose and that nothing is wasted. All encounters have potential good in them. All experiences bring growth as well as freedom. Further, that which appears to be a stumbling block to one individual will seem a "piece of cake" to another.

Because we all have our own weaknesses and strong points, that which is easy to some is difficult to others. All is relative to one's perspective on the path. And though we still experience pain if we choose, we understand that learning comes through love and awareness of the simple truths of nature and spirit.

We know we can choose to learn in the light of our awareness, or we may stumble in the dark. We'll reach our goal in either case. Learning in the light is more pleasant. Learning in the dark because we are ignorant of the laws of truth causes us pain, which we tend to remember within the soul. This pain is an assurance that we'll remember our lesson. Our new awareness becomes a part of us. We don't have to find it in a book or hear it from a teacher. It is there within us. While learning each truth, we take another step up the ladder, bringing us closer to the goal of self-awareness and empowerment.

Learning on the path helps us to be more tolerant of others. As we learn our lessons, we glance over occasionally to see what others are learning. We all have to pass the same tests, so we are not apt to judge another's lesson or their progress. That which is easy for us may not be for others, and vice versa.

Further, we all have our own goals, so our learning will depend to a great extent on what our goals happen to be. We are all nearing the end of our need to return back to earth. This doesn't mean that we're perfect, but it means that in the large scheme of things, our time here is becoming limited. This means that many of us are "cleaning house," so to speak. It means that we are clearing out the junk in our minds, bodies, and our spirits. It means we are changing our attitudes, our habits, and our emotions. Though we can become angry, for example, we don't stay in our anger for a long time as we might have earlier. We are cleaning up our act, because it's time. We are on schedule and moving forward, each at our own rate and in our own time.

Many are leaving the earth at this particular time in history. They're leaving through death from war, illness, natural disasters and other causes. The rest of us are here learning how to cope with the large masses of people leaving, as well as with our own assignment that involves taking care of ourselves, healing our past, and coming to terms with our work for the future. Learning is intense because time is short. We learn quickly now. What took the adults of today twenty or thirty years to learn, their children are learning often in a matter of months.

What are we learning? We're learning to be better human beings. We're learning to love ourselves and others. We're learning to care for our neighborhoods and our planet. We're learning to go with the flow and accept our responsibilities as they are given to us. We're learning to open to spirit and seek within for guidance. We're learning to depend on ourselves, where we used to depend on others. We're learning to be aware of who we are in relation to the whole. We're learning to understand our place in nature and our environment as well as to bring healing to both. We're learning to share what we have with others, being careful not to interfere with lessons they may have chosen for their growth. We're learning to share that which we receive in the silence, so that others may prepare for what lies ahead. We're learning to trust in our Creator to bring us to where we need to go physically, as well as psychologically and spiritually, so that we will be at the appropriate place at the right time. We're learning to trust in our abilities and talents so that we will blossom forth, giving where we are able and as it is necessary. We're learning to stand firm in our beliefs, not doubting the inner voice or that from without that rings of truth.

We are being led, and we must recognize the voice of truth as it calls to us. We may hear it in a book or see it in the sky. It's telling us the time is right to get our act together. We are all one, and now is the time to recognize it. And as we do, great things will come about as we visualize together a world that is healed of hunger and pain. Further, as we visualize this great healing which is taking place, we can see our own lives being healed. We can sigh a great sigh of relief with Mother Earth as she too cares for her wounds that have been cut deep due to man's ignorance. And as we visualize a new earth, a new time—a better time for all, let's send love and gratitude to God for the opportunity to be part of this great transformation.

ON UNIVERSAL LAW

What does Universal Law mean? Just as we have physical laws like the law of gravity, we also have laws of the universe. These laws never change in any respect. It doesn't matter if one is aware of them, or if one necessarily believes in them, they are always in effect. Once a law is broken, the transgressor pays the price, even though he or she may not be aware that a law has been broken.

There are many universal laws. Every religion claims some part of the Truth. No one religion could contain all of the truth that exists. Therefore, all of the religions and philosophies of the world help to disseminate a portion of truth which can be added to the whole. As we become familiar with these different bodies of knowledge and experience, our soul is expanded.

Further, as we learn to live the truth, we become one with our Creator and our soul becomes fulfilled.

The master Jesus studied the universal laws as a young boy and learned how to put them into practice. He developed a great understanding of the laws and fulfilled his mission by teaching, healing, and even dying in order to demonstrate their effect. Jesus knew that as the laws were broken, he who broke the law would pay for the transgression. He attempted to show to the people that if they lived in harmony with God's laws, they would prosper. On the other hand, if they didn't, they would pay the consequences.

However, He also taught us that God doesn't punish us. He taught that God loves us and wants only the best for us. However, because He loved us, He allowed us to learn in our own way. If we chose to break the laws and do things our own way, we would pay the price by drawing the appropriate conditions to ourselves that would help to make us aware of our mistakes. Unfortunately, many of us are slow learners. It took us a long time to understand that we were bringing about our own misfortunes. We are very accustomed to putting the blame more outside of ourselves. We have blamed God, our parents, our teachers, our environment, and society for what we are now discovering are our mistakes. "As you sow, so shall you reap." By the law of karma, which means that that which we send out, either positively or negatively, in thought or in deed, will be returned to us, we set up conditions in our lives which are either positive or negative. It often takes a long time for us to understand that this is how it works. We're very accustomed to thinking in terms of more blatant, immoral acts such as stealing, adultery or murder. We're often unmindful of the more subtle ways in which we can bring negativity into our lives.

For example, by the Law of Attraction, the quality of our thoughts will determine what will be drawn to us. If our thoughts dwell on fear, we'll draw fearful situations. If our thoughts dwell on love and success, we'll draw opportunities for both. There is a limiting factor here, in that while the law will bring us that which we desire, it has been up to us to create—to act upon what is presented to us. Therefore, remembering how potent the power of thought is, we can become mindful of how important it is to be positive in our thinking. It is by this means that we create beneficial conditions in our lives through positive affirmations and visualizations.

Similarly, by surrounding ourselves and others with Divine Light while sending love to ourselves and those we care about, and by placing all in God's hands, we can then let go of the control of our lives. Thus, we are better able to help ourselves and others through knowing that we each have our own spiritual help which may be called upon for assistance.

Therefore, it is the ignorance of the laws that exist and the help that is available to us that causes us to "sin" or to make mistakes, thus falling short of our goals. It is often through experience that we "catch on" to these laws and the way in which they operate. And even though we often hurt, Christ has taught us that learning through pain is unnecessary. He taught that we could learn through love and understanding. Learning through pain is a choice that we make, and eventually we discover our mistakes and how we are bringing negativity into our lives. Often this is done not just through our misdeeds, but through our thoughts as well. Simply by thinking negatively about ourselves and others, we can bring about our own misfortune. Therefore, it is knowledge, acceptance and living in accordance with the laws that will help us to know the truth, and it is the truth that will set us free.

For those who believe in reincarnation, becoming free enables us to get off the wheel of coming back to earth again and again. For those who believe in just one lifetime on the physical plane, it means becoming free most often on the inner planes through learning in the spirit world. We are free when we have obtained perfection. Until that time, we will continually attract people, situations, and conditions in our lives which will help us to grow. Further, being mindful of how the laws work helps us to work in harmony with the laws, rather than against them. And as we learn to work with this divine energy each day, we will eventually become Masters as the Christ taught. When speaking of His miracles He said, "And these things you shall do, and greater." Further, He stated that through the Divine Energy that flows through each one of us, we would learn to live the greatest law of all—the Law of Love; and as we learn to live in harmony, peace and love, we would be healed and our world would thus be transformed.

ON STUBBORNNESS

One stumbling block that can beset us along the path is our own stubbornness. Stubbornness is not necessarily a bad thing. There are times when we need to be firm. We need to stand on our own two feet and not allow ourselves to be walked on. On the other hand, we can be stubbornly intolerant, impatient, and unwilling. Because of our inflexibility, we don't allow ourselves to be open to others and what they have to offer. Thus, we miss opportunities that might otherwise be there for us, all because of our stubborn attitude.

When we are stubborn, we are narrow-minded. We create a tunnel vision attitude in which we don't allow ourselves to see the full scope of what is there. We limit our opportunity for growth and new experiences. Further, as we limit our experiences, we limit our ability to accomplish all of the goals that we previously set for ourselves. We may be aware of our goals and we may not be. Nevertheless, when we go to the spirit world following our sojourn here on earth, we will be able to see what our goals had been. Further, as we look back, we will see how opportunities came to us that we passed up because we determinedly held to our narrow perceptions and our fears, never freeing ourselves enough to experience all we could have.

Often one experience we have leads to another that in turn leads to another opportunity. Therefore, if we miss the first or second link in the chain of events, we miss the end result. Fortunately, we are given more than one chance for an experience, but if we keep turning opportunities down, they don't continue to be manifested. We are making our choice by our unwillingness to see things differently. Therefore, we close the door to fulfillment in a particular area of our life that could be ours if we were more open to it.

Another way in which we can be stubborn is in our resistance to change. Many of us fear change. We can be very comfortable where we are, even in the most unpleasant circumstances, all because we resist change. We stubbornly hold on to the old, and as we do, prevent ourselves from experiencing the inflow of new creative energy available to us. There can be change all around us, and as we resist the flow we create blocks for ourselves. These blocks may show up in the physical body as stiffness and soreness in the muscles, as well as pain in the joints and other areas within the body. We wonder what is wrong with us.

After awhile, if we decide to go with the flow and do whatever is appropriate for us at the time, our pain goes away. Pain may be caused by our negative attitude toward an experience we have had. It may be a block in energy due to our fear of moving ahead on a project. It may be due to a resentment we are carrying around with us. In any case, it is because of our stubbornness that we are unwilling to let go and go with the flow, just as a river flows downstream. When we stand up in a river that is flowing freely, we feel the current of the water against us until sometimes we are pulled over by the pressure. The same thing happens when we refuse to bend in our attitudes. When we are inflexible and unwilling to flow with the current, we expend tremendous energy in our will to stop the flow. This often ends up in some kind of pain that may be physical, mental, spiritual or all three.

On the other hand, stubbornness can be our ally at times when it is important not to give in. There are times when we must stand up for what we believe in at all costs. This doesn't mean not listening to the "other side," but it does mean not allowing ourselves to be influenced or persuaded to change our view or our stand on something if we believe we are right. In this case, we are not being stubborn; we are simply holding to our truth, whatever that may be. We are being true to ourselves, and this kind of honesty is essential if we hope to progress on the path. We set ourselves back as we compromise our beliefs or our goals. Therefore, when we learn to discern when we are being stubborn and when we are simply being true to our own values, we can learn to become more open to new experiences. Of course, we realize, too, that we must not compromise our integrity in the process. However, when we are willing to listen to other points of view, as well as experience new opportunities as they are presented to us, we will indeed expand our horizons. Further, as we learn to be flexible in our thoughts and attitudes on life in general, we will become more tolerant of others, thus opening the way to having others accept us as we are. While becoming willing to expand our awareness—to stop, look and listen to the signs of direction and guidance being given to us—we will become aware of the wondrous ways in which our Creator speaks to us. Each of us will hear this voice differently and at different times. We'll receive His messages through nature, through the birds, through our pets and other animals around us. We'll hear Him in the brook and through the waves lapping on the shore. We'll see Him in the flowers and in the children on the playground. We'll see Him in the look of pain in the eyes of another in sorrow. We'll see Him in the sky as the clouds clear, bringing the sun on a warm summer day. His messages will be clear to us. Because we have asked for Divine Light, we know no harm can come to us, and as we seek to know His Truth, it will be made known.

ON CHANGE

How well do accept change? As we grow, we are changing constantly. We are also asked to accept change as an inevitable aspect of human existence. Change is the one constant in our lives that we can count on. Change is continuous within the Universe. Nothing stays the same, and as we can accept that fact and learn to go with the flow, we can invite change to be a part of our lives. It's going to be anyway. But as we invite change instead of resist it, we will be happier.

We are constantly subject to change. We can be aware of the cycles of nature as fall turns to winter and winter to spring. Further, change is as inevitable within our own being as it is in nature, for we are part of nature. The same Divine Universal energy we call God moves through us as it does through the wind, the trees and the flowers that bloom in our gardens. The same energy flows through the animals, the fish, and the birds in the air. Everything that is alive is a part of nature and is therefore subject to the cycle of life.

Everything has a beginning as well as an end: a time to be born and a time to die. Where there is an up there must be a down, and where there is sadness and sorrow there must be joy also. Nothing stays the same. Where there is discouragement there is also room for hope. Where there is laughter, pain hides there also because this is the way it is. The yin and yang of life moves us forward. We don't have one without the other, and where there's hatred, love finds its way there also.

Learning to accept change is learning to accept life as it is. When we can truly say we accept life as it is, we have experienced much growth and peace. Peace only comes as a result of acceptance—accepting ourselves and others. When we accept ourselves and our life conditions, as well as accepting others as they are, we are living in harmony with the universal laws. We are in the flow. Furthermore, as we accept change as part of life's process, we are better able to maintain our balance and equilibrium as we undergo the experiences of life.

Accepting change is a necessity if one chooses to live a life relatively free of pain and conflict. It is always resistance that causes pain, rather than the acceptance of the negative conditions in our lives. If we would learn to accept the things we cannot change about ourselves and other people, we would be able to experience our lives relatively free of pain. This doesn't mean that we sit back and allow ourselves to be walked on, but that when something comes that we can't do anything about, if we learn to first accept it, we will be far better off.

Then as we sit in the silence and ask for guidance, we may become aware of what this condition is doing in our lives. Perhaps it's bringing us a message or lesson we need. If so, let's accept it as an opportunity for growth. We don't always know the reason why a particular person or situation is with us, but if we keep asking, we will know in time. Again, as we speak of change, timing is important. Each piece of information we receive and each experience we have comes at the proper time. This requires, then, that we develop a great deal of patience. We can't always know everything when we want to. Our lives unfold naturally, just as our awareness comes to us in its own time. We will know what we need to know when the time is right.

Perhaps we need to develop faith. In order to become strong in our faith, we must let go. Letting go sometimes means not knowing. It may mean not knowing what job we will have, if any, when we are required to let go of the one we are now in. It may mean not knowing where we are going to live as our home is taken from us in a flood. It may mean not knowing if a son is going to return from war. If we had all these answers, where would our faith come in? To be on the spiritual path one has to develop faith. To be able to accept change in our lives without necessarily knowing what is to come is an excellent way to develop faith.

Change comes in many forms. We change as we grow and

watch our children grow as well. We change physically, emotionally, mentally and spiritually. Our bodies change as we change our perceptions about ourselves and our world. We go through change, some of which we view as positive and others we resist. There is one thing we know for sure. That which we are attracting will be for our good whether viewed by us as positive or negative.

All negative experiences can be looked upon as blessings in disguise if we are open to the learning that is available to us. In resisting a new situation, we close ourselves to that opportunity and find ourselves "stuck." We can stunt our growth by acting like stubborn mules that sit down in the middle of the path and refuse to move. Others may make their way around us, but we refuse to follow the flow of the river or to continue our trek up the mountain. At the same time, we wonder why life isn't "happening" for us. We may think we're attempting to find peace—and we may succeed to some extent—but life has become dull because we dare not change.

Change may come in the form of a new trend or sport—or just a new hairstyle. It may also come in the traumatic loss of someone close to us. As we learn to accept this kind of loss in our life, we make way for a fresh kind of experience. It is true that we will miss a beautiful and loving relationship, but maybe we can now more fully discover who we are and appreciate what we find in the process. It is true that things will never be the same, but are they meant to be? No, without change there is stagnation of the soul. We are forever moving upward. We've had many loves, many relationships of all kinds, and we will continue to have them until we are finished with our human experience. Therefore, let's enjoy each new gift of awareness brought to us when we accept change as an inevitable and welcome part of our lives.

Jill Downs

ON TRANSFORMATION

The word "transformed" signifies total change. A total change involving values, beliefs, attitudes, and behavior is required if we are to be transformed; i.e., we must shift from what we were to what we are to be. That being the case, we have a great deal of housecleaning to do. Further, in order to clean house we must first ascertain what needs to be done. We have to look at the mess we've created and establish the order in which the rooms need to be attacked. We take care of the big things first.

In other words, if someone were in the habit of robbing banks, that "defect of character" would be taken care of before he would be required to work, for example, on his patience. We take care of the blatant, more obvious, and most troublesome flaws in our personality before working on the other less obvious shortcomings.

As we clean house and make amends where we need to, we learn new ways of thinking and looking at life so that we don't find ourselves locked into the same old behaviors. The reverse can also be true: our patterns of thinking and our moods can change as we change our behavior. If, for example, we are in a low mood, it sometimes helps to put on a pretty dress, heels, and a new hairdo and walk out the door with a smile on, even if we don't feel like smiling. As we pretend to feel good, we actually convince the world and ourselves that we are content with our lot today. As we change our thinking, we begin responding to life in new ways. We set up new goals and discard the old. Letting go of the past sometimes presents problems for us, but as we realize how important letting go is to our spiritual growth, we become more willing to do so. When we resist the letting go process, we bring pain to ourselves—and sometimes others as well—because we slow up the natural process of things. Learning to let go is a wonderful tool we have on the path. Those who have ascertained its importance and are aware of means to let go are fortunate, indeed. As we pray to release the old, we open the door to the new opportunities, relationships, and experiences that await us. This is essentially what transformation is about.

Transformation can be partial or total, depending on how much a person is willing to let go of his old patterns of thought and behavior. We are in different phases of our evolvement as spiritual beings. Therefore, we are all working on different aspects of ourselves. Some choose to progress at a faster rate than do others. It's important to reiterate that appearances are deceiving. Therefore, we can't make a judgment about where someone else is on his or her path—nor is it advisable.

What comes when we are totally transformed, as we all will be one day? For one thing, it means that we will be healed from our past. We will no longer be inviting experiences into our lives as growth experiences, for we will already "be there." We won't attract negative situations, throwing us off balance in their attempt to get our attention. Our experiences, instead, will be those we create in the positive attempt to either enhance our own lives or serve others.

These experiences may be as varied as appreciating good music or going to heal a friend of a headache. They won't include having a nasty encounter with one's boss in which we are left heartbroken and humiliated. There will be no need to experience the pain of such a meeting, because whatever the lesson may have been, it will have already been learned. As we are transformed, our experiences appear positive to us and we are able to appreciate the joy that life brings.

Further, because we've learned to accept life as it is, including the negative as well as the positive aspects of it, we do not create painful conditions through our resistance to what is happening. We are open to the flow. The negative can move through us without affecting our attitudes or feelings, while the positive attitudes of our life continue to uplift us. We can be happy because we no longer fear that joy can be taken from us. Further, we no longer fear abandonment in any form because we feel whole within ourselves. This brings us a security we haven't known before. Again, while healing our doubts through having developed our faith in God and ourselves, we fear nothing.

Can we imagine a life without fear of any kind? We would feel free to experience anything because we would always trust that everything we need would be available to us. These things we need might be, for example, words given to us in a public speech, or they might include protection in a fall on a ski hill. Moreover, when we are transformed, we will send out help at the same rate that we receive it. Consequently, the flow is uninterrupted.

We will know how to work with the laws of the universe. Our soul will recognize the power of thought and will use our minds to create our world. We will understand how to create through affirming and visualizing. We will be able to heal ourselves, as well as others. We will have a clear understanding of Divine Order and will know we are not to tamper with the laws of nature and spirit. We will not suffer from limited vision but will be able to "see" the unseen and feel the pain of others when it means we can help to heal them. We will be open to hearing the voice of spirit and will obey the voice that speaks to us in the silence. We will send out thoughts of love to others because our own cup will always be full. We will often go unrecognized as the Master we have become. Humility will be a part of who we are. The transformed person could be a taxi driver, our barber, the checkout girl at the supermarket—or we ourselves. We don't know them by their loud voice or their fame. We recognize them only as our own healing has been accomplished and the veil has been removed from our eyes. Then we will be allowed to see truth as it is. So be it!

ON SERVICE

All who are consciously on the spiritual path will be serving humanity in one way or another. There are many ways to transmit that which we receive from God. We may serve simply by being an example to others. We may serve by listening to another's problems. We may serve by being who we are and sharing our experience to encourage and bring hope to others. We may serve by being available to others in time of need. Sometimes a person just needs someone to pick up the phone—to be there, to listen with an understanding heart.

We may serve by counseling in one form or another when we are in a position to do so. Any kind of counseling should leave options open to individuals so they may make choices for themselves. A wise counselor does more listening than anything, making some observations, and then giving feedback as well as options for a course of action based upon what is heard. No one can make another do something he or she doesn't want to do. We are all free to make our own decisions. We need to support each other as best we can as well as respect the choices people make in their lives, even if we don't agree with them.

There are times when people choose to learn the hard way. This is often difficult for others to watch because they seem to make one poor choice after another and don't seem to turn themselves around. It may help to remember that on a higher level there may be a good reason for what may appear to be very slow progress, if there appears to be any progress at all. The individual is gaining much needed experience to insure certain lessons are learned thoroughly.

As we experience, the soul records these events and we do, indeed, remember the learning, though it may not be conscious. Sometimes certain lessons have to be repeated over and over again to make sure that they are assimilated properly. A house has to have the proper foundation so that it won't topple to the ground. Therefore, each aspirant along the path will have to have any and all experience required to insure this doesn't happen. We all need a strong base if we're serious about moving ahead in accomplishing our goals. Further, in order to be of service to others, we need to work on ourselves.

Another purpose for service along the path is to keep ourselves balanced. Once we have made the decision to go forward in improving our lives, we begin to receive as much help as we are ready to receive and use. Therefore, as we take in all that is available to help us, we need, as well, to be giving out. This balance is important for our well being. When we are unbalanced, we will often sense that fact. If we are receiving and not giving, or if we are too wrapped up in ourselves, we will start to feel uncomfortable. As soon as we start giving, our balance is restored and we begin to feel much better, much less irritable and self-centered. It's wise to keep this in mind.

We may wonder how we can be giving to others if we are working all day and home at night, or otherwise wrapped up in our own daily routine. One way in which we can be sure to reach many people is to have our own list of individuals or even groups of people who could benefit by our sending love and uplifting thoughts to them. Love is the most powerful force in the universe. If we think about that statement awhile and ponder its significance, we can see how sending love to others has the potential of doing a great deal of good. Love sent to others may be just what they need to help them out of a crisis or move them forward so that they may be encouraged to take that next step. Love can heal relationships and break barriers of deep hatred and misunderstanding. It can heal physical ailments and bring balance to the spirit, mind, and body.

We are accustomed to thinking we have to be "out there" doing something that appears significant and important and takes lots of our energy. However, let's remember that by simply sending out positive thoughts to others we can do more good than we can by exhausting ourselves trying to "do good" out there in the world.

There is a place for both kinds of activity. But let's not put ourselves down by doing what may appear to be the lazy man's method of serving. It's the old tapes in our minds that tell us we have to be out physically accomplishing something that looks good to others. After all, God knows all that we are doing and not doing. We each have a recording angel who keeps a record of all the good deeds that we do. Furthermore, we will be repaid for all the good that we do in the world. In fact, when we give of ourselves, our return will be one hundred times greater.

Giving and receiving keeps the balance in our lives and is important to how we feel physically, emotionally, mentally, and spiritually. We need only to try it sometime when we're not quite up to par in order to see the difference it makes. As we become too self-centered, we become out of balance, so the balance has to be restored. Often it's the last thing we feel like doing. However, it is often the answer to our dilemma.

As we give to others, we will find our lives changing. The more we give and send out love to all around us, the more that comes back into our lives. We will find that if we can bring light to a negative situation and send love to those involved, it can be resolved very quickly. We will find more people being attracted to us as we send out this positive energy, and our world will open up as it never has before.

Therefore, as we look at our lives and take note of how we can best serve humanity, let's remember that as we serve others, we are serving ourselves as well. As the Law of Attraction records each act, the good that we do will be returned to us. We know, too, that as we maintain a balance between giving and receiving, we are serving God and humanity as well as healing ourselves.

BOOK TEN

ON BELIEFS

Our beliefs are unique to each one of us. Because we are all individuals, our beliefs will vary according to our background, culture, religion, and political viewpoint. As we grow and change, our beliefs change. What we believe to be true one day may change the next: we are evolving spiritual beings.

We are living in a time of great change upon the planet. As a result, many individuals will be changing their viewpoints concerning themselves and the world. There is a maturation process taking place. Some of the older, more traditional ways of thinking and doing things will be discarded in this process. We need to find new ways, new methods to reach the individual. We have become lost in our attempts to serve ourselves through science, technology, and bureaucracy. Though many of our accomplishments have been worthy in and of themselves, we have lost the ability to connect, not only with each other, but with ourselves as well.

In our attempt to serve ourselves, we have become lost in the mire of red tape that alienates us from one another rather than bringing us together. Further, as we have tried to help ourselves through our religious beliefs, we have become isolated, often through fear, intolerance, and hypocrisy. These issues are now being addressed so we can no longer hide behind that which we have been calling truth, but which is not.

Our attempts to help others to "see the light" by means which attempt to control the individual will be exposed. Further, where we have been hypocritical and self-righteous, the mask will be removed. Again, in those areas in which we have been dishonest with others and ourselves, we will now have to get honest. As the walls of bureaucracy come tumbling down, new methods and avenues of connecting ourselves to each other and the world will be established. Traditional values and attitudes will be scrutinized and stripped of their power when they no longer serve humanity. We are entering into a new time. Where there has been discord, peace will rule. The walls of artificiality will be torn down. Now is the time for the real values of man to be reborn.

How do we decide what is real and not real? That which lasts is real. That which passes away is not. That which supports man in his journey up the mountain—his spiritual journey—will last. That which goes contrary to spiritual progress will wither and die. That which separates us from each other in values, beliefs, and attitudes will be dismantled. That which brings us together, supporting our similarities rather than our differences will survive. As we move into this new time, those who attempt to hold on to old values and traditions which are not meant to work any longer will suffer for refusing to let go and go with the flow. As we resist, we cause pain to ourselves and others. It's time now to let go—to be open to new ideas, new thoughts, new ways. It's time to remember that we're all individuals, and each of us has our own path to take.

There is no right way up the mountain. We all do things differently and that is how it should be. If we all followed the same religion and belief system, we would not be true to ourselves. Therefore, if we think there is only one way, we will be shown that this is not true. As Jesus once said, "By their fruits you shall know them." In this time there will be many persons from all religions and belief systems who will exemplify the truth. There is only one Truth, but many ways to that Truth and many means of expressing it. The more open we become to others and their framework of values, the easier this transition will be for us. As we close ourselves off from each other, believing our way is the only way, we slow up our progress.

We will all have to come to this place of unity in time. By "unity" is meant our ability to allow others to believe, think, and feel as is appropriate for them. As we allow others, we will be allowing ourselves. As we restrict others, we restrict ourselves because that is the law. Remember, when we see our neighbor in his beliefs and his struggles, we have been there too. Further, when we notice his lack of tolerance and rigid belief system, we must recall that we also have held ourselves down. And when we become aware of another's inability to be open to our philosophy, we have also walked in his shoes.

It's only as we have learned to discard our fears that we are able to reach out to others. It's only when we have discovered that there is no need to fear what may happen to us as we express ourselves that we can feel whole again. Many have come forth to help us in this time of transition. There are those who teach and those who heal. There are many who are the decision makers in government as well as in business and industry; their task is to point the way to new and better ways. There are others who come of their own accord to help in the area of environment and health in order that we may save ourselves from destroying that which we set out to preserve. There are those who come quietly in the night from spirit who help show us the way. As we each take our direction—our assignments—upon us, we must learn how to banish any residual fears which may be left over from the past, when our attempts to express the truth were squelched by our fear of others. Now we must come forward again, not fearing the power given to us to take our rightful place as healers, teachers, communicators, musicians, artists, writers, and ministers.

We must not allow ourselves to be overcome by fear. We must learn that as we express ourselves and meet the challenges presented to us along our path, we will eventually eliminate any stumbling blocks. As we persist, our work will become a labor of joy to us. It doesn't matter what image we project or what group we belong to, our job is the same. It is to bring people together with respect for all. Everyone has a right to be here and express him—or herself in a unique way. It is our job as leaders to bring truth to the people.

And what is this truth? It may perhaps be better described by what it is not. It is not controlling, rigid, or hypocritical. It is not intolerant of others' beliefs or impatient with the progress of others. It is not artificial or steeped in values that are not lasting. It is not close-minded and unsympathetic to the needs and situations of others. It is not inappropriately expressed.

Instead, truth speaks for itself and abides in all who listen for it. It speaks of harmony and peace. Its values are lasting and do not express fear of any kind. Truth accepts the viewpoints of others, perhaps not as its own, but as a means to an end. Truth is not afraid to express itself, regardless of the consequences, because it knows it will win out in the end. Truth has compassion for those who fall by the wayside. Truth never dies. It has followed us this far and will continue to speak to us until we begin to live it. And as we do, the transition that has begun will be made as gently as possible.

As we each take our assignments, however we see them, we help complete the design which allows this plan to work out as it was intended to do, thus bringing together the correct forces to bear upon the earth at the appropriate time. As this Divine intervention is upon us, we can thank God that we have been allowed to be here as witnesses to this great transformation.

ON SPIRIT

How may God speak to us? God speaks to us through spirit, which takes many forms. The form it assumes for us at any given time depends on many things. Regardless of appearances, however, we are constantly being made aware of spirit around us. We must acknowledge its presence.

On the other hand, we may close ourselves off to the manifestation of spirit in our lives if we choose. There are some persons who believe it important for them to live without acknowledging this tremendous force. They seem to feel that to do so is showing some kind of weakness. They fear that dependency on something greater than themselves is in some way demeaning to them, so they often block the very energy that can help them in their lives. Sooner or later, at some point in everyone's evolution, there comes a time when we will all have to acknowledge God's presence: that is the purpose of life as each individual comes to know and understand his place in God's kingdom. It's comparable to a child's coming to acknowledge the presence of the head of the house—the person who makes the rules and "holds the cards," so to speak. The child may rebel and not want to obey his father, but he can't deny his presence.

Spirit speaks to us in many ways and through many forms. As we are open to the messages it brings we can gain great knowledge, insight, and guidance for ourselves. Further, we can add a new level of enjoyment to our lives as we see how these messages can come to us. Such awareness brings a sense of fulfillment to those who are open to it.

The process is something like a game in which many clues are given as the players attempt to win. As they attempt to reach the goal and defeat their opponents (who may represent challenges), the players are given signposts along the way to guide them. As these clues are taken into consideration and reflected upon, and as the various warnings are heeded which keep the player in line, great advances can be made. The person who chooses to ignore the clues closes himself off to help and seeks to make his way on his own, without the hints and secrets that may ensure his success. Therefore, he often doesn't make the entire journey. He doesn't finish the game. His challenges overcome him and he can go only so far on his own. He may be pleased with the great efforts he has made and the degree of success he has had. Nevertheless, he may not understand that there could have been more for him. He may think he won the game, when in reality he's only half-way towards his goal.

We expend much effort when we "go it alone." Our challenges do, indeed, become work as we shut spirit out of our lives. We make our own decisions with no assurance that they are the correct ones. We worry about everything, because we don't have the desire or the faith to ask for help. We exhaust ourselves in an effort that could be shared if we would but allow our co-creator to assist us. Life becomes a struggle. However, as soon as we come to the awareness that inviting God's power or Divine energy to flow through us, we find that we are not weak at all, but have simply adopted a new and different way of operating. It doesn't have to be labeled good, bad or indifferent; it simply exists.

We must choose between these modes of action. Whichever way we choose to go becomes part of the experience that enables us to continue our journey.

Perhaps a person needs to go it alone for a period in order to understand the feelings that come from doing so. One can't appreciate God's power unless he's been without it. We take driving our car for granted until it runs out of gas. The same may be said for spiritual power. We appreciate what God can do for us only when we understand through experience what we can't do for ourselves.

Many people try very hard to take care of themselves in their own way. They may even study religion and spirituality. They may be able to quote the Bible at length. They may even have become ministers and priests proclaiming God's power, and yet not have a clue as to how to let go and allow it to work for them. It's always sad to see such a case. There are individuals who have spent much of their life seeking spirit and never finding it because they have not allowed themselves to open their hearts. They are still locked in their fears and prejudices and can't open the blinds for even a moment to allow the light in. They are forever in their intellect, expounding their views and their beliefs without exploring for themselves what meaning they have in their lives. They are controlling in their attitudes and behavior and yet feel controlled at the same time. They are bound by their obsessive need to be right and to dominate their environment, whether it is their home, their business, or their church. The thought of being wrong is so frightening to them that they hold tenaciously to their opinions for fear they themselves may soften. Further, if they do soften, there is a fear that they may bend; if they bend, they may allow someone else's beliefs to affect them. And if we should become tolerant of another's way of looking at life, what could happen to us? Do we die? Do we simply annihilate ourselves? Or could it be, instead, that we are led to believe as is appropriate for us?

Once we open the door even a crack, we allow God to slip in a gift to us. Instead of being a bomb that might explode in our hands, it turns out to be a butterfly that we can admire and set free. We don't hold on to the butterfly. But we may examine its beauty from all angles and then let it fly away. Wherever it goes is God's business. It may fly out the crack in the door or it may land on our head. It may disappear or it may remain with us.

So it is with the awareness that is brought to us by our spirit. We needn't be frightened by it, but as we examine it and see it for what it is, we then allow God to decide if it is for us or not. If it is for us, it will remain with us. If not, it will be taken from us, but we'll still be allowed to exist.

We all have a purpose, and if we allow spirit to bring us its gifts, and if we allow God to choose what to hold fast to and what to let go, we will be led right. Remember, too, that we are constantly seeking balance: if some individuals appear to you to be becoming too involved in some activity or pursuit, they may be seeking to balance what was not there before. The middle road will be found eventually as nature continues to seek for balance. All souls will find their rightful place in time, whether they go by way of spirit or on their own for a period of time.

As we choose to work with spirit, we invite its presence in all that we do. Angels and divas may visit us. We may open ourselves to the nature spirits that tend our plants and the fairies that abide in the woods. Archangels and avatars may visit us. We may be blessed by the White Brotherhood, whose mission it is to inform and uplift the souls of those who are ready. We may speak to the spirits of our animals and come to see the roles our pets play in our lives. We may become open to all of life as we read the pain in the eyes of those we meet on our journey. We know the right words to say to help others regain their strength and we can laugh as prompted from within by those in spirit who are there to help lighten our load.

Indeed, the gifts are there for each one of us to experience if we choose. We must be open to those many and varied forms that knock on our door to shake us out of our complacency. It's true, we "entertain angels unaware." And as our awareness becomes greater, more will be shown to us. We don't die, and spirit never dies. As long as God is, we are. We may choose to be open or we may close ourselves off from the beautiful world that exists around and within us. The spirit world is for all of us to explore as we choose.

ON ILLNESS

As we seek to discover the role that illness plays in our lives, we are reminded that disease means just that: dis-ease. When we are ill, we lack ease; we are not in harmony with our true nature. What does this mean?

It means that within each of us is contained a perfect pattern which represents our wholeness. As we think, so we are. As our thoughts are harmonious, so are our physical bodies. All illness begins first within the mind. We cause our ill health through our thinking and our attitudes toward ourselves and life in general. If our thoughts are positive and in harmony with the God force, we will also allow that energy to pervade the cells in our bodies so that health is maintained. Conversely, as we allow ourselves to be controlled by negative thoughts from within and around us, we invite disharmony to become a part of the physical body as well. This is another area that those who are on the path come to see as a part of the responsibility we take on when we refrain from placing blame outside of ourselves. Often we don't know the cause of a particular illness we have invited into our lives. Yet it's important to know that at some level of our being we've chosen to experience this disharmony within the body in order to learn something. There are times when we are aware that our nerves, for example, are making us ill. Sooner or later we know we'll end up with ulcers if we stay on the same course we're now following. We also know that if we insist on driving very fast because we are angry or upset we are inviting an accident to slow us down. Sometimes various twitches within the muscles can be trying to tell us something; if we learn to pay attention, we can develop the ability to ascertain what these spasms are indicating to us.

Illness is always there to teach us something. The next time we complain of a bad cold, we can ask ourselves what we have been experiencing lately that might make us feel run down. Perhaps we also have the need to sit and have a good cry about something that we have not yet acknowledged. In this fast-paced world we live in, we often don't allow ourselves to feel our hurts and nurse our wounds. Therefore, we come down with a cold instead. This entitles us to take care of ourselves in another way that is more acceptable to us than crying.

Our diseases mask what is really going on within us. Often, for example, our rigid attitudes and behaviors, and in particular our lack of tolerance for others, may come out in the form of illness, particularly of the joints. Every part of the body has a way of speaking to us of our attitudes, beliefs, and values about the world and ourselves. As these perceptions become distorted, they manifest themselves in some area of the body that relates to that particular attitude, belief, or value. Further, as we become whole and spiritually aware, we learn to keep these perceptions harmonious with the God force. As we find ourselves out of balance, which is part of the human condition, we attempt to discover what it is we need to change, reevaluating where our problem is located and how it can best be treated.

Meditation can help greatly along this line. We need not discover exactly why we have this particular symptom or ache or pain, but we can seek to rid ourselves of it simply by asking for its release. It is a good practice to affirm this release of negativity from areas within the body that are painful or otherwise out of harmony. We can simply lie down on our bed and say, "I now release all the negativity from within me that has caused this pain in my toe," for example. If there is not a particular physical problem, its good to say, "I now release any negativity I'm carrying in mind, body, or spirit and fill myself with Divine Light and love." This is an affirmation that is highly effective when done with visualization. This practice helps to keep the body from developing conditions within itself that are difficult to release.

Because we allow these conditions to build from time to time within the body, we need to be patient with ourselves as we go through the process of being ill, whether we're confined at home or have to go into the hospital or other facility for care. Perhaps the change in attitude toward our illness would be a good idea.

Having respect for ourselves and our illness can be helpful. Instead of just wishing it away, we can first of all congratulate ourselves for accepting the challenge our condition has brought. Illnesses, as well as accidents, may be telling us that we are willing to be slowed down to look at a problem. When we're stopped short by a car accident and have to go to the hospital, we have some time to think. As we lie there, perhaps it might be good to ask the universe what brought us to this place. Being open to the truth speeds us on our way to getting well.

The answer may not come as a bolt of lightning. It may not be that we will hear God boom out, "You're afraid to take that new job! That's why your heel is sore." However, because we have opened ourselves and asked for knowledge and help, it will come to you, perhaps in a much more subtle way. You will learn about your illness and begin to heal because that is the law. "Ask and you shall receive."

We can face our illnesses and physical handicaps and learn to respect their place in our lives. We can accept the challenge of working with our dilemma and learn much about ourselves in the process. Further, while we are making discoveries about ourselves, we find much we can share with others to help them along the way to recovery.

People who have major handicaps in their lives are in some ways very blessed. They have chosen a route by which to learn a great deal in a relatively short period of time. Even a lifetime is short in the large scheme of things. The more debilitating the handicap, the greater the advancement, especially if the condition is undertaken with love and acceptance. Acceptance is the key to living with illness. It doesn't mean accepting the illness without working with it, but it does mean accepting the challenge it brings.

Each debilitating illness brings with it its own corresponding conditions to be dealt with. And whether they are dealt with or not, they represent the appropriate challenge to the person who is suffering. For example, if we have broken a leg, we will be in a cast and have to ambulate on crutches. We are slowed down. We are more deliberate when we have to deal with our foot, our leg and our crutches. Every movement is carefully planned. Pains must be taken so that further damage isn't done. As we make it into an easy chair and finally get our foot propped up on the pillow and stare out at the calm lake in front of us, we ask ourselves if we take the same care in examining our own life and ultimate destination.

Again, what about the person who must spend much of his life in the care of others? He must wait until others are ready to help him with his physical needs. Thus he develops patience. He may not like all of those who attend him. Thus he develops tolerance. He may find he has to work hard every day on his rehabilitation so that perhaps someday he can walk. Thus he develops perseverance, hope, trust, and faith; not only in the Almighty, but in himself.

As we look at the role illness plays in our lives, we must have respect for ourselves and others in the process. Sometimes we choose an illness for the opportunity that can bring us to spiritual growth. So let us not judge ourselves or others on appearance: we don't know why this condition has afflicted us or those we love.

On a higher level, we do choose all of our experiences, including illness. Therefore, we can stop thinking of ourselves as victims. Moreover, we have every right to choose what comes to us as well as to understand our choice. In other words, we have the right to learn all about our condition and what it can do for us. We already know how it hinders us. But let's learn to focus on how it can help us. What can we learn and how can we advance ourselves in what we know?

Working in this way, we can help ourselves to get well and to stay healthy. When we find ourselves in a crisis, whether it be in the mind, body, or emotions, let's congratulate ourselves on the courage to overcome the challenge.

ON SPIRITUALITY

Spirituality is that which pertains to the spirit. We all have a spirit, therefore spirituality pertains to everyone. That which is of the spirit is universal, and universal means "all." Religion, on the other hand, has to do with dogma. Religion tends to be more specific because it pertains to a set of beliefs that are adhered to by a particular person or group. In order to be religious, we have to subscribe to the beliefs of a particular religion, while spirituality includes everyone.

We all have our own brand of spirituality. We each use our God-given spirit in a different way and express ourselves according to the way in which our spirit sees the world. There is only one truth, but as many ways of viewing and expressing that truth as there are individuals. Each has his or her unique brand of spirituality, which may be expressed in any number of ways. One may desire to be a staunch Methodist, while another may be a "wayward" Catholic. Another may be a respected priest while another may prefer not to go to church at all.

Each is still expressing him—or herself in a distinct way. The fact that we do or do not attend church does not indicate our degree of spirituality. There are many individuals who express their spirit beautifully, but who do not attend church. Church attendance generally indicates our desire to belong to a particular group that expresses its faith in God. Others have great faith in God, but have never seen the inside of a church. The American Indian, for example, has his own unique way of acknowledging the Creator through his involvement in the sanctity of nature and the power derived from it.

God is everywhere and is everything. How we choose to acknowledge and express God's power depends on our culture and background as well as our perception of what it is to be spiritual. Often people change their religion because they need to incorporate a new aspect of learning into their experience in order that the soul might be more fulfilled.

We see with only limited vision, and often what we might regard as a reason to leave a particular church may not necessarily be the "real" reason. Perhaps we are disgruntled at the minister's asking for money, or maybe we find his sermons boring, and so we leave the church. However, on another level there may be something entirely different going on. It may be that we have spent a good deal of time with formal religion and deep down we have a desire to explore within our own being. We've come to a place in our life and in our spiritual development or "spirituality" where we crave a deeper meaning for our own existence. Further, perhaps we wish to see how others worship. Then again, maybe we feel the need for ritual, which we feel has been lacking in our spiritual life. There are many reasons why we may desire to change direction, and all of them can be valid.

Just as we need a change of clothes for variety and to be comfortable in different kinds of weather, we may find we need different forms of expression in spirit to make us feel secure and fulfilled. Do you ever hear people say, "I like to go to such and such a church for the most part, but once in awhile I go back to the one I used to go, to for the ritual," for example. We often need different ways of expressing ourselves and sometimes this means going back for a time to what we have left behind. We need to see whether we were wise to leave that with which we had perhaps grown up. At other times we go back because we still miss a certain aspect of the spiritual community that was meaningful and important to us.

Often as we evolve spiritually we need to find our own answers. The churches and spiritual communities to which we belong can come just so far with us, and then we may develop a strong desire to obtain our own answers. The church can tell us only so much about ourselves, and we find we want to know more.

We want to discover who we really are and where we are going. We wish to discover our purpose in life and if we have a mission to accomplish. Furthermore, because most of us are curious, we have many other questions relating to our lives and the means by which we can accomplish our goals. Organized religion and doctrine can give us some tools to use, but ultimately our answers must come from within. We must ask and seek within our own hearts for the answers.

No one can tell us what our purpose is. They may, if they are gifted, be able to discern something about our goals in life, but they can't "feel" it for us. We must feel our own purpose. To have knowledge of what may be is only of the intellect, and we need to feel it so that it becomes our desire to fulfill it. We must seek within ourselves and begin to feel the spirit respond within us. In this way, we can begin to get in touch with who we are and where we may be headed.

We have control over our lives—at least over our spirit. We are the only ones who can stop us from fulfilling our goals as we have defined them from the spirit side of life; i.e., if our goals are realistic and in line with our purpose, no one else can prevent our achieving them. However, how we decide to get in touch with our spirit to find our answers is a very individual thing. To judge another's path only brings judgment on ourselves. Therefore, let's keep our options open as we look for ways to express ourselves spiritually. Further, as we become aware of who we are and how we got to be where we are, we can accept where others are on their journey up the same mountain. We are all one family, but, like a wise father with many children, God allows each of us to experience life in a different way.

Therefore, as we glance over at what our brothers and sisters are doing, let's support them in their effort to know themselves as we seek within our own hearts to discover our own unique spirit and how it may best express itself in the world.

ON JUSTICE

While we humans seek for justice in the world, the universe has its own way of providing us with the conditions we need to learn our lessons. Man's inhumanity to man cannot and should not go unpunished, and yet often we fall short of our goals in educating people not to turn to crime in their frustration with life. Naturally, there need to be laws to protect the citizens of the world, and there need also be measures taken against those who break the law. This is the way it must be in the physical reality.

However, in God's world there is a different set of rules. As we break God's laws, the soul is aware of the transgression and immediately sets out to correct it by setting up a corresponding situation that will bring upon the transgressor that which he has inflicted on another. Even when we have hurt ourselves through drinking too much or working too hard, we will get another opportunity to do it differently—to make new choices. Therefore, as we break the natural or spiritual laws we will always have ample opportunity to make up for it in new situations which will be set up for the purpose of testing us. As we test ourselves, we may make a new choice to think and act differently—to change our ways and try something new.

Sometimes it's very difficult to try new ways. It can feel frightening and uncomfortable to start a new way of life, for example. To leave a job or family and to take on another such challenge, when we have seen that the old way is not working, is unsettling at best. While starting over can be a joy, it still carries with it, as well, an element of risk which leaves us feeling insecure and scared. Nevertheless, how fortunate we are that new opportunities come to us.

Have we ever thought about what it would be like to never have another chance? What if we were never able to be released from our self-made prisons? Many of us have come into this lifetime with challenges that require us to release old habits and old ways of thinking—old patterns which have been ingrained in the soul. We knew these challenges before birth and we agreed to take them on in our lifetime.

For some it may mean healing a relationship which had caused much conflict in the past. For others it may mean healing an addiction. For still others it may mean taking on a responsibility which was met with opposition in earlier times. Again, perhaps one has a tendency toward sadness and loneliness and needs to develop ways of overcoming such feelings. Still another may need to deal with a very complex situation involving several relationships simultaneously. Again, another may need to heal his past entirely and become transformed in order to help lead others into the new age—the Aquarian Age, which is now upon us. Then again, there is the possibility that one person may play out all these scenarios. This could be one individual's assignment as he "chose his classes" for the coming lifetime. If it sounds like an accelerated course, it may be.

Many are choosing just such challenges so that they may get their "act cleaned up" in a hurry because much will be expected of them as time goes by. A great many others will perhaps not be electing to advance quite that rapidly: they have chosen to learn carefully the lessons they have prepared and they understand the importance of getting it right this time. Repetition of the same old mistakes is unappealing to them because they have decided to make some rather drastic changes this time. They intend to better their lives and make use of their talents and abilities that perhaps they have let go by the wayside in past times.

Where conditions and circumstances are difficult at best, we often don't use the gifts God has given us because we are too busy trying to survive. We're too busy just trying to cope with the world and our problems and can't see how playing the violin, doing creative writing, or swimming the English Channel is going to help our situation.

Instead, we are spending sleepless nights worrying and fretting over our dilemmas. Therefore, though perhaps we'd love to put on elegant parties, we're too busy fighting with our spouse and arguing with ourselves to even imagine, let alone plan, such an affair. And though we'd love to play baseball again, how can we possibly, when we're so in debt we have to work night and day to make ends meet?

Is this justice working itself out? Maybe so. We bring upon ourselves these conditions so that we may learn from them. Earth is a place of great learning. It is a place like no other to gather experience to put into the computer we call our brain, which in turn feeds the subconscious mind. As we keep making the same mistakes over and over again, we record each experience we have, pleasant or unpleasant.

Finally, one day when we've had enough of the same repetitive unpleasant reaction to life, we say, "Enough. I've had enough." We don't really know how long we've been doing the same old thing. It may be weeks, months, years, or lifetimes before we arrive at the moment when it's over.

Suddenly we know we're on a new path—a new way. The old cannot be repeated. We now have learned that in this area of our life we are going to learn to respond to this particular situation in a new way. It may be right, or it may be wrong. We're at the point where we know that to go back is not possible. We are on to a new course—a new way of thinking, believing, and acting. No more will we react in the same old way. We have been shaken shamefully out of our complacency and put on a new road. We were given another opportunity and we took it. We packed our bags and got on a train, and there's no turning back.

Justice in man's world seeks its own revenge. Justice according to universal law will meet itself. That which we send out will come back to us. If we harm ourselves or another, the deed will come back to our own doorstep. Further, while we keep making the same mistakes and reacting in the same old way to life, it will treat us accordingly. We will be treated as we asked to be treated. Therefore, when we seek to change our minds and our behavior, our world will change. We will set into motion new conditions that will play back to us that which we have programmed.

The fact that that which happens to us is created by us serves to let us know that we do, indeed, have control over our lives. Therefore, there is much we can do to change what we don't like. As we learn to work in harmony with our Creator, many things can happen very quickly to change our present circumstances. We need not wait around forever to stop worrying and start living. All we need do is ask for Divine help and intervention. Further, that which we have let ride for days, weeks, or months can be changed overnight if we ask.

Spirit won't help us unless we ask. We have to take that responsibility as we assume this role of co-creator. If we allow God to be the director, we'll be all right. As soon as we try to direct the play, we start making mistakes again. So it's okay to make mistakes: that's how we learn. We needn't worry because we'll always correct ourselves, and we have ample time to do it. Just as soon as we've erred, we've set into motion a new opportunity.

Therefore, let's thank God for His mercy on us as He shows us what it means to be patient with His children. The universe can wait while we get our act together, and our Creator will always see us through the hard times.

ON FRUSTRATION

Frustration along the spiritual path is common. Often there is enthusiasm as one begins this journey, and then somewhere along the way, not too far down the road, we hit a snag and we become frustrated. Either we don't know what to do about something, or we feel as though we are blocked in some way and can't move it any further. As a result, we become discouraged.

Indeed, it would be amazing if one never felt frustrated. We have, many of us, high goals and we wish to do a good job at whatever we attempt to accomplish. As a result, we have set up situations which have the potential to be frustrating for us. If we didn't care to accomplish much of anything in the way of improving our lot, or if we were not caring, particularly, what kind of a job we did, then we would not be disappointed at our failure to adhere to high standards.

On the contrary, many of us are perfectionists, a fact that makes it difficult to succeed easily because we expect so much of ourselves. It is best not to be a perfectionist, but still aspire to relatively high standards. When we expect too much of ourselves and everyone around us, we are apt to be very hard on ourselves as well as on others. We create disharmony when we expect everyone, ourselves included, to toe the mark. When things don't match our expectations, we become upset with the conditions around us. Then we become upset with ourselves because we've allowed the situation to get us down—to destroy our peace.

Perhaps we wake up one day—the only day we've had off for a long time and we have to go back to work tomorrow. We have great expectations and have planned the day carefully so as to make the most of our time. We plan to do a little shopping. There's a dress we saw that we'd like to buy. Then we plan to have lunch with a friend. Following lunch we planned to sit outside the rest of the afternoon, or perhaps go to the beach to enjoy the beautiful day. Unfortunately, things don't seem to go as we had planned. Someone bought the dress just five minutes before we got to the store. Our friend forgot her lunch date with us, and the weather turned. It began to rain just as we got settled at the beach. Are these not situations which would cause frustration? Of course they are. Anyone could be thrown off by such disappointments.

What then is the answer? How do we handle frustration? And how do we approach our life to avoid unnecessarily frustrating conditions?

First of all, it's best for us to remember that we aren't directing the play. If we put ourselves in God's hands each day, asking that we do that day all that would be best for us, we're less apt to make mistakes. As we ask for Divine light and guidance each day, and as we ask to be in tune with our intuition, which can tell us if a particular action seems appropriate or not, we'll be better able to make choices.

There are times when we feel we want to go out and get all sorts of things done, and yet if we consult our intuition we may be surprised. It may tell us to spend our day quite differently. It might be that we should be staying inside to take care of things in our home. Learning to follow our intuitive sense in making decisions is often a good way to avoid frustrating situations.

Another way to avoid frustration may be to change our attitude about these situations when they do occur. Instead of becoming completely upset, we can learn to be more patient when things don't go our way. We can learn to be gentle with ourselves and keep our sense of humor. It's important not to take ourselves too seriously. When we do, we get thrown when things don't come off as we planned. Therefore, being patient, maintaining a sense of humor, and taking life in a lighter vein all help in not becoming frustrated.

There are times when we will be tested in this area. We challenge ourselves to see how patient we are. Are you ever aware of going through a day when you are constantly waiting for your turn? You may be at the grocery store and the person in front of you has several coupons that the check-out person has to process. Sometimes it can seem like an eternity while you wait for this transaction to take place. Then you get into your car and the person in front of you is driving very slowly. Next, you get home and the phone stops ringing just as you walk in the door.

These kinds of situations help us to build our character. It's often the small experiences we have during our day that can make a difference in the rapidity with which we can move on our spiritual path. As we pass each little test, we allow ourselves to move up the ladder another step. We often think of the larger, more powerful experiences in our lives as being indicators of how we are doing, but actually it's the small things that count.

These seemingly insignificant daily encounters we have with people during our day tell us a lot about where we are in our growth. It's the way we handle the rude lady in the department store or the smile we give to the lonely person at the bus stop. Then again, perhaps it's helping someone with heavy packages that makes the difference. The larger, seemingly more obvious events and crises in our lives are important, but it's the little things that pave the way to our successful handling of larger problems.

Another reason for frustration on the spiritual path is our desire to advance farther and faster than is good for us. Our Higher Power knows the best timetable for us; if we would remember that, we'd be better off. There are times we think we should be further along than we are, but again, with our limited vision we can't see all the facts. There are many other factors involved of which we are totally unaware.

In order for us to take another step up the spiritual ladder, many conditions have to be in perfect order. It's just as if we were to open a brand new store or restaurant. Everything has to be completely ready before we display the "Open" sign.

Because we don't know what all of these conditions are, it's best to simply trust that we will move along at the rate chosen for us. We're not being forgotten. We're being watched over carefully and protected so we don't move too fast before adequate preparations can be made for us. So, let's remember that we are in good hands, and trust that we will know when the time is right to make our move.

It pays to be gentle and patient with ourselves. Let us learn to enjoy life and the people around us, being aware of who might need a smile or kind word. Further, let's hold to our high standards while learning not to expect too much of ourselves or others. Let us place all in God's hands with the knowledge that because we're being watched over and cared for, doors will open and we will advance as the universe is ready for us. Finally, let us realize that because we have an understanding of these principles, we can and will be able to avoid situations that could be potentially frustrating. We can allow ourselves to calm down, cool down, and trust in our Creator.

BOOK ELEVEN

ON PERFECTIONISM

How can perfectionism be a stumbling block on the path? Having the compulsive need to be perfect can be very hard on anyone. Often people aren't aware that they are perfectionists, unless it is pointed out to them or they begin to recognize the trait within themselves.

Often, the reason people fail to see it is that they often feel they are coming up short or not making the mark. Because they aren't able to bring about the perfect conditions that they desire, these people tend to view themselves not as perfectionists, but as failures. They feel devastated, believing that they are not succeeding in reaching their goals. Convinced that they are lacking in some way, they are compelled to work harder and harder to make things come out perfectly. Unfortunately, they also expect the same of others.

This situation causes great anxiety and turmoil in the people around a perfectionist. It may be that others don't share that drive for perfection, and they can't see what all the fuss is about. They can't understand why anyone would want to become so upset about something that seems so insignificant to them. They can't understand how someone can make him—or herself virtually sick over some trifle that doesn't really matter much in their eyes.

Therefore, being a perfectionist creates problems, not only for the individual who suffers from it, but for those around them. For example, working for a boss who is a perfectionist is hard on everyone in the office. People walk around on "eggshells," not knowing what to expect. They're constantly waiting for "the other shoe to drop," which in most cases, it does.

Where does this need to be perfect come from? Maybe we grew up with a parent who had the problem. This sort of thing is often carried on down to the next generation. As a child begins to feel he or she is inadequate due to their inability to live up to the standards of the parent, they tend to enter the same cycle of working hard in order to please. This becomes a compulsive inner need, and if we asked them about it, they probably wouldn't have the slightest idea why they have such a drive. In most cases, they wouldn't even recognize it because they don't see themselves or their situation objectively. Further, because they focus on what is lacking instead of what is there, their cup is always half empty instead of half full. This is unfortunate as it tends to take the joy out of life.

Always seeing what needs to be done rather than looking at what has been accomplished can leave one feeling incomplete and exhausted. Further, if we're always seeing the flaw rather than the beauty of the whole design, we cheat ourselves and others by not giving credit where it is due. Instead, we're always looking for what is wrong. There is also the feeling that we are always inadequate because we are constantly comparing ourselves with others. Feeling our job is never good enough no matter what it is we're doing can leave us feeling negatively about ourselves. Even if we do accomplish something that seems perfect in our eyes, it is only a drop in the bucket.

When we expect perfection it is usually in many, if not all, areas of our lives. So even if we do achieve one thing well, it gives us very little comfort: there is always the next challenge to meet. The real fact is that perfectionism never ends. Consequently, we are perpetually looking ahead, feeling frustrated at our need to go through life never making mistakes and whipping ourselves when we do. Growing up in this kind of environment is unhealthy for children and can be harmful to their self-esteem. If we learn to be gentle with ourselves and realize that it's okay to make mistakes, even if others are not happy with us, we become much healthier, self-accepting people. We also go easier on others, and consequently we're much more enjoyable to be with.

As we learn to accept ourselves with our mistakes and to welcome God's will for us on any given day, we relax. Relaxing is important on the spiritual path. As we relax the personality—the brain and the mind—we can allow the spirit self to take over. We then allow ourselves to pick up the intuitive thoughts that try so hard to reach us through our anxieties and our fears. Further, as we stop trying to control, we allow our higher power to run our lives. It will direct our next move and comfort us when we err.

There's nothing wrong with making mistakes—big or small. We're on the earth to learn. If we were truly meant to be perfect, we would not be here. We're not here to demonstrate how we can control ourselves and everyone around us so that the world can be perfect in our eyes. We must remember that we have limited vision, so our view of what is perfect may differ from God's view.

Therefore, we shouldn't be dismayed when we see our imperfections, whether they are physical, mental, emotional, or spiritual. We are all human, and we need to recognize the humanity as well as the humility in ourselves and others. If we are perfectionists, let's be glad that we have ample time and opportunity to grow. We'll be happier if we see ourselves from a new and healthy perspective.

So let's leave the prospect of being perfect to the Creator that created us. Further, let's begin to understand that this trait is something we can overcome as we allow ourselves to be who we are. At the same time, we must allow others the same privilege. We will be far more content when we allow ourselves to relax and let the spirit within bring things to their proper conclusions. Leaving the results to our Higher Power, while we take care of the footwork, is a good policy to follow. And...well, if things don't turn out to be perfect in our eyes, maybe they weren't meant to. Let's trust in the God of our own understanding to know what is best both for ourselves and for others.

ON NEGATIVITY

How do we deal with negativity on the spiritual path? What do we mean by being negative? There are times when it feels appropriate to be negative: perhaps we're sad, worried about a loved one, or perhaps we've lost our wallet and are concerned about losing all of our money. We can feel negative, too, with momentary bouts of jealousy and fear.

Again, perhaps we're disappointed because plans we made fell through and we have to give up a trip we've been looking forward to. Then again, maybe we're tense because a child is sick or we're having to work hard over a certain period of time. All of these things can cause us to feel negative for a while. However, when the situation or condition has passed, we become our normal, reasonable, contented self again.

However, when people are said to be very negative, it usually implies that they are negative about life in general. They complain about everything, from the food in the restaurant to the weather. They seem to have a habit of nit-picking, finding fault with everything and everyone. They seldom see the good in things and they're masters at finding the flaws in every situation. Instead of just brushing something off, they tend to focus on another's mistakes. In doing so, they exaggerate the error, if there was one at all, and make the situation worse than it really was.

Negative people can be dangerous because they can get everybody else involved. By making situations sound worse than they really are, they can cause people to change things that perhaps didn't need to be changed at all. Through their negativity, they manage to gain power to bring things around to where they would like to see them. A very negative person can usually manipulate others, because people tend to shy away from the strongly negative approach to life. Others tend to give in to the very negative person simply because they find it easier to do so than to confront the negative energy emanating from such a person. Therefore, by being negative, demanding, and nit-picking, people often get their way.

It takes energy and some courage to stand up to someone who is easily angered and obstinate. Often people would just as soon give this type of person the upper hand. However, capitulation is unfortunate, because it encourages this type of behavior. If a person comes to know that he can manipulate others by bullying his way through something, he's apt to continue this type of behavior until someone stops him.

Negativity also attracts further negativity. If we wake up "on the wrong side of the bed" in the morning, feeling crabby and out of sorts, one could say we were negative. There seems to be no known reason for our hostility. We simply feel like being a grouch. We all have days like this. If this kind of behavior continues day after day, however, we may want to look to a deeper cause for our unpleasant attitude.

What may some of these causes be? Sometimes a physical problem could be causing our "blue mood." Perhaps we have low blood sugar or a pain somewhere in our body. Then again, perhaps there's some other physical cause that may be disturbing our equilibrium.

Also, we can look as well for an emotional cause. Perhaps we're worried about something that has turned out to be a chronic condition, so that a short-term cure looks out of the question. Often this type of worry can make people chronically negative. If this is the case, the individual needs to learn how to let go and leave the worry in God's hands, knowing that the best will come out of the situation. Often this is easier said than done. But with practice and diligence, "letting go" can become a very beneficial practice.

On the other hand, a person may be fearful due to a problem of low self-esteem. If we feel poorly about ourselves, we're apt to project a negative outlook. Sometimes this is to keep people at a certain distance from us so that they can't see how unhappy we really are. Thus, the person tends to "bark" at people or simply reflect a negative attitude about everything and everyone. Once this person is ready to be honest with himself and understand that his negativity (if he recognizes he is being negative), is due to his poor self-image, he can begin liking himself. As we learn to like ourselves, our attitude toward the world changes and we become more positive and pleasant to be around.

Another reason for being negative is that we may be under constant tension. If this is the case, the individual, if he chooses to change himself, can perhaps alter his lifestyle. Such a person may wish to take a look at why it is they think they have to work so hard. They may also want to look at what may be making them so tense. Is it the work itself, or someone at their workplace, that is causing them to be chronically tense?

In any case, it is wise to sort out the causes for our negativity if we suspect that we may suffer from this chronic syndrome. As we sort things out, we can help eliminate the cause of our troubles by turning our troubles and situations over to our Higher Power, asking for help and then leaving things in God's hands.

It's important to remember that while we are negative, we will attract further negativity to us, both in the physical plane as well as from the spiritual realms. As we decide to change our attitude toward ourselves and life, and as we work on being positive, we will attract positive people and spirit forces around us who affirm our own attitudes.

If we choose to remain negative, most likely the friends that we do manage to find will all be negative as well, carrying many of the same attitudes that we do. How come such people are not aware that they project this kind of attitude—particularly if they are surrounded by others like themselves?

Negativity can be subtle as well. We can be negative in our humor, projecting a sarcastic or cynical view of life. Once in a while this kind of joke or amusing story is harmless, but as we continually see other people and life in general from this type of viewpoint, we will soon be considered chronically negative.

It is true that we attract more of whatever we are. It is important, if we wish to be positive and attract positive conditions and people to us, to ask for Divine Light—and that all that comes to us be for our Highest Good each day, even before we step out of bed in the morning. It is true that if we send out negative thoughts, we attract more negativity to us from the unseen world. We are all connected spiritually, so that if we are unhappy or sad or worried, we will attract other such thoughts and attitudes to us. Thus, we compound our problem.

One way this situation may be solved is by our learning to be patient and gentle with ourselves while we trust in our own process and remain persistent in calling upon Divine Light to be with us. By doing so, we surround ourselves with only the highest spirit energies and guides. We may call upon angels, Jesus, and the other Masters, as well as our own guiding forces, to aid us at any time. Never feel unworthy or hesitant to call on the Highest. Sometimes people feel uncomfortable calling on Jesus, for example, because they feel they aren't ready to call on such a high energy. This is false. We are always worthy of all the Masters, and as we send out a cry for "help," which, incidentally, will be heard all over the heavens, the appropriate forces will be there to aid us.

The point here, however, is that we must take responsibility. Negative forces won't leave us alone unless we do our part to love ourselves. Further, as we become more positive, kinder to ourselves, and freer of fear, we will begin to feel happier and have a brighter outlook on life. It is important to know that all of us have to deal with negativity at some time in our lives. It's not an unusual occurrence, nor is it unusual to have to deal with negative energies from the spirit realm. It is part of what it means to be human. Anyone who has made this transition in conscious awareness of both worlds, knows it's a "battle" well worth fighting. Yet somewhere along the path we come to realize it's not a battle at all. For as we learn to let go of our negativity, both in the physical plane and in the spirit realm, we can bless these energies that have come to challenge us and help us grow. Without these dark forces we would never need to affirm and walk in the light. We would remain weak and vulnerable and would be unable to progress along the path. It's only as we become strong in our faith and our ability to master ourselves that we can remain in the light and manifest the perfection that is ours.

ON SUPPORT

People seem to receive varying degrees of support as they consciously embark on the spiritual path. There are those who seem to receive a great deal of support from family and friends as they have perhaps made a drastic change in attitude and behavior that has relieved all who have been concerned about him or her. For example, perhaps someone has received the help they needed from a sensitive and intuitive counselor who was instrumental in inspiring that person to help him— or herself, thus dissuading him or her from a potential life of crime.

Again, perhaps the illness of alcoholism was discovered in another, and adequate treatment was offered to and accepted by the sufferer. Then again, perhaps a young man was persuaded to get further education, thereby getting him off the streets and into something in which he could use his great talents and abilities. Sometimes in these kinds of cases, much support will be given. It will be of great help to the person making this kind of transition in their life.

Support from those around us can be crucial and can help make the way smooth for us. It is as though we are being lifted up and carried by many persons who believe in us and approve of the way in which we are handling our lives. Everyone's applauding our efforts, and we can feel proud of ourselves. Although there may still be adjustments that have to be made by all concerned, people are only too happy to comply with the new rules—the new situations—which arise as a result of this change in our behavior.

On the other hand, there are times and situations in which support seems to be lacking. Often when we make a decision to change our ways or lifestyle, it can be threatening to those around us. Perhaps our family and friends are not ready to accept this kind of a change. It may be very uncomfortable for them as perhaps it forces them to look at their own lives—which may be something they have been avoiding. It's often much easier to stay where one is.

To make a change, particularly in one's perspective towards life with its ensuing behavioral change, takes readiness, courage, energy, and strength. Not everyone is willing and able to make such changes; it may not be their time. However, to watch someone else make the decisions this step requires can be very helpful to anyone who may be contemplating the same or similar moves. Still, because any major change can be threatening, family, friends, and acquaintances aren't always as supportive as we would like them to be. One obvious reason for lack of support is the change that is required on the part of others when one person alters the pattern. For example, when an individual has been very ill over a long period of time and suddenly gets well, it is often difficult on the part of those who have been caring for their "patient." The fact is, everyone involved begins to play a role when the person is sick, and as that individual recovers, it's difficult to adjust to new behavior. Each member of the family must find a new role—a new way to relate to this individual for whom they have cared. Their services are no longer required, so a new relationship must be developed. The caregivers must relinquish their roles. This means having to let go of perhaps a considerable amount of control which they have previously experienced in their relationship.

Another reason we may feel a lack of support comes from a spiritual perspective. There are times in our lives when it is entirely appropriate for us to have to make it on our own. As we experience this solitary walk, we gain great strength. It feels nice to have support, but when we are being carried we don't exercise our muscles and we become weak as a result. If we find that we are experiencing little support on our life journey, most likely it is because, on a higher level, we have asked that this be so in order that we can gain strength, courage, independence, and self esteem. If this is our lot, let's accept it and be grateful that this is our time to gain more attributes. We have something to look forward to as we see ourselves emerging into the self-confident, talented and creative persons we really are.

None of us is meant to be overwhelmed by fear, anger, addictions, illness, poverty, or any of the countless other human afflictions. We may appear that way to ourselves and others, but that is not our true self. The real self is quite different. Most people would be astounded to see the true identity of people they know who are showing only their weak, vulnerable natures at this present moment. Once again, we need to be careful not to judge another. We are all working through conflicts and issues that each one of us will have to face at one time or another. As we witness the true nature of ourselves unfold, it is a most miraculous phenomenon.

However, it's really not a miracle that brings about this kind of change within human beings. It is only a decision made at a deep soul level that indicates that it's time that another step be taken up the ladder. From that decision, forces are gathered which correspond to the new emerging pattern within the individual. New ways are learned to use this energy, which is Divine Light coming from the Creator. In other words, we learn new attitudes and behaviors that are appropriate to the Higher Self (i.e., the spiritual self). The real person begins to emerge as the old begins to die. This is called growth, or spiritual growth, and represents our journey up the mountain.

Sometimes we have support along this journey and sometimes we don't. Whether we do or don't is immaterial in a way. We still have to do the work. God knows when and how much support we need, as well as where it should come from.

We receive support from God through many sources. We

may obtain support from Jesus, from angels, other Masters and Wise Ones in the spiritual hierarchy. We receive support from our spirit guides and teachers and other sources who work with us, particularly as we ask for help. Divine support comes to us as directed by our Creator through people, through animals, and our own spirit as we are open to the signs and messages brought to us to aid and assist us.

As we ask for Divine Light each morning, we can be open to all the ways in which our Higher Power chooses to help direct us. Further, the more interested and willing we are to work with guidance which is being brought to us, the more beneficial it will be for us. For as we follow our intuitive thoughts and trust in the universe which directs us, we will find ourselves being led to a new place.

While making this transition, we may or may not have the support of our family and friends. But in any event, Divine Power never lets us down as we make an effort to live in the Light and walk a new path. We never have to fear being alone on our journey, as we are always watched over very carefully and help is always available to us. Whether it's for a big problem or small decision, help from the Source will be there for us.

This kind of support is always permanent, non-judgmental, trustworthy, loving, and good company. Isn't it exciting that we can count on Divine assistance to guide us through each moment of every day? Further, isn't it great that we never have to feel alone again when all we need to do is call on the nearest angel to help us? When we learn to talk with the divas and the plants in the woods, we know we never have to feel deserted. All that is spirit is connected in consciousness, and as we become aware of this divine connection, we have all the support and companionship that we need.

ON HOPE

Hope is especially important on the spiritual path as it uplifts us and helps to keep us going when we might be tempted to slow down or even quit our journey up the mountain.

Hope is different from faith, which is a "knowing." It's been said that anything short of knowing is not faith. Faith has to be complete if it's going to bring about the desired conditions that we seek in our lives. Jesus, for example, taught that we had to have absolute faith (knowing) that we could be healed in order for our healing to take place.

When we talk about hope, on the other hand, we're talking about expectancy. We're talking about a feeling which comes from the heart. "I hope the sun will shine tomorrow. I hope I pass my test." If one should say, "I know I can pass my test," that would be a demonstration of faith in self. Hope, then, is to wish or desire something with some expectation that it will come about.

Why is hope important? Hope is important on the spiritual path for the simple reason that life is not easy. We can, in fact, quite easily become discouraged, particularly if we feel we are embarking on a journey that is going to give us anything but a smooth ride.

As we consciously accept our role in life with the desire to fulfill our goals as planned by the Higher Self, we really need to commit ourselves to an adventure which can be rather harrowing at times. If we are dedicated and willing to go the entire way, we will be taking many risks that will require much faith in ourselves, our activities, our abilities, and in God. We will be required to jump across the abyss more than once. Furthermore, where the average or unaware individual would most likely sit complacently near the edge of the cliff, the aware and conscious spiritual traveler would have the understanding that this is not the end of the road. We can know that there is more on the other side, and we must make that leap to the other side even though we may not know precisely what awaits us there. We simply know we must take the risk.

Therefore, in order to have such faith, we have to have hope enough to bring us to the edge. We need to be inspired, to know that there is more, to be hopeful. We must feel confident that something exists beyond our present awareness that gives us a feeling of excited expectation. Otherwise, how could we carry on? How could any of us live without hope? We would, indeed, die without some kind of hope in our lives, however small.

The injured person in a rehabilitation unit wakes up hoping he will be able to walk down the hall today. If he were really fortunate, he would have faith that he could make it. But hope is better than nothing. We need hope to survive. Those who have lost all hope lose their will to live. Sometimes when an elderly person loses a spouse he may have lived with for many years, he loses his desire to carry on. The reason is that he loses hope that there is anything for him without the loved one on whom he has depended so long. He has a feeling of hopelessness as well as helplessness, especially if he and his spouse have been very close. It can, indeed, be a challenge to find that little ray of hope that will carry him forward.

The same holds true for all of us. Our challenges can sometimes overwhelm us to the point we don't feel we'll ever be hopeful again. Even though we know we're never given more than we can handle, we fear feeling hopeless as the conditions in our lives begin to feel like punishments rather than opportunities to learn. But eventually, as the gray sky parts and the clouds show signs of dispersing, we do look forward to the sun's peeking out at us again. Yes, we do look forward to a new day. This may surprise even us: we thought our hope was gone for good.

How can we regain our hope once we feel it has been lost to us? How can we bring back that spark of happy expectancy? One way that hope may be rekindled within us is by our doing something creative. When we are creating, we are using our spirit. We're opening ourselves in a way that allows Divine energy to flow to us and through us. Then as we do, we open the door for hope to be made alive within us once again. That feeling of joyous expectancy returns as we delight in using this Divine energy to create something out of nothing.

Another way may be to listen to music. Music of all kinds, depending, of course, on whether we are attuned to its vibrations and find it pleasing, can arouse hope within us. Music can be a great tool in and of itself to help us in our spiritual awareness. Certain kinds of music can bring a feeling of hope to just about anyone because it is universal—its tones reach our spiritual ears and uplift and inspire us.

Other music may make us feel hopeful for different reasons. Perhaps it reminds us of something inspiring, or perhaps because of its lively nature it cheers us and can even prepare us for the day ahead. People listen to music for all kinds of reasons, and seeking hope is one of them, whether the listener is consciously aware of it or not.

We can also regain hope through nature. Sitting by a running stream and gazing at the water rushing over the rocks can help to stimulate hope by giving us a feeling of stability. Nature can help us to feel secure because it is constant, dependable, and truly lasting. We can become tranquil in nature as we partake in its gifts; as a result, we begin to feel surges of hope well up within us. We cannot move from despair to hope until we've reached a feeling of stability. From there, we become hopeful and even develop a strong faith, if we have the will to progress that far. So nature can play a very direct role in helping to provide hope to our sinking spirits.

Another way to become restored is through meditation. As we learn to still the mind with its attendant doubts and fears, we can allow the spirit to come forth just as when we paint, draw, sing, or dance. We restore hope when we return to the Divine gifts that are there for our edification. Our ability to get in touch with the Divinity within us is indeed a gift. Whether it is accomplished through meditation or creativity doesn't matter. As long as we begin, once again, to feel at one with our Creator by stabilizing our mind and emotions, there is a chance for hope to be renewed within us.

It is also helpful when going through a dark period to recognize the impermanence of all things. We hear the expression, "Time heals all wounds," or, "Nothing lasts forever," or "What goes around comes around." All of these statements serve to tell us that things do change: people change, conditions change, and our moods can change. Everything changes, no matter what our attitude happens to be. If we would only remember this truth, we would be better able to accept periods of depression, knowing that things will shift with time. It is only when we try to hold on to the present, unhappy as it may be, that we bring pain to ourselves. When we recognize the impermanence of our situations and the conditions around ourselves and others, we can look forward to a shift in the wind. However, conditions must be allowed to change themselves. When we attempt to control what is to be adjusted naturally, we cause unnecessary pain to everyone.

Attempting to control how we feel oftentimes clouds the issue. We need to feel pain, grief, and loss, and then let them go as we begin to experience the sunrise that is sure to follow. Therefore, through accepting ourselves as we are and accepting our life conditions, we can be assured that things will change for us. As we learn to facilitate the natural flow of things, we find ourselves in harmony with who we are and all of life; and because we are at peace with ourselves, we can allow that joyous expectancy to build within ourselves. We have hope for a brighter tomorrow.

ON STRESS

A certain amount of stress occurs in everyone's life. We are all here to grow, and because we are all growing, we will experience stress. We all have challenges. Challenges will differ depending on who and where we are on our path.

Often, people seem to experience some of the same kinds of stress. For example, because we all have physical bodies, we are all subject to various conditions, both positive and negative, to which the physical vehicle is prone. We all have certain needs, desires, comforts, and complaints. We are all responsible for our bodies and understand that it's up to us to take care of ourselves because no one else is going to do it for us. Consequently, we have to learn to eat well, exercise, and get plenty of rest and adequate sleep. As we take care of our basic needs, we find we feel good, physically.

However, if we fail to care for the physical body in one of these areas, we don't feel as good as we'd like to. If we wish to do something about it, we set about to discover what is wrong. Are we suffering from a food sensitivity or allergy? Often these sufferers may go through their entire life unaware that their discomfort or ill health may have been coming from this relatively simple condition. Again, perhaps we're tired all the time and we discover that there is, indeed, a physical cause behind our complaint.

Through the study of healing, it has been discovered that the mind is responsible for the problems we find in our bodies. It is our attitudes that cause our physical problems. Further, we now understand, that though the mind may be the cause, we still have to correct the physical as well as the mental and spiritual. Therefore, in order to stay well and healthy, we are required to exert ourselves mentally, emotionally, and spiritually.

The work that is required to stay healthy on all of these levels creates stress, whether we're consciously aware of it or not. If one area gets out of balance, we have to compensate in another area—so we are continually attempting to maintain harmony between the physical, emotional, mental, and spiritual bodies. No wonder we can feel tired at times. Keeping this complex mechanism in order isn't easy, and demands much of us as we continue to grow. Thus, there are pressures from within that keep us busy. We create our own internal stresses caused by our beliefs, attitudes, emotions, and reactions to ourselves and the world around us.

In other words, because of the way we choose to perceive life, we decide whether we are going to add stress to our lives, or, instead, attempt to keep stress at a low level. If we maintain a harmonious attitude and positive outlook, we eliminate much stress that would occur if we were negative and resisted the flow of life. Staying peaceful and serene by accepting ourselves and life as it is isn't easy. Furthermore, knowing when it's time to make appropriate changes and take action is difficult as well. Not many of us are able to do this easily.

Therefore, we add stress to our lives because we are learning. The more we're willing to learn, the more stressful our lives can become. But there is a more positive side to this. The more we're willing to accept the help that's available to us, the more help we get and the calmer we become. We are then able to take on great challenges we never dreamed we were capable of simply because we've learned to rely on Divine help, which comes instantly, without fail, and with love.

Let us imagine that as we sleep at night we make certain decisions about the day ahead. Perhaps we set up a situation that may be a bit challenging to us, just to see how we will handle it. As the condition presents itself to us, whether it is a necessary confrontation with our boss or co-worker, or whether it is the loss of our pet, let us imagine that a part of us already knows that these things are going to occur. Therefore, when the event actually happens, we may say to ourselves, "Well, here it is. I must have planned this; now how am I going to handle it? Am I going to pass this little test I set up for myself, or am I going to feel like a victim and blame others or God for putting me in this position?"

Sometimes life can feel like a play if we allow it to. It is as though we have rehearsed our roles and suddenly we're called upon to play them out as we had planned. If others play their roles as well as we play ours, the scenario works out very harmoniously indeed. The most difficult-seeming situations can be resolved as people are attuned to the play and their part in it.

Could this be why we are so often surprised when someone's behavior changes so positively to fit the situation? Suddenly Dad allows us to have the car when in our wildest dreams we never expected it would happen. Perhaps this time we want to test our sense of responsibility with the car out late at night. Intuitively, Dad knows this is the time, and all goes as planned. The father may not consciously know why he allowed the son to have the car; he probably thought he was just "in a good mood." However, in reality he is playing out his role in the play in order to help develop responsibility within his child. And, most interestingly, he knew it was the appropriate time when there was perhaps no other indication that his son was prepared for this experience. He just knew.

We're continually testing ourselves as our spirit sources guide and direct us so that we may advance, not only spiritually, but materially as well. The material life, which encompasses our work, family, financial affairs, and other concerns of a more physical nature, is just as important as the spiritual. We need to balance both aspects of life. There cannot be spiritual advancement without material conditions improving as well.

Overcoming our material challenges helps pave the way for our spiritual advancement, but keeping a balance between the two can create a great deal of stress for us. Further, the manner in which we handle that stress indicates what we need to improve on so that our lives can become more pleasant and serene.

There are many answers for stress. Some methods for handling stress are healthy and some are unhealthy. The unhealthy methods leave us potentially worse off than we were before the stressful condition. Excessive smoking and drinking are two common ways people handle stress. Overeating and spending money irresponsibly are other ways in which we handle the uncomfortable feelings that stress causes. Sleeping a great deal or watching television constantly are other methods people use to "calm down." The list can go on and on. None of these ways helps us in the long run. They only add to our problems, because they affect us negatively in other areas and do not allow for our full potential to be realized.

Yet in regard to these areas, we need to be gentle and patient with ourselves and once again trust in our process. Attempting to force these so-called negative habits out of our lives only attracts them further to us.

There are, on the other hand, other, more healthy methods for handling stress. These means may involve or at least begin with the mind, body, or spirit. We may choose to exercise in order to relieve stress. Any form of exercise or sport we choose that we like can help relieve tension. Sex also helps to relieve tension, provided that the conditions within the relationship of those involved are love-filled, peaceful, and stress-free. Eating when hungry can help to relieve stress: perhaps the body is in need of certain nutrients.

All these methods should be used in balance and not to excess. When, for example, we find that we are eating more than our body actually needs in order to relieve our stress and that it's becoming a habit, then we're into a more negative approach to handling our problems.

Mentally, as we change our attitude about life and change our thinking in the process, we can do much to eliminate old, stressful reactions. Further, as we learn to let go and let God, new patterns emerge within us that project a new approach to life. Our thinking changes, thus bringing about new, more positive conditions to us. Then again, as we become interested in delving deeper into the spiritual, we discover that learning to be still greatly reduces tension on all levels, and we become peaceful as we learn to enter into that calm place within us.

Further, once accustomed to this space where we can come for serenity, comfort, guidance and direction, we begin to develop trust in our Creator as well as in our ability to make such contact possible. As we work together with our Creator, learning to listen as well as to obey the inner voice, stress begins to feel like a condition of the past. Although we may continue to experience it periodically as we test ourselves, we don't remain in a tense situation for long. For we know that all we need to do is seek within for all that we need, whether it be comfort, love, guidance or wisdom and it will be there for us as we have asked. Further, because we've remembered to ask for God's Divine light and that all that comes to us be for the highest good, we will be safe and secure. Therefore, let's look upon the stresses and tensions in our day as indications that we are indeed in the play, and the way in which we respond to each situation will determine whether we are ready to advance. Our goals are before us, but how we reach them is up to us. The amount of peace we have during our climb up the mountain is largely determined by how well we can form this union with our Creator. The more "involved" we are in our relationship with the divine intelligence that orders the universe, the smoother and more peaceful will be our journey up the mountain. The more we can trust, the more we can let go; the more we let go, the more we let God.

BOOK TWELVE

ON POWER

What can we learn from our experiences in life about power? Many of us have issues concerning this subject. It is wise to learn where we have power and where we don't. In other words, we can have power in our own lives, but we don't have power in the lives of others. We can attempt to control others, but in the long run it doesn't work. We will eventually have to pay the price for power which has been abused.

It may look, upon appearance, that an individual or particular group is getting away with abusing God's energy as it is given freely to us. But that particular state of affairs will never be allowed to continue indefinitely: sooner or later we pay the price. It may not be for a long time, but eventually we must pay our karmic debt and the tables will be turned as we wonder why we find ourselves in situations in which we are the objects of abuse. The scale must be balanced, just as it must in all other areas of life in which we have done harm to ourselves or others. For our own learning, then, we choose, from a higher level of ourselves, to experience that which we've put others through.

Lust for power can be very subtle. Often people would be horrified to think that they enjoy having power. Often people who have this problem in their lives deny it fervently. Very often such individuals don't feel that the characteristics typical of those who desire power fit them at all. Perhaps others see such an individual as appearing "power hungry," but the individual him— or herself would never describe themselves that way, even in their most honest moment. They neither see nor feel it. There are some, however, whose quest for power is obvious, it would be difficult for them to deny it, but usually they do.

What kind of behaviors and attitude are we talking about? Abusing power needn't be a very obvious trait. In fact, many won't recognize it unless they have become aware of their right to exist as spiritual beings. We sometimes are not alert to the fact that we not only have rights, but that we are, indeed, quite separate from even our closest friends and relatives.

This means that we came into this world alone, and we will go out alone. And though we spend much of our life often in the company of others, we still have our own identity, our own goals, and our own purpose. Further, though we may be married, which may be the closest of all relationships, we still are our own person. When the spouse dies after many years of marriage, we still have to be with ourselves. We still have to work out our own karma and our own lessons and learn to live life for ourselves.

One of life's biggest lessons can be to learn to separate oneself from one's spouse, for example. Many times we become confused in marriage because we don't understand what our boundaries are, if we even acknowledge boundaries at all. We tend to "slide" into the other person, thinking we know what's best for them and not being honest with them for any number of reasons that are all based on fear.

We begin to attempt to control the spouse so that we may feel more comfortable. It's as though we can't operate comfortably on our own without being affected by what the other partner is doing or not doing. We live in fear of the relationship, a situation which is demonstrated by the fact that we're constantly telling the partner what to do and attempting to control how he or she thinks, feels, and behaves. We may even tell them what to wear and what they should eat. We may become angry when they smile at an attractive person at a party and we react when they don't like our new hairdo. It is not a relationship of responding to each other's needs, but of reacting out of fear. As one tries to control the other, resentment flourishes. The relationship continues to exhibit an unhealthy mode of interaction that leads inevitably to co-dependency. This is just one example where power issues can get out of control.

In truth, we have no right to control another through any means and we will eventually learn that it is impossible anyway. We simply can't make another do something. We don't have that kind of power. Furthermore, if they do obey us out of fear, we will pay the price down the road. Once again, we don't have ultimate power in the lives of others. This can be a very painful and difficult lesson to learn.

On the other hand, parents have a duty to set limits for their children. Children need boundaries and discipline. But as any parent of a rebellious teenager knows, we can't make a boy clean his room if he really doesn't want to. Many such children would rather run away than succumb to the will of the parent, especially after they reach a certain age. It may be that they are rebelling at the controlling authoritarian attitude of the parent rather than whether or not they want their room clean. Often as parents let go of such issues that are really not that important, the child comes around on his own.

"Letting go and letting God" works wonders when we deal with many aspects of our relationships with others. And as we let go we can allow others to be and to live freely within the boundaries of society and the law. Obviously, we have to have certain rules, laws, and moral codes in order to be comfortable living together on the earth. But when it comes to attempting to dominate another by physical or psychological means against their will, we find ourselves getting into trouble.

"Live and let live" is a good philosophy, and as we practice it in our lives we will begin to feel a freedom that we allow others, too, to experience.

We can, on the other hand, have power in our own lives. That is, we have the right and ability to create, thus allowing ourselves to experience the fulfillment we so desire without harming others.

As we learn where we have power and where we don't, we begin to make wiser choices regarding the best places to put our energy. We realize it's foolish to try to get our husband to dance or our son to take a class with us if they don't want to. We simply don't waste time and energy on such things. We may mention it and then let it go, knowing that our Higher Power will take over and make the rest of the decision. We learn to leave things in God's hands, rather than trying to control every situation that presents itself to us. We find it's much easier and doesn't take so much out of us. We put our concerns "in the Light" and ask for help, and then leave them alone. The rest becomes history as we sit back and watch the play unfold.

We must remember that we have the power to create. We also have the power to forgive ourselves when we have misplaced our power. Perhaps we've tried to control another. On the other hand, maybe we've allowed another to control us. We've given our power away to someone we think is better than we are because we have yet to see our own beauty and abilities. Therefore, we need to forgive ourselves as well as others. We have the power to maintain a forgiving attitude because we know God forgives us.

We may also use our power to accept ourselves, other people, and life as it is. Further, we may accept our lessons as opportunities, which come to help us to grow. We have the ability to do this. Further, we have the ability to love ourselves and improve our life conditions.

The power we use to accomplish that which we desire to manifest positively in our lives comes from our Creator. It is through this Divine energy that we become co-creators. Jesus said, "You will do all these things and greater" as he spoke of the miracles He created. Jesus was well aware of man's potential to explore and use God's energy as it was meant to be used. He told us we would be healers as well as teachers. He also told us of the good we would accomplish through correct use of His Divine energy. Moreover, as we learned to use the power we were given to benefit ourselves and mankind, it would be increased in order that we could demonstrate our ability to love as well as to heal ourselves and all mankind.

Therefore, let's take upon ourselves this great responsibility and be grateful for God's energy as it is given to us each day; and let's seek for guidance as we set about to manifest the perfection we seek within ourselves and the world around us.

ON AFFIRMATIONS

What does it mean to affirm something? Affirmations are positive statements we make about ourselves and our world. Why are they important to our growth? They are important because they help put into place that which is to be. As we affirm who we are in a positive manner, we set the stage for what will be in the future. If we affirm our goals, we will help bring them to reality. We set in motion the conditions by which things can come about naturally.

For example, if we say, "I am happy," we set in motion the forces that will help bring about that state of mind within us. However, we can't just say, "I am happy" and expect things to change for us. This message must reach the subconscious where it can be internalized. We can know something intellectually, but to believe it at a deep level of our being is another matter. If we just say something over and over without feeling it, it doesn't become a part of us. We have to feel it in order to believe it.

Affirmations can be very powerful if they are said, felt, and internalized properly. We can convince ourselves of just about anything and change our patterns of thinking through their continued use over time.

There are many ways of internalizing affirmations. One simple way is to repeat over and over that which we wish to believe about ourselves. We must then add energy to it by feeling that which we say at the same time. Further, as we do that, if we visualize ourselves as "being happy," for example, if that is our goal, we add another dimension which makes our affirmation even more powerful and ready to be internalized.

We may even read short paragraphs or several affirmations put together about ourselves, saying them over and over again with feeling, and visualizing ourselves projecting whatever it is we are attempting to affirm. This technique has helped people make changes within themselves quite rapidly. If done several times a day, it adds even more to the power of the technique.

There are other methods of internalizing affirmations that involve body movement. These help to integrate the right and left brain in order for the internalization process to take place. These techniques can be found in books that talk about "Touch for Health" and other holistic practices involving right and left brain integration.

Still another method for internalizing affirmations may be through hypnosis. Learning to put oneself in a semi-hypnotic trance for the purpose of integrating positive principles can be a very worthwhile practice. A qualified hypnotist may do this or we ourselves may accomplish it. In order to effect hypnosis, we may, after requesting that Divine Light be placed around us, count down to ten. As we count slowly, we imagine ourselves sinking deeper and deeper into the subconscious. Imaging going down a staircase is sometimes helpful. As we go deeper and deeper we feel slightly sleepy as if in a semi-trance. When we have reached "10" we begin to repeat our affirmation over several times, feeling it as we do. Again, visualization adds to the power of this technique. After repeating it several times, we can count ourselves back up. When we come to "1," we affirm that we are wide-awake and fully returned to our original physical setting.

Repeating affirmations is also good just as one is drifting off to sleep or when one is waking up in the morning. When our minds are in the alpha state we are in a position to internalize these wonderfully positive image messages.

Another way in which we can help ourselves is through prayer. The God force alone can help to bring the desired changes we wish to see take place within ourselves. But let's remember also that sometimes our Higher Power will lead us to a person who can teach us what we need to know. Sometimes we expect God to magically do everything for us. Yet, there are times our Creator sends a messenger and thus has us consciously do our part in our own healing.

Our Higher Power has its own reasons for whatever method is chosen for us. We need only keep our eyes and ears open and not always expect that everything will be done for us without any effort on our part. (Although at times God seems to work that way as well.) Even though we have to do our own work, sometimes it is so subtle we're not aware of the changes taking place within us. We simply notice that what used to be a problem for us doesn't seem to create difficulty anymore. We are at peace.

Thus, all situations are different. We may be led to a person, a book, a class or workshop, a doctor, therapist, minister, or counselor for help in solving our problems. On the other hand, it may appear that prayer alone seems to be enough to solve the difficulty.

Whatever the case, after we have asked for help, we need to let go so that we may be open to the answer. And if someone comes by and starts talking about something in relation to the issue we are concerned about, we must be alert. It's important to listen so that we get the message. It may be that God, through our guides and angels in spirit, is giving us information through another person. Therefore, we must learn to be on our toes as we go about our day, listening to information from various sources. It may be a notice on the bulletin board or something we see in the newspaper that puts us on to something that will be helpful to us.

There are times, however, that we can be misled. This is where meditation and discernment become especially valuable. We must "take in" what we see or hear and see if it is appropriate for us.

Occasionally we may ask the guidance of someone we feel

might be "clear enough" to help us sort out our own affairs. But this is risky business, and we should be very circumspect and careful before consulting others for guidance. We must always make sure that the person we choose is as reliable a source as we can find for our particular need. Then we have to make sure to meditate on what he or she tells us, testing its effect on us before we go ahead with our decision.

We can also ask in prayer for roadblocks if there's a situation on which we are hesitant to take action. And though we can receive help from others, we must always remember that we are attempting to develop ourselves and our own intuition. Any teacher or spiritual guidance counselor who encourages us to seek within ourselves is probably trustworthy because their intent is appropriate. Friends, counselors, and others intent on helping us should be there to encourage our independence rather than our dependence on them.

At times we may run into "helpers" who are co-dependent. In other words, they need and desire our dependence on them. This sets up unhealthy conditions for both parties. It's wonderful to be able to help someone else, but if we find we want them to depend on us so that we can feel good about ourselves, then we have problems. Instead of helping, we're creating a dependency that in turn creates new problems for both parties. Therefore, we must be careful to whom we go for guidance.

So, then, we must keep asking for help and listen, listen, listen. It may be that we will find someone or something that can indeed get us back on track. We will know if something is right if it feels positive and comfortable. If it begins to change, then we leave it and seek for further guidance.

Our affirmations can help keep us on track as we confirm our ability to always be at the proper place at the right time. We can affirm our place in the universe as well as our goals and our ability to accomplish them. We can affirm that we are loved, protected, guided, and directed, and that our thoughts will be in harmony with the God force. This will put us in the right spiritual framework as we begin our day and it will keep us there as we repeat aloud these thoughts several times throughout the day. Affirming that we are in God's hands gives us the security we need in order to project our true nature into the world. Therefore, as we claim our right to be who we are, we affirm our identity as spiritual beings capable of manifesting God's love and perfection in all that we are and all that we do. Where we are weak, we affirm our strength; where there is discord, we seek for harmony within ourselves; where we are ignorant, we ask for knowledge; and where there is misunderstanding, we see only love.

ON LETTING GO

Why is letting go important? How can holding on to old issues keep us from enjoying our life today? How does letting go help us to grow?

Letting go is one of the most necessary tools available to us on a spiritual path. If we don't have the ability to let go of the past, for example, we can't move forward into the future and carry out the goals we've set for ourselves. If we cannot let go of our hurts and resentments, there is no room for the positive feelings of acceptance and love to enter our being. If we are unable to let go of old attitudes that are no longer appropriate for us, we cannot be ready to take on our new responsibilities and the joys that come with them.

If we are resistant to leting go of old pain, we stay in that pain, which can raise havoc with our mind, spirit, and body. If we refuse to let go of old issues, we can't heal ourselves of the past. Therefore we may remain stuck, unable to move forward to accomplish that which we have set out to complete in this lifetime.

Before coming to earth, we set up certain goals and plans for ourselves with the help of wiser souls who guide and direct us.

We choose our families and certain other significant people to share in our life dramas with us. We also set up certain situations and scenarios, which will challenge us and help us to grow. Some of the people we choose to be in our "play" will present us with opportunities for this growth.

Very few people grow up in families in which there is total harmony and peace. We choose to be surrounded by people with whom we find it both easy and difficult to get along. The easy ones are like gifts. They're wonderful to have with us, but don't give us a great deal of opportunity for growth. There is no need to stretch ourselves in order to be with them. In other words, we are not forced to learn a great deal from them. They are just there as friends, supportive and nice to have around.

The more difficult souls for us, on the other hand, can present us with great challenges and opportunities for tremendous growth. They often turn out to be individuals who are very close to us. They may be a parent, a spouse, a son, or a daughter. Actually, we have much to thank these people for because they have agreed to play a part in our lives. Without them, we would not be able to climb up that mountain.

We have certain tests to pass as we pursue our path. These challenging individuals and situations in our lives provide the opportunity for us to pass our tests. We may be testing ourselves on patience, tolerance, or the ability to believe in ourselves and stand up for our rights. We may be testing our ability to be honest in our relationships with others or we may be testing our self-esteem. Are we still jealous or selfish? Do we give too much in emotional relationships while not paying attention to our own needs? Have we learned what it means to have healthy boundaries or to take care of ourselves physically, emotionally, and spiritually? Do we still look to others to make us happy or tell us what to do? Do we still need the approval of others and do we give our power away to another whom we regard as better than we are for one reason or another?

Do we react instead of respond to situations that tend to

threaten us? Do we see our lessons as opportunities, or do we look at the difficult times as punishment for who we are? Do we like ourselves as God made us, or do we wish we looked like someone else?

Are we happy with our talents and abilities and have we even given time to ourselves to explore God's gifts to us? Do we dare take risks, or are we too locked into old patterns and rigid ways of behaving and looking at life? Are we satisfied with our lives and do we recognize our need and our ability to change that which we find unacceptable to us? Furthermore, are we able to accept what we can't change about ourselves?

There are certain things about us that we must learn to accept. We cannot change our parents or the place where we were born. We are unable to change our physical appearance beyond certain limitations. Further, we cannot alter our lessons. We all have certain weaknesses we have come here to work on, thus making ourselves more complete and whole. Like bruised areas on a ripe peach, these shortcomings call out for healing so that the soul may be more fulfilled.

At a deep level we know what these patterns are, but on a conscious level we are largely unaware of our weaknesses until we decide to take the time to learn about ourselves. We may go for a long time without discovering what these areas are. However, all the while we are attracting people, situations, and circumstances in our lives to help us to release that which is no longer appropriate for us.

We begin these lessons as early as the period before our birth. While waiting to be born, we are subject to certain influences and perhaps emotional trauma that can set the stage for what is to come. Perhaps our mother is feeling tension and stress with our coming into the world. As feeling entities, we pick up her uncomfortable sensations and may even develop a sense that we are responsible for her unhappiness. So there may develop within the child a great feeling of responsibility to make things right—to be pleasing to everyone so as not to cause any problems. Consequently, this child grows up not speaking his or her mind, unable to be totally honest about his or her emotions, and being drawn into the mold of being "a people-pleaser."

There also may be guilt for having caused problems that they feel may not have arisen had they not been born. There may develop a fear of abandonment that becomes evident years later, after the child becomes an adult. Further, there may be a sadness that develops as a result of all these negative feelings that can be difficult to overcome. These feelings are, for the most part, buried and hidden well within the personality and often go undiscovered unless there is an opportunity to bring them to the surface to be healed.

This all appears very tragic and can make this child or adult seem to be a victim. However, could there not be something going on here that brightens the picture? All of these feelings the child experiences tend to lower his self-esteem and cause him to discount himself as a spiritual being capable of positive experiences and enjoying life to the fullest. Could this not be a major lesson in his life? Could it be that as this child experiences these feelings throughout his life there may one day be the possibility that the light may go on in his mind? "What's wrong with this picture? Why am I feeling so poorly about myself? There is nothing wrong with me. I'm a nice person with high goals and ideals. Why do I feel guilty, alone, and afraid? Why do I feel responsible for the problems around me? Why am I jealous and why do I fear being left alone? Why am I unhappy? Could I not turn this around? I see no need for this to be part of me any longer. I'm tired of these feelings and I think I've had enough." And the healing begins.

God gives us all equal opportunity to heal ourselves. This child who grows into an adult has the appropriate experiences when help heal an old pattern of low self-esteem. If the issue had not been brought forward, it could not have been healed. There is great value in our weaknesses in that they sometimes cause us to endure very painful experiences. These painful experiences instigate our healing and thus create great beauty within the soul. We learn from each experience, whether positive or negative. And, as we learn, we let go of our old patterns.

The letting-go process can be easy or difficult, fast or very slow. For many people, letting go can be a long, difficult process. We hang on because of fear. It is only fear that forces us to cling to the way things are. We will often stay in the most uncomfortable, unpleasant, and even tragic circumstances simply because they are familiar to us. Further, we will resist looking at a new way because it is unfamiliar and causes us to feel even more insecure than we already are.

Little do we know that if we would only take that leap to the other side of the abyss, we would find joy and security. We would discover the appropriate place for us. When it's the right time for us to make any kind of a move forward, things will always work out well because our timing is right.

Resistance and hanging on causes pain. We must let go and trust as we gather our resources in an effort to learn our lessons. Once we've had a glimpse of a new way, we must let go of the old. The longer we hang on, the more uncomfortable we'll be.

Often we are unaware that we are going through this process at all. We may develop pains in our bodies, instead. A massage therapist would tell us we need to let go of something. Therefore, it helps to be aware of our thoughts, as well as what's going on in our bodies.

What lesson might we be learning? Is it time to try a new way? Is it time to let go of an issue that has been bothering us? Is it time to send love to the person who has been aggravating us? Is it time to quit the job that has been dragging us down and trust that a new opening will come? Is it time to forgive my uncle for sexually abusing me as a child? Is it time to put some plants in my apartment to spruce it up a little? Is it time to have a new hairdo? Is it time now to take off ten pounds? Is it time to start feeling good about myself? Is it time to forgive my ex-wife? Is it time to tell my child I love him? Is it time to bring a new pet into the home? Is it time to take out the garbage—all the garbage?

Once we're on a spiritual path, we attempt periodically to clear our minds of the garbage it collects. However, time is passing rapidly, and we need to keep ourselves current with our issues. We need to be aware of being on a schedule with our spiritual process—letting go as it is appropriate and being willing to take on the new responsibilities and challenges as they present themselves to us. We are all taking our assignments now, as we come into this very significant time in history. Therefore, letting go is a crucial issue that faces all of us so that we may get on with the opportunities that await us. Further, as we learn to let go and let God, we will find our lives changing rapidly. Old doors close and new doors open for us. If we resist, we will find ourselves being uncomfortable, although we may not know why. If we are ill at ease, we must ask ourselves, "What do I have to let go of, and what am I afraid of if I accept this new responsibility?"

If we replace our fears with faith, and if we feel we are trying to make the change we know is inevitable, and if we are certain the change is necessary, we find we have nothing to lose by taking the plunge. Furthermore, we will be glad we did once we've taken that leap into the unknown. Then we can look back and ask, "What was I afraid of? I feel good here, and I am in the appropriate place. All is well. I feel secure." Indecision causes us to feel very insecure. Once the decision has been made to move forward, we feel whole again.

Letting go is a process, and there are many ways of accomplishing it. We need to find out what works best for us in each situation we encounter. Our Higher Power is more than ready to help us as we ask for help and direction. And as we learn to meditate each day for a few moments, asking in the silence for help and guidance in taking that next step, we will be led forward appropriately. We may be uncomfortable at times, but that is all part of the healing process. One day our life will be over and we can look back and say, "I'm glad I made the journey and now I can rest for awhile. I can enjoy myself and my surroundings in peace and love. I am grateful that I had the courage to let go and risk in order to accomplish my goals."

ON OBSERVATION

Observation is one of the tools that we need as we make our way through life. What is meant by observation?

As we learn to observe ourselves and life itself, we come into a greater realization of who we are and how things work within the universe. We begin to become aware of the universal laws, whether we make an effort to study them formally or not. Through our experiences, as we encounter them in a more conscious fashion, we begin to see certain truths emerging. We learn from watching ourselves and others struggle along life's highway.

We begin to see that we pay for our mistakes, whether anyone else notices them or not. Further, we begin to see that our opportunities for growth, as well as for rest and enjoyment, seem to come in cycles. As we pay more careful attention to these cycles, we may take advantage of the opportunities that present themselves to us on a rather regular basis.

Also, as we begin to observe ourselves, we can see that much of what we encounter in life is there for us to learn from. We also come to understand, sometimes painfully, yet with some relief, that the effect of all of our experiences depends on our perspective. In other words, no matter what happens to us, we always have to "bring it home" and see what our part is in the situation. If we feel we have no part in what has happened, that we were merely victims of circumstances, we then must look at how we respond to what has happened.

Perhaps we have drawn this situation to us as a learning experience, just to see how we might handle it. If we can come out of the situation accepting with love what has happened, we have done ourselves a great favor. We won't always know the reasons why certain things are the way they are. But if we can accept circumstances and their outcomes, believing that God has prepared something better for us as a result of our experience, we will have passed the test.

It makes it more difficult when the curtain has been drawn and we are not allowed to see the causes of all of our situations, but we can be sure that for everything there has been a cause. We are never "victims" in the spiritual sense. Certainly, in the physical world, we can say someone has been a victim of rape, for example. But on the spiritual level, other things of which we are unaware are going on. They account even for the assault. Even through death, there can be victory for the soul at this higher level. When we have faith in this truth, it is easier to develop a more detached view of life that can be extremely helpful in dealing with life's situations.

Just as one can develop a strong belief in life after death, one can also come to believe in a higher explanation for all that we experience. Where there has been an early unfortunate death, of a teenager through an accident, for example, all those involved with the victim will be a part of the drama. Each will have an opportunity to respond to what has happened. How each responds will depend on where they are in their growth, as well as their relationship to the deceased.

The victim who chose to make his transition at that time will be playing out his own role and doing what he needs to do for himself at the time. It may be that the young person had fulfilled his purpose and his death was to be a catalyst for the spiritual growth of many souls around him.

An untimely death often jars people into a new reality. It forces them to look at things they haven't yet had to face. It gives an opportunity for further awareness that only that type of experience can give. Those deeply affected needed the experience, and those who do not seem to be affected as much didn't need that particular occurrence to motivate their movement forward. They will, perhaps, be shaken by something else that will put them where they need to be.

Our experiences can literally transport us from one place to another—that is, they can either move us in consciousness or place us in a new environment or situation where we find ourselves doing something entirely different. We may even move physically as well. It may be necessary to relocate, find a new occupation, or a new way of looking at life. We may find all three things happening at once as a result of some experience we've undergone.

As we learn to observe ourselves and life, we begin to read the signals and become aware of the process of learning and what our experiences can mean for us.

We begin to see how they form a pattern, and we start to develop the faith to go with the flow, not fearing the depth of the river or where it is going to carry us as we keep going in spite of the obstacles that appear. We understand that if, without offering resistance, we simply allow ourselves to brush against the rocks and branches that appear in our way, we will make our way down the river quite nicely. However, we discover that if we put our hand out in an effort to stop the boulder that appears in our path, we hurt ourselves and interrupt the flow of our journey. As we drift along enjoying the scenery, not fearing what lies before us, our attitude remains peaceful and we can enjoy our ride. But as we anticipate trouble, we tense up and begin to focus on the large rock ahead in our path, meanwhile missing the smaller events and circumstances in our lives to which we should be attending. We miss, as well, the lovely scenery along the way that is there to bring us joy and comfort.

Therefore, as we seek to discover the ins and outs of life, and as we learn to observe the cycles that set us on our course, we are in awe of all over which we have no control. We become humbled as we observe God's attention to detail and nature. We are equally humbled as we see beauty and devastation alike.

We see good and evil existing side by side in a world that is chaotic, but struggling for harmony and peace. As we see beauty and truth in nature, we notice the balance God's universe provides. We realize that because man has been invited to share the earth with nature, he, too, has to be kept in balance.

The universe will always provide opportunities for us to balance ourselves. Further, the more willing we are to go along with the flow, not resisting the lessons that are presented to us for our own good, the more smoothly we will move back on track. However, as we resist, our lessons become increasingly more painful and difficult. Therefore, detachment, observation, and awareness are the keys to keep us open to what our experiences are teaching us.

The more aware we are, the less apt we are to "miss the boat." The more faith we have in God and the ways of the universe, the more we can let go and trust; and the more we can let go, the faster and easier is our ride down the river.

We will go far if we learn to observe ourselves and not blame others for our unhappiness. As we learn to bring each experience back home without obsessing about other people's behavior, the better off we'll be. It's a wise practice to ask ourselves, "Why did I draw this experience to me? What can I learn here? What is the best attitude for me to have in this situation?" If we can introspect and experience our feelings as we need to, we will begin to see our pattern.

Our learning comes in cycles as well. If we pay attention, we can be alert to new opportunities for growth. Accepting ourselves as we are and being grateful for this opportunity to spend "another year in school" enables us to make our journey worthwhile. Furthermore, observation of the world around us affords us the chance to respond rather than to merely react to our experiences. In truth, we may feel blessed that our conscious awareness has brought us to a place of greater understanding of what it means to be part of all that is.

BOOK THIRTEEN

ON HEALING

Healing begins as soon as there is recognition that something needs to be healed. If we break a leg, the healing process begins with our acceptance of what has happened. The same holds true for healing other parts of the body, as well as the mind and emotions. It is acceptance that provides the proper conditions or environment for change, and this applies to healing of all kinds.

Acceptance may be on the conscious or unconscious level. Sometimes we are healing when we aren't even consciously aware that there is a need to be healed. While our conscious awareness may include only a portion of what we know to be true, some level of our being is keeping very close track of all that goes on with us. Spiritually, we can operate and carry on all sorts of functions, while the mind may be totally unaware of what the spirit is doing. It's as though two lives are going on at once. The spirit body, however, is aware of the physical, but the mind is generally unaware of the activities of the spiritual body.

For example, when we go to sleep at night, the spirit body leaves the physical vehicle and travels to other dimensions where much work and activity is carried on. The two bodies are attached by what is called the "Silver Cord." At death, this cord snaps and the spirit body is free, never to return to the physical. The term of life on earth has been completed, so the spirit is free to carry on in the spirit realm doing whatever is appropriate for the soul at that time.

We are not all the same, so our experiences at death will be somewhat different, depending on where we are at all levels of our being when the two bodies separate. Where we go at death depends upon many factors, and we may advance rapidly through the various planes until we have found "our home."

We don't change at death—that is, we are not transformed: we stay much the same as we were at the moment of death. But we continue to learn and to grow in the spirit world, just as we do here. It is said our learning on the physical plane is more rapid. In other words, our opportunity for growth is greatly facilitated on earth and our lessons are often learned at a faster rate here than in the spirit world.

There are some things that must be learned on the earthly plane. For example, if one has physical addictions that he wishes to relinquish, earth is the only place where that can be accomplished. In the spirit world, it is true that our addictions can fade away with time, but we will have to face the temptation as we return to earth again. Most likely we will pick up the habit again because it is "in us" to do so. It is a part of our nature.

We came with our physical weaknesses ingrained in the soul. They formed a "blueprint" that indicated what was going to need work in the lifetime ahead. That blueprint might have included impatience, intolerance, misuse of power, or greed. It was all there waiting to draw experiences that would expose the issues to be worked on. Whatever the individual, with the help of other wise souls, chose to work on in this life, the lessons would be appropriate to the weak area.

If we are terribly impatient, we will draw experiences that will bring this issue into the light. We will be faced with situations that test our patience over and over again. Then again, if we have a problem with believing in ourselves, we will encounter individuals and conditions that challenge our faith in who we are and in our abilities and talents. Somehow the issue needs to be exposed. If we never have to face the problem, we are unable to grow out of it. It may even go undetected, unless we have someone or something to point it out to us or in some way call it to our attention.

If we need to learn to love, we will most likely be born into a family that is not very loving. Otherwise, how would we become aware of what is lacking within us? If our family is always supportive and loving and accepting of everything we do, how can we become aware that we have an issue with love? There would be no need to look into the problem because there wouldn't be one. It is in the unloving atmosphere that we test ourselves with love; and it is in an atmosphere of negativity that we test our self-esteem; and it is in an atmosphere of fear and challenge where we test our faith in God and in ourselves.

So as we come to earth we have our assignments cut out for us, although—because an angel places a veil over our eyes—we are unable to see or remember why we came. We are taught some things in our Sunday Schools and churches about religion and how to be good so we can get to heaven, but usually we are not totally certain why we're here and what our purpose is.

We don't usually know our goals beyond those that pertain to an occupation or hobby. We may be aware of a few talents and we have a vague understanding that perhaps we'd better use them. But beyond this, we are often at a loss regarding the personal spiritual goals that we set before our birth.

It is analogous to being in school. We sign up for courses that we need to take in order to graduate. We need so many credits of humility, for example. Then we need to take a course in tolerance, and of course, acceptance. (That one's a humdinger!) Then we need to take some credits in being balanced, along with several courses in patience.

While in the spirit world, we feel excited about our lifetime ahead and we feel confident that we will be able to pass our courses. From all perspectives there, everything looks rather easy. Sometimes we become overly enthusiastic and take on what later appears to be too much for us. However, we are watched over carefully by our guardian angels and guides who protect us and lead us aright as we sometimes stray from our chosen path.

Having chosen our lessons, we finally make our descent and are born back into the physical world. And as though in a hypnotic state, we forget all of our wonderful plans, hopes, and dreams. We find ourselves, instead, lost and bewildered as to the meaning of it all. When we stumble and fall, which we will do, our spirit forces which are naturally a part of God, attempt to pick us up again. As we accept our "fallen condition" and our need and desire for healing, the perfect pattern within us begins to emerge, replacing the old, worn out pattern.

As we let go of the old, the new appears in its place. Just as we have weaknesses imprinted on the soul, so do we also have the perfected Christ pattern within us. Total healing means total perfection. Healing, then, doesn't come from an outside source. Healing is the emergence of the perfected pattern within us that may be activated by someone or something outside of ourselves. No one heals us. But others may facilitate our healing process. We heal ourselves, and only when we're ready. Sometimes we need to keep our negative conditions for awhile until we learn what we need to learn.

As we become more conscious of our healing process, we begin to pay more attention to the body and what it is telling us. All physical conditions begin with the mind, so we take a look at our attitudes and thought patterns to see what may be causing our difficulty. Then we can learn to release the emotional condition or attitudinal problem that may be affecting us physically. Restoration comes only as we're ready for it. Our growing awareness of how we can facilitate our own healing process is exciting, indeed.

Our need to run to the doctor is lessened as we develop a greater understanding of how we bring upon ourselves our own health problems. Of course, a visit to a doctor is recommended for anything that appears to need a doctor's attention. Using many healing methods, including a doctor's advice, is a part of holistic medicine.

More and more, we are seeing people taking responsibility for their health. Relying on one's intuition, as it feels appropriate, can also be a good thing. Learning to be attuned to body, mind, and spirit together is the ideal in being able to maintain one's health. Also, asking for Divine Light and guidance each day helps to ensure that we will be able to face the challenges that await us. When we find ourselves out of balance and our body in disharmony or dis-ease, we may send out the thought, when we are ready, that we wish to be restored to perfect health.

Jesus, the principal source of healing power in the spirit realm, is awaiting our call for help. Christ Energy is the most powerful and profound source upon which we may call when we are in need of healing. As we call upon this Divine Energy, let's give thanks, always, for its availability to us.

We receive according to our faith, as well as our readiness to be healed. God is in charge of when and how we shall be healed, so let's leave the outcome to Him. Meanwhile, we can do our part by learning to accept ourselves and our inadequacies as they are.

We are ill as long as we think we need to be. But when we're ready to bring forth a new pattern, and when we're ready to accept responsibility for what that means to us, then we may be healed. Further, when we're healed of all fear, we can know the meaning of unconditional love and our healing will be complete. And so it is.

ON SOUL

The soul is that portion of ourselves that represents All That Is. It is the higher part of our nature and as such it is both perfect and permanent. The soul, being everlasting, is unchanging and is a reflection of the God Force. We represent a portion of the soul as we come to earth as human beings in order to gather experience so that the soul may be fulfilled.

The soul is relaying messages to us constantly. We hear people say, "Deep in my soul I knew it was true." Or we may hear, "My soul yearns for a better tomorrow—a new dawn." Anything that has to do with the soul has a distinct depth to it. In other words, the soul is profound. "From the bottom of my soul," we hear people say. The soul represents the essence of our being and from it stems all that we are or ever will be. The soul is without judgment. It just is. And because it is permanent, it is not fickle and is not influenced by the temporal nature of life in the world as we know it.

The personality, on the other hand, is ever changing and dynamic. It changes as the individual grows. As the personality experiences life, it feeds the soul, making it larger and more complex. Each experience brings to it a new dimension from which the personality may draw as there is need. "As you sow, so shall you reap." The soul draws conditions and circumstances to itself, depending on what is created by the personality. If the personality commits a crime, for example, the soul will attract an experience somewhere along the line that befits the crime that was committed. In other words, we pay for our mistakes.

The soul is the mechanism by which we attract our experiences in life. The soul knows what the personality needs in order to experience proper growth and development. The personality, then, in an effort to better itself, responds to the experiences that have been attracted by the soul.

If, for example, we fear something or someone and hold that fear in our consciousness, the soul will more than likely attract whatever is feared by the personality so that it may deal with the fear. If we dread seeing a particular individual, we can be sure to run into him or her, especially if it is pertinent to our growth at this time to face the fear. It behooves us to be careful of our thoughts, because we are prone to attract that which we are and that which we think about. If we have a fear of being raped, for example, it's wise to deal with the fear rather than allowing it to grow within us: we are more likely to attract the experience due to our fear.

As we grow in the belief that we are watched over and guided by the God of our own understanding, we will also grow in love. Our ultimate motivation for action is not fear, but our desire to learn the lesson of love.

The conditions we fear, then, are really there to help us. As we release our fear, we will attract fewer negative situations to us. As we hold on to fear, we will attract the feared situation in order that we may face and release it. We may also attract negative situations as we send out correspondingly negative energy or commit an act that is contrary to God's laws. It is the natural and spiritual laws that dictate our boundaries and tell us how properly to use the Divine Energy we are given each day.

As the law of gravity dictates what happens when we drop a dish to the floor, the universal laws tell us what happens when we think and act in certain ways. And it is the soul that monitors all that goes on within the personality. The soul knows when the laws have been transgressed and it responds accordingly. It will then, at the moment of transgression, set into motion a corresponding condition in order to balance what has just been created. The soul acts as the balancing agent, continually attracting necessary experiences to the personality so that it may learn about universal law.

Most of us learn about life by doing. Knowing isn't enough. We need to experience in order to believe the wisdom that has been handed down through the ages. It isn't enough, for example, to be told that we should eat right, exercise, and take care of our bodies. Sometimes we have to experience poor health in order to believe the truth.

Often, we can't just be told that we must learn to forgive those who hurt us. To really understand the meaning and wisdom of this teaching, we may need to know what it feels like to experience years of built-up resentment. Similarly, sometimes we must experience the pain of rejection in order to believe that we must learn to love ourselves. Being told is not enough. We're here to experience life and release our fears so that we may grow in understanding and love.

Thus, it is the soul that is responsible for monitoring all that we do. We have the proper experiences in our lives to enable us to grow in wisdom and strength. It is the soul that knows our every hope and fear and makes our growth possible. Again, it is the soul that grows in beauty as we gather experience after experience in our quest for greater knowledge, wisdom, and truth. Lastly, it is the soul that teaches us to love as it fulfills itself through all that we experience.

ON COOPERATION

What is meant by cooperation on the spiritual path? With whom and what do we need to cooperate? We are living in a time when working, living, and playing together are vital. What does that fact mean to our spiritual life?

We are attempting to move into a long period of harmony and peace where disharmony and confrontation used to be commonplace. We will be experiencing conditions based on peaceful solutions to everyday problems. What used to be the norm in behavior will be unacceptable as we learn to love ourselves and others. We will be connected in consciousness as we are now, but through bonds of love and acceptance rather than fear and discord.

As our fear of each other lessens, we will become increasingly open to finding peaceful solutions within our relationships. We will find it easier to communicate as the walls built upon fear begin to crumble. We will close the door to bigotry and hatred from without. Cooperation will be commonplace because the lessons from the past will be learned and wisdom will prevail.

As we embark on the spiritual path consciously, we can be aware of this move toward cooperation in many areas of life. We see it all around us as people begin to take responsibility for themselves as well as for their environment. Cooperation involves not only our relationship with each other but with nature as well. As we learn to take care of our planet, we are cooperating with God, the universal laws of nature, and all of the spirit forms which oversee the plants, trees, and animals. Further, as we learn to cooperate with nature, we will be in harmony with forces that bring the wind, rain, snow, and all of the elements that make up the diverse conditions we encounter on earth. As we connect with these forces, we find ourselves in tune with All That Is. We need not fear nature, because we will understand the purpose of all that it brings to us. We will be in harmony with the flow of nature and will seek to use it expeditiously. We will use what is meant for us in terms of energy and will not waste this universal force given to us by our Creator.

Subsequently, as we each come to terms with the natural as well as the spiritual laws, we will work, play, and live in cooperation with each other automatically, without giving it much thought. We will have the proper mindset—brought out by the healing of ourselves. For as we are purified, we will be brought into alignment on all levels, physically, emotionally, mentally, and spiritually, with the universal forces. This alignment is taking place now.

Many of us presently are feeling the pains or uncomfortable pressures that accompany this process. We feel the tugs and pulls as we desire to smooth our path, even by the tiniest bit. We become torn between temptations to flow with the mass consciousness and our desire to adopt the new consciousness that is characterized by love, acceptance, and non-judgment.

We hear some terrible news on television and are tempted to get into a discussion of how awful it is, when we know that that only adds to the negativity already there. When we would be better off to change the subject, we stay with it just to have something, at least, to talk about with family and friends. We get into "Ain't it awful?" and wonder why we feel pulled down by all that's going on in the world. Yet we all know better as spiritual students.

We know the earth is cleansing itself, just as we know that negative as well as positive energies are out in full force. We are being asked to look at both and make our choices. We know, too, that all we see out there in the world is but a mere reflection of who we are. And we know that it is our response to what we see that tells us whether we are going forward or backward on our path up the mountain. We know that it is our response to the conditions we find in the world that will either help to increase or decrease the power of negativity in the world.

It isn't the negativity itself or the things we don't like in the world that comprise the problem. It is the approach we take to these things. Our manner of thinking can give negativity a power that makes it come to life. If we ignore a child's negative behavior, it will eventually go away, especially if it is there only for our attention. It is the same with the negative forces that wish to take hold of our consciousness. If we were to hear about all the terrible crimes being committed in our society, but refuse to give what we hear an ounce of energy, this type of negative behavior would decrease.

It is the negative force behind a criminal act that responds to our effort to ignore it. Actions are all thought. If we refused to give a place in our consciousness to horrible crimes, they would cease. Naturally, this has to be the work of mass consciousness. But this is how we contribute to the collective mind in a positive way. In other words, through giving power and attention to negative forces, we invite them to continue. It doesn't matter that we don't like what is happening. Our attention alone is enough to keep the activity going.

In our great attempt to heal ourselves and thus align ourselves with the Christ Energy, we are making an effort at eliminating the fear of these dark forces. The only way to release the fear of evil is to bless it. We need to face it when it comes and understand that it is there to help us heal ourselves. It is there for us to look at and say, "You have no power over me. I thank you for coming and showing me what I need to learn. I realize you are here to teach me something about myself and I bless you and release you because I now understand. There is no need for you to come again into my consciousness." If we work in this way with the "shadows" in our lives, we will find our fears vanishing. Further, as we learn to cooperate with the negative and positive forces that are all around us and with us, we become masters of our fate and co-creators with God. Further, as we cooperate with one another and with nature in our alignment with the natural and spiritual forces that have always existed, we will find peace and total acceptance of ourselves and those around us. As we seek harmony with the God of our own understanding, we will gain in trust and remain faithful to our path that leads us forward on our journey up the mountain. Lastly, as we merge with the Higher Forces that help protect and guide us, we will, indeed, be blessed.

ON CREATIVITY

Why is creativity so important to our growth as human beings? We have been endowed with many gifts, and as recipients of these abilities and talents we are, by God's grace, expected to use them.

Many of us have abilities we have never used and don't even know exist. Often we don't know all of our talents until we are faced with the opportunity to use them. Many times we are very surprised that we are more than able to do things we never thought were within the realm of possibility.

There are times when we are held back from doing certain things because of karmic obligations. At other times, it simply isn't time to use a given ability or the need is not there. However, we must never underestimate our ability to do anything until we've tried it. Further, we sometimes have to give ourselves a second try later on in life in order to see if we have the ability for a given task, sport, or whatever the effort is. Maybe it's painting a picture. When in school as young children, perhaps we felt we did poorly in art. But as we grew to adulthood, this talent blossomed within us and we felt free to express ourselves, finding our new hobby exhilarating as well as relaxing.

Our abilities will blossom forth as we allow ourselves to experiment with different things. If we don't try, how can we ever find out what we like to do and have the ability for? Being creative is important because it is a way in which we can express ourselves.

Self-expression is essential because it is through expressing how we feel that we begin to heal the inner self. If we have no way to express how we feel, we will block ourselves, and our ability to heal will be stifled. We see people, occasionally, who are very withdrawn. They look very sullen and quiet, but one has the feeling that they have a great deal of emotion bottled up within them. If they could have an outlet for their feelings, a way of expressing themselves, they would soften up, smile and maybe even laugh. We need to be able to let out the excess energy within us.

We also find we add balance to our lives by becoming creative. Many people spend much of their waking hours in their left brain; i.e., their intellect. They are always thinking and figuring things out. Perhaps their job demands that they compute numbers all day long, or maybe their work requires that they make decisions based upon many facts that they have had to sort out and analyze. This is called left-brain work and is very necessary to our thinking processes, but needs to be balanced by the right brain or the creative mind.

When we create, we use God's energy. This energy flows through us. Consequently, as we use it we don't become tired. The truly creative person simply relaxes and allows spirit to flow through him as he sews things, plays the piano, paints a picture, or goes wherever his talent leads him. He doesn't have to "work" at it. As a result, interesting and beautiful things happen as he allows creative energy to flow through him. This process helps to create the balance necessary to our feeling whole. In being creative, we relax and enjoy what we're doing. We're releasing tension as we allow spiritual energy to flow through us, healing and restoring our minds, bodies, and spirits.

Being creative also brings perspective to our lives, particularly if we're worried, uptight, or tense about something. And if we're having difficulty letting go because our minds are obsessed with our problems, we can find great relief in singing with a group if we like to sing, or getting lost in making poetry or doing a watercolor. We are going from using our minds to our spirits in moving into the creative mode. As we do, we tend to forget our worries and get lost in our creation. Then, when we come back to "reality," often our problem has lost its hold on us and it just doesn't seem as bad, or perhaps we have a new perspective on it that we never had before. In any case, we feel more balanced and we have a healthier view of our situation. Thus, being creative can add stability to our lives as well.

There is also a need for the creative mind in solving the problems in the world today. We have been a left-brained society, using the intellect alone for solving the issues that confront us. With the coming change from the Piscean to the Aquarian Age, there is a great need for the creative mind. We need new solutions stemming from the feminine energy or creative source.

Planetary healing will result from the feminine energy that waits to soothe the troubled earth. It is the creative thought—the spiritual mind that will bring the appropriate ideas to the masses. No longer will we look only to logic and reason, but will find balance as we allow the feminine energy to share the healing process. Without the Christ Energy, the world could not heal itself. We need both the masculine and feminine—reason and intuition will combine to bring about the transition for which we are waiting. To keep ourselves in balance so that we may walk through this potentially tumultuous period, we need to express ourselves creatively in many different ways.

What does it mean to be creative? It means that we allow new ideas to become a part of us. It means that we stay open, to listen not only to others, but to ourselves as well. We must hear our intuition speaking to us. If we live only by what others tell us or by what we read in a book, we are blocking our ability to become whole. If we are living the way others want us to live, then we are not being true to ourselves.

God gave us the ability to think for ourselves as well as the ability to receive thoughts that are given to us from spirit. Again, we may receive differently because of the point we have reached in our evolution as spiritual beings. If we don't allow ourselves the privilege of seeking within for our answers, we are turning down one of God's greatest gifts to us. The use of meditation is one way in which we can get in touch with that creative spiritual source. Learning to use our own intuition that God has given us will be essential in days to come, when much of what we hear and read may be dated or inappropriate.

There is much truth "out there," but interpretation of that truth is another matter. For example, there are those who feel the Bible should be taken literally, word for word. Others feel this is not so at all. They feel that the Bible is symbolic and contains a great deal of hidden meaning. Thus, there are differences in opinion when these written sources are studied. However, as we seek within ourselves, we will find only one Truth. There is only one God and we are all His children. As we each seek to know the Creator, we will each find our way.

If we all, no matter what religion we are, seek guidance each day from the Higher Intelligence within our own being, we will merge harmoniously, forming a beautiful tapestry with many blended colors. We will not be concerned with dogma because we will have found peace within. And as we find peace we find love; and as we love, there is no fear and all is well. So let's allow ourselves to feel, to hurt when we must, to think creatively as we listen to the messages the Wise Ones bring to us. And let's listen to each other and learn to accept...accept...accept. Acceptance is contrary to our need to control. As we learn to accept, we keep the channels open and our creativity alive.

Jill Downs

ON DEATH

Death may be called the final stage of growth. As we conclude our sojourn here on earth, we prepare for our transition into the next dimension. There is a preparation period that can last for a number of weeks or even months as the mind, body, and spirit prepare for the spirit make its journey into the next realm.

All must be ready in order for a smooth transition to take place. The more prepared a soul is on all levels, the easier will be the transition process. If the dying person is ready for his release, all will go smoothly—even if those closest are not yet prepared for his release. When we hang on, we make it more difficult for the loved one to let go. However, this is a normal situation: it's difficult to let go of people we care about. The thought of not seeing them again is hard to bear. We want to hold on to them as long as we can before releasing them to go on their way.

Another term for death might be "graduation." In some cultures, death is celebrated and the dying person is released with great ceremony. This seems to be appropriate: a person's time here on earth is ending. He has completed his scheduled period here in the world and has passed through all of his trials, as well as the joys, of his stay here on earth. He has, indeed, accomplished something.

It is not up to us, however, to judge what he has or has not accomplished, because we don't know what his actual goals were. Only the Higher Intelligence knows what the person was meant to complete while on earth. We may praise people's accomplishments, however, and recount what they have done for us and how they have affected us in our lives.

Celebrating a life just ending is important for each of us to do in our own way. This effects closure and helps surviving friends and family members deal with the loss. As we go into the final days of a person's life, it is important that things be said that need to be expressed to the one who is leaving.

Its important, also, that the dying be allowed to say their piece as well. Unexpressed thoughts are carried with us and tend to burden our mind and emotions. So it's best for everyone to get out what need to be said to our loved ones before saying good-bye. The dying person needs to know he is loved and appreciated for whatever he was—and is—able to do. Even the tiniest favor can help ease his mind if it is mentioned with gratitude. If we are holding back things that need to be said or taken care of, they "hang in the air," and everyone knows there is yet something to be completed.

Death can be a very healing experience for the dying as well as for those left behind. As we are forced to let go of something that was part of our past, there are many emotions and other considerations that go along with such a release. Letting go is not always easy when we are forced to think ahead and imagine what life is going to be like without this person in our midst. What changes will have to be made, and will we be able to carry on without the loved one?

Particularly where there has been a very close relationship, we find it is often difficult to face these issues. However, as the crucial time draws close, we are forced to think about these things which begin our healing process. As soon as we accept the inevitability of the death, the healing process begins for both the dying and those left behind.

Saying good-bye is never easy where there has been a loving relationship. However, it helps if we have faith that assures us that this is not a final ending. If we believe in a life hereafter, we can know that we will, indeed, have a reunion following our own death. Our good-bye then becomes temporary, until we meet again at a future time. It can be as though the dying one has moved to another state or location and we will have the opportunity to see him or her again. And depending upon how "tuned in" a person is or how sensitive one is to vibrations from the spirit world, we can become aware of our loved ones as they come near to see us while they are living in the spirit world. They are really only behind the veil in another dimension, but they can come as near to us as we allow them to.

If occasionally we feel a slight pain in our body that we can't understand, it may be that we are picking up the physical condition of one who has left the earth who has stopped by to greet us. If our grandmother had arthritis, we may be picking up her aching joints. It feels like our own body, but in reality it is hers.

The same holds true for emotional states. Occasionally if we feel overwhelmed with sadness or happiness, the emotions may belong to loving spirits in our midst. We can bless them and thank them for stopping by. If, on the other hand, we feel uncomfortable with an invisible being in our midst, or if we suspect our space is being invaded by an uninvited guest, ask them to leave in the name of Jesus Christ, and tell them, firmly, to go to the Light. We don't have to allow anyone, physical or non-physical, to invade our privacy if we don't wish them to be there. We all have rights and boundaries and it is up to us to uphold our right to privacy.

Sometimes a loving person will open up to many in spirit, but we should understand that if we ask for only the highest appropriate forces to be allowed into our space, we can save ourselves some trouble and confusion. Otherwise, we are tuning in to several different frequencies at one time. That can be overwhelming as well as draining. If we ask Divine Light to be with us, we allow our guides and spirit to monitor what comes into our force field.

As our loved ones come to visit us, we bless them and acknowledge their presence. It should be remembered that if we are in an emotional state of any kind, we will not be apt to sense their presence. It will more likely be when we are calm and content that we may notice their coming..

We need to develop faith in ourselves. Spirit communication can be a beautiful experience that can bring great fullness to life as we keep relationships alive that are meaningful to us.

But just as we have to live our own life here, we also have to live and let live with those who have gone beyond. In other words, we don't hold people to us, but allow each to go his or her own way. When we let people go, they will come back to us if the relationship was meant to be.

So let's live and let live, and allow and release. In this way, we can each grow in our own way and in our own time as we make our way up the spiritual ladder. And as we cross the threshold to a new adventure, our loved ones who have gone before us will meet us.

It is important as we are preparing to leave the physical body, to remember to go directly to the Light. It is helpful to instruct those who are leaving in the same way. As we go to the Light, we will find ourselves in the place appropriate for us and will be greatly uplifted.

People sometimes get lost as they allow themselves to be tied to earthly considerations. It's best to make the break as completely as possible; heading directly for the Light will allow this to happen. Then, as we are reintegrated and settled into a new and appropriate situation, we can come back with the proper perspective to visit those left behind. And as we adjust to our new life, whatever that may entail, we can look back on our earthly experience with gratitude for the life just ended.

Further, as we take all that we have learned from our sojourn on the physical plane and apply it wherever we find ourselves, we will discover that we'll be making new plans and creating new opportunities to experience joy and fulfillment. Life will be a new adventure. And as we leave behind old friends and acquaintances, we need not be sad because we understand the law of love. We know there can be no separation from those we love. We comprehend the meaning of death, seeing it as only another step taken as we press forward into the Light. And to those we've left behind, we don't say good-bye forever, but only "until we meet again" as we come together in another place and time.

Therefore, let us not fear death, but celebrate its meaning for us, whether we are leaving the earth or being left behind. Further, let's appreciate the healing which comes from acknowledging all we've gained from our relationships. Let's thank God for those who ha ve helped teach us what we need to know as we make our way up the mountain. And let's be grateful for the opportunity for life and all it brings, knowing it will never end—it only changes.

So as we discard the physical body, we put on a spirit or ethereal body that becomes the new vehicle with which we identify. As our new life takes shape and form on another level in a new dimension, we'll continue to grow and to experience and to help those who need our wisdom. Thus, life goes on and so do we. Just as love never dies, neither do we. We continue to live, to learn, to laugh, and to love, forever climbing into higher dimensions. "My house has many mansions," says the Lord. And, as we graduate from one level, we move up to the next, ever climbing to higher levels in consciousness.

Finally, one day—one moment in time—we will reach the home from where we came and from where we began this journey. As we began—a spark from the Source—we will, again, return. A circle in eternity will be completed—another soul fulfilled in time and space. So be it!

BOOK FOURTEEN

ON CHOICE

As we grow in spiritual awareness, we become more aware of the importance of choice in our lives. Where there is choice, there is opportunity. Without choice, there is no opportunity to grow and to learn.

Choice offers us the opportunity to err. We learn through making mistakes. If we never made a mistake, we couldn't learn anything. If we did everything perfectly, there would be no need to be here. We're here on earth to learn, to experience, to grow, and to make mistakes in the process. Being allowed the opportunity to get on the wrong path at times helps us to see the benefits of being on the right path. How can we appreciate doing the right thing if we've never done the wrong thing? How can we help others to do the right thing if they haven't the benefit of our experience? How can we teach effectively if we haven't "been there"?

The most effective teachers are those who teach from experience. As we experience life, including our mistakes, we equip ourselves with wisdom. If we are controlled by others regarding what we can and cannot think, do, feel, or read, we cannot possibly make a decision about what is right and appropriate for us. If someone is attempting to control our attitudes and our beliefs, he is interfering with our rights as spiritual beings.

We all have the God-given right to think and feel as we choose. We also have the right to share that with others. No one needs to accept our opinions or beliefs as their own, but they have a right to hear what we have to say if they so choose. No one has the right to limit another's learning. And that includes parents as well.

Sometimes we like to control our children. We like to shield them from harm and protect them from unhappy experiences.

But when we do so, they often rebel against our authority. Could it possibly be that they were meant to have certain experiences even though those experiences may be unhappy ones? Could it be that some experiences may be extremely beneficial to their growth and what lies ahead for them? Could it be that without the unpleasant experience, they might not be able to continue successfully on their path, because they have missed an important lesson?

There are some things we have to learn in order to continue upward on our journey. If the needed experiences are interrupted, the person can't continue to grow. It's difficult to watch people go through what may appear to be tragic circumstances. On the other hand, the more severe the circumstance, the greater the learning and the more room there is for joy at the other end.

If we always try to protect people, including ourselves, from life, we fail to permit them the opportunity to make choices. Further, if we have no decisions to make regarding our fate, we can't know the meaning of discernment. If you lock a child in a closet for several years, taking care of only his basic needs, he will come out understanding little about life. He will be emotionally and mentally stunted. Even physically, he will be unhealthy and immature due to lack of exercise and proper nutrition.

In much the same way, as we "protect" others' experiencing what they must for their growth, we take away their chance to unfold naturally. This doesn't mean we can't express our opinions, feelings, and desires. It simply means we don't use measures of control, whether psychological or physical, to prevent someone's right to choice.

Sometimes, we attempt to control people emotionally by showing approval or disapproval in our facial expressions and body posture. We may think we are allowing that person the freedom to make their choice, but we're still attempting to influence them by controlling them emotionally. Perhaps we tend to be jealous. We go to a party with our boyfriend, determined not to nag him if he starts to flirt with someone at the party. We get through the evening successfully, not saying a word, but all the while we're scowling at him, letting him know how we disapprove of his behavior. Wouldn't it be better to tell him how we feel about it, and then allow him to do what he wants? Then we can go off, enjoying the party, leaving him to do as he pleases.

We can be honest with our feelings and set boundaries where we need to with family members and all those persons with whom we come in contact. However, we would be well advised to refrain from attempts to control another's freedom.

Actually, we are unable to control people anyway. We're seeing that fact demonstrated in countries that, until recently, lacked freedom, but are now getting their first taste of democracy. Once the door is open even a crack, there can never again be any shutting out of the light. Sooner or later, the human spirit longs for freedom of choice once more, and the door swings open again. The fresh air rushes in and the sunlight shines on all that has been dark for so long.

The same things happen as we attempt to control how people think and believe. Sooner or later, the mind that has been controlled for so long allows a ray of light to enter and the cobwebs begin to clear away. The old dogmas and thought patterns that had been so prominent for so long begin to disintegrate, and new ways of thinking and processing begin to take shape. Further, a new level in consciousness is reached as the creative mind reaches toward the Light. Again, once this Light rushes in, the door cannot be closed successfully again. Once on our way, we can't turn the clock back and become what we once were.

When we have opened ourselves to the greater consciousness, we become a part of that stream and we cannot return. Once we've experienced the Light and all that means to us, we can't return to darkness. And without being able to choose what is appropriate for us at the time, whether it be a happy experience or what may appear to be a great set-back, we prevent ourselves and others from gaining headway on our trek up the mountain.

If we are carried every time when the going gets rough, we won't gain the strength we need to finish the journey. And again, if we're not given the choice to experience the situations that are presented to us on the way, we will be lacking in knowledge and wisdom. If we are not allowed to determine our own direction and guidance along the road, we won't know who we are.

We must be given the opportunity to know ourselves. If we can't experience life, we don't know what our capabilities are, and if we aren't allowed to choose our thoughts, we don't really know how we believe. Further, if we can't make our own decisions, we don't have the confidence to become a mature adult; and if we don't have the ability to choose our friends, we can't know ourselves. For who are we but a reflection of all we see around us? If others make our choices for us, we aren't being true to ourselves.

We can remain truthful to who we are only by following our own path. As we allow others to control the expression of our true nature, we will never unfold as spiritual beings, thus denying ourselves the right to inherit the kingdom of heaven that is within. "A house divided cannot stand." Therefore, as we compromise ourselves for the sake of others, we prevent ourselves from knowing God. "The only way to the Father is through Me." And the only way to the light is through making choices available to us along our journey. Without the choices we don't go anywhere, and without the freedom to make our own decisions, we remain spiritual invalids. Afraid and unable to move, we hide alone in the world while others live for us and choose what they think is best for us to do.

As we ponder life's journey, let's remember that no one controls our destiny but ourselves. No one controls us unless we allow someone to do so. No one causes us to fall short of our goals unless we, ourselves, allow it to happen. So let's go forward in freedom, knowing that our choices are ours to make.

And as we come to the fork in the road, let's ask our Creator for guidance that we may make the choices that will enable us to continue on without taking unnecessary detours along our path.

As we make our mistakes, let's be grateful for all we learn and not judge what appear to be our misfortunes. For what appears to have been a wrong turn may have been a totally appropriate side trip. Therefore, as we take all that we have gained from our experiences and assimilate the learning into our being, let's thank God for the ability to be master of our fate and co-creator with a higher intelligence which knows us so well. Let us also ask for guidance and Divine Light each day so that we can be sure that all that comes to us will be for our edification. Finally, let us pray to choose wisely and go on our way, not questioning ourselves or doubting our path. For as we doubt, we draw experiences which will accentuate that doubt.

Instead, let's affirm our belief in ourselves and seek guidance from within, especially when we do not know where to turn. For as we listen in the silence, our path will be affirmed and we can move forward in power and in strength, knowing we are right in our choices and strong in our knowledge of who we are and where we are going. If we stumble, we may pick ourselves up again, forgiving self and moving on, taking what we've learned to help another who may need our wisdom. Growing in strength and in faith in ourselves, we gain the knowledge to move even further into the light, taking our experiences with us as we learn to love ourselves, to forgive our mistakes, and to trust in our ability to choose.

ON DISAPPOINTMENT

As we embark on the spiritual path we are apt to experience disappointments along the way. Sometimes we aren't prepared for this because we're attempting to improve ourselves and our lives. Therefore, we feel that our life should be smooth and easy. Unfortunately, or fortunately depending upon our perspective, we find that the road is difficult and we are faced with one disappointing experience after another.

Especially as we begin this conscious healing process (i.e., deciding to go the spiritual route in full awareness of our choices), our life can be tumultuous at times. How rocky the road becomes depends upon what obstacles have to be removed. If we have several large boulders in our path, it will take much strength, endurance, and patience to remove them. If we have only a few small rocks, our beginning will be easier. But we will all have our challenges, regardless of who we are.

Everyone is in relationships of one kind or another. Some of these relationships will remain intact, while others will be torn apart as is necessary in certain situations. There will be times when we will be happy to let go of some issues or people in our lives because we will be ready. At other times, we will want to hold on to what we have, even though it may not be in our best interest to do so. Some relationships will be discontinued for a time, only to be picked up again later on.

In the healing process, there needs to be time for regeneration that is best done away from the issues, circumstances or people who were a part of the tearing-down process. It is as though we want to avoid hearing an old song that reminds us of our former loves. Or perhaps we want to move to a new city if we have had an especially unfortunate experience. The new environment seems to offer a new potential for a fresh start without all the reminders of our old life all around us. So relationships come and go depending on their value to the person who is attempting to change his or her life.

As our circumstances change, we encounter some disappointments along the way. There are times when we think we know what is best for us, so we have in our minds a vision of what we want. Perhaps we see someone who we think would be the right husband or wife or girlfriend. We're certain this is to work out for us, only to discover that this was not in the plan for us. We become disappointed and disillusioned, feeling that perhaps our decision to change our life isn't worth it after all. Again, perhaps we have our heart set on going to medical school, convinced that this is the answer to our problems. However, we later discover, to our great disappointment, that we are not accepted. Then again, maybe we find a new apartment we love, only to discover that we can't afford it.

As disappointments mount, we wonder if we have made the right decision to go a new way. "Is it worth all this? I've worked so hard to get where I am. Is it worth going any further?" The problem is that we've forgotten about limited vision and our trust in our Higher Power to provide for us. Sometimes the things we desire would be disastrous for us down the road. Again, perhaps that which we want would have amounted to a waste of time or energy when there was something better all along, waiting for the appropriate time to appear.

If there's one quality that's necessary if we want to get all we can from life, it's patience. Learning to have patience is one of the most valuable lessons we can encounter. When we are patient, we are willing to wait until we know we have found what we're looking for. If we lack patience, we're bound to cheat ourselves out of our dream house, the best available job for us, or the right marriage partner. Often just as we're unwilling to wait any longer for something, that which we desire appears. If we would allow ourselves to wait just a little longer, to stretch our patience just a little further, then we wouldn't be disappointed and settle for less.

Still, at other times our disappointments are blessings in disguise. If we could have faith in the blueprint of our life, if we could see, feel, and understand that there is a plan for us that we will be pleased with, we would be willing to wait for an indeterminable amount of time to allow this wonderful plan to unfold. If you know that a beautiful apartment was to be yours later on, you'd be willing to forgo the one that is appealing to you now.

In other words, if we could only see down the road, we would accept the will of the Creator and forgo our own wishes. If we understood that certain things have to be accomplished before new conditions can appear on the horizon, we would be willing to wait for what is right for us. If we could only come to believe that it is not always appropriate to know everything today, we would then be willing to wait to comprehend what was happening in our life or what we are to do.

Similarly, if we could learn to trust, we would come to see that our disappointments are blessings in disguise for any number of reasons. Perhaps others have to learn life's lessons. Often we become disappointed in the behavior of others because they are not doing as we want them to. We forget that those around us have things to learn, too.

When things don't turn out as we hoped, we may not know the reason; we have to accept that too. Understanding may come to us down the road, or we may never know until our life is over. In any case, if we have faith that our Higher Power is looking after us, guiding and directing our lives, we can relax. Also, by understanding that we are living in accordance with God's laws, we may find some measure of peace.

Further, though we may be brokenhearted at the loss of what we thought was to be, we can take that pain and bring it into our new awareness that what is to be will be. In the same way, we come to know that what is not to be will dissolve or not come together for us as we would wish. In other words, if we could see the whole picture, we would be happy to do things God's way. For the spiritual path is our way now that we have decided to join ranks with the higher forces that have taken command of our lives.

Coming to know and believe there is a plan for us assures us that if we will allow things to unfold naturally, trusting in the Creator to point the way, we will become more peaceful. By observing the flow of the river without getting caught up in the tides and eddies of our emotions, we will be carried downstream to our destination. Having faith in the process and accepting our disappointments as part of life's experience will bring us that same sense of freedom. We will find courage as we look to the future with great anticipation. And lastly, as we trust in the Creator, we will turn our discouragement into joy and our failures into triumphs.

ON SELFISHNESS

One of the stumbling blocks that we confronted in life is the quality of selfishness. Whether it is within us or the people we know, selfishness robs us of the ability to really know ourselves. For it is only in reaching out and giving ourselves to others and to life that we come to know who we are.

If we insist on remaining in our shell and taking care of only our own needs, we can't see ourselves in the mirrors of other people. When we deal with the world and the people around us, we learn much about ourselves. We learn what we react to and come to know how we respond to certain situations.

We see our abilities and talents as we strive to give ourselves to the situations that present themselves to us. We're attempting, always, to be open to others—to their thoughts, their beliefs and attitudes, observing at the same time how they correlate with our own. We come to see our likes and dislikes as we open ourselves to the world. We learn to integrate all we do and experience so that we become a whole and healthy human being.

However, if we opt for being selfish in our lives and in our attitudes, we don't allow ourselves to experience the richness life has to offer. Because we are narrow in our perceptions due to our lack of experience with the world, we are apt to miss the subtleties of life around us. Looking after our own needs becomes a time-consuming project, and we're forever trying to protect ourselves from having to expose our vulnerable sides to the world.

This self-protection takes energy and we can actually become tired from having to plan our lives so that we will be totally comfortable and secure within our enviroment. Our protective walls become thicker the longer we remain within our enclosed space. The more we try to keep the world out, the greater our chances are of isolating ourselves from experiences that might prove frightening.

Selfish persons often have an air of grandiosity, but in reality they are pathetic and ought to be pitied. They haven't yet learned to put their pride aside and learn to be human. Instead, they're busy feeding their egos and images. They have to bolster themselves up because they know that if they took a good look they would see the pain that lies there beneath the arrogant exterior.

Selfish people don't usually think they're selfish. Usually they just feel they are right. They're also aware that they have rights as human beings. One of these is the right to live the way they want to. Then self-centeredness is used as an excuse to "be an individual" or to exercise the "right to privacy." These, indeed, are rights that each of us has, but when they are used to keep oneself from experiencing life, they become a handicap rather than a privilege.

We are all tempted at times to close the door on the rest of the human race as fear or boredom overwhelms us. Sometimes when we are attempting to figure out our lives, or when we need to just be alone for awhile, we like to withdraw from the world. For awhile this may be all right: we need to readjust our priorities or figure out what our next step is to be. However, if we continue to remain aloof from the rest of the world, we hurt ourselves and actually defer our progress rather than enhance our growth. What could be a constructive time to regroup and restore one's spirit becomes a habit, until we find ourselves locked in a pattern we find difficult to change. Once we get ourselves into that comfortable environment where we refuse to stretch ourselves for fear of breaking, we don't want to leave.

After reclining in an easy chair, we find it difficult to get up. Our muscles are stiff, and we don't have the energy to get moving again. So we sleep on, ignoring the world around us. Then when somebody comes to wake us up to try to encourage us to do something new and different, we grumble.

Our selfishness forbids us to be grateful, so we accept what others have for us without giving in return. In this way we can punish ourselves if people give up on us. So we continue to complain about everything while the weeks, months, or years drag on. We, in the meantime, impose a great challenge to those who are concerned about our welfare.

If we are confronted with our problem, we shrug it off. After all, we're right, aren't we? Occasionally in our moments of openness, we glance at others around us to see how they operate. Certain that we can never find joy in our lives, we wonder what makes them different. Usually we decide that the Creator, if there is one, has clearly given them a break we didn't get.

Armed with that perception, we close the door again and go back to our self-imposed hell on earth. For, in reality, that's what it is. There is no place to which we go when we die that doesn't already exist right here on earth. We make our own hell wherever we are. If we are still in the physical body, we can make our hell here if we choose. If we had made our transition and carried with us selfish attitudes and lifestyles from our earth life, we would make our hell in the spirit world. Hell is hell, no matter where we choose to establish it. And selfishness is hell.

As we close ourselves to the channels of light that can give us what we need to edify our lives, we have created hell for ourselves. Further, as we refuse to accept our gifts, talents, and abilities to help ourselves and others, we are halting our own progress. Again, as we refuse to recognize the beauty of others, we fail to see anything good in ourselves. The more selfish we become, the less faith we have in a Higher Power that can sustain us, because we take pride in using our own power in meeting our needs.

Once we have so thoroughly embraced the darkness, we are afraid to turn on the light lest we might see something too frightening to comprehend. As we sink further into the night, we become certain that there's no way out. We then are both relieved and frightened. For in that dark space we are saved from having to cope with the world: we know we can't. Yet, we are frightened to see others doing so well. We are caught in a dilemma of our own making and we know it—and this is the greatest hell of all.

Once we have recognized our situation as it really is, we have the first inkling of truth that we've had for a long time. Suddenly we know we've done it to ourselves and we have no one else to blame. For the first time we admit defeat and say, "I don't know." As we search in the pit we've dug for tools to help get us out, we find ourselves alone. No one is there to help us or to take care of us, and we are lonely. And for the first time in a long while, we pray.

At last our prayers are heard, and a ladder appears over the side of the pit. We scramble over to the ladder and hold on with both hands, struggling to pull ourselves up. We look up and see that there are faces smiling down at us, cheering our efforts to climb out of the hole.

One who has been watching climbs down the ladder and holds out a hand to us. We take the hand and hoist ourselves up onto the ladder. Everyone claps and the climb begins. When we near the top of the ladder, there is a new look on our face. There is a smile that wasn't there before; the worry lines are gone; and our eyes shine with bright anticipation of the future.

Hope has been reborn and faith is solid. Further, love is renewed within our heart as we give our hand to others who have fallen down the hole after us, repeating our same experience. We realize that we keep hope alive through sharing what we have with those who need to learn from our experience. Moreover, as we keep our eyes open to the light, we needn't fear returning to the dark side of our nature. For that is all it is. The hell we create for ourselves is there only because we think we need it. Therefore, once we discover that the light is preferable to the darkness, we give ourselves permission to choose humility over greed, the light over the darkness, and love over fear. When we learn to turn away from our selfish nature and embrace the positive side of who we are, we allow ourselves to face the sin or shortcoming and be cleansed by its light. There, as we linger in the light, we heal our wounds of the past, forgiving ourselves for our mistakes and vowing to help those who can benefit from our experience.

ON SIN

To sin means to fall short of one's goals. Formal religion and doctrine often imply fear when talking about sin. We get the impression that punishment is associated is with sin. But really, the only punishment resulting from sin is what we do to ourselves. God does not punish us. If we have transgressed the natural or spiritual laws of the universe, our soul will automatically attract conditions and circumstances that help to get us in line by balancing what we have done. In other words, if we have hurt someone, we will in turn be hurt, in order that we understand what it feels like. God isn't sitting on a big throne handing out punishment to law-breakers. God is love.

However, in order to understand how to become loving, we have to learn to live in accordance with the spiritual laws of the universe as they exist for everyone, regardless of what religion or spiritual philosophy we adhere to. It doesn't matter if we are Protestant, Jewish, Catholic, or atheist, or if we belong to an eastern tradition, all are subject to the laws of the Creator.

The situation is comparable to our working with the law of gravity, which is also universal. It doesn't matter whether we believe in it or even know that it exists; it is still there. If we pick up a china dish and let it go, it will drop to the floor and, most likely, break. The fall is inevitable. Moreover, no matter who drops it, it will fall. Can we imagine a God Who has different rules for each of His children? We all adhere to the same, universal rules to help ourselves to learn to love all of life.

It's as though we are in one big school. There are several courses of study and many, many classes. When we graduate we all have to pass the same tests. There are some basic requirements that all must have in order to get diplomas. We may specialize in some area, but our foundation must be the same.

In life, for example, we all must learn patience, tolerance, faith in God and self, and on and on. These are tests we all must pass in order to make it back home to the Source. "By their fruits, you shall know them," Christ told us. In order to reach perfection, we must perfect ourselves. This process applies equally to everyone, no matter where they live in the world. How we get there is not important.

To judge another's process or religion is inappropriate because this is a long "course," and many avenues and many dimensions of learning go into completing it. Just as we have to take science, English, and another language to get through college, we have to have specific areas of learning in life in order to become whole. We are also always balancing the scale.

If at one point we turn totally away from the Christ, for example, at another time we may be totally into His teachings. If at some time we are without spiritual practices of any kind, we may later find great comfort in ritual. We may enjoy the secure feeling we get from engaging in certain specific religious or spiritual practices that give us a "hands on" connection with our spiritual philosophy. Perhaps this is something we have always had and therefore want to continue.

There are many persons who like a certain amount of ritual to augment their beliefs, no matter what religion they choose. Ritual can have the effect of cementing our belief system, making it tangible and allowing us a means of expressing ourselves at the same time. It supports us when we perform certain functions that keep us centered and balanced. Yoga, or tai chi, for example, are excellent examples of practices which help align the physical, mental, and spiritual bodies in a way most respectful to the Almighty. As one completes a session of either of these practices, there is a sense of oneness with the Creator.

What does this have to do with sin? Sin does the opposite. As we abuse God's Energy, knowingly or unknowingly, we become off-center. We are uncomfortable, though we may not always be aware of what is happening. Sometimes we feel guilty, knowing that we have erred.

In any case, there needs to be a balancing of the scales. Corrective measures must be taken. Sometimes we impose these on ourselves, and other times they are imposed on us, seemingly from outside conditions. However, nothing happens to us that we don't know about at some level of our being.

Being corrected or realigned can be painful, or it can be barely noticeable, depending upon the nature of the condition with which we are dealing. If we have engaged in excessive drinking, for example, as a way of covering up pain or running from one's responsibility or being unable to cope with life, we will pay the price. However, many persons can be healed or brought into balance when we seek help. Very often those around us need help as well, so all have the opportunity to heal.

By healing, we mean coming into balance. The seeming tragedies in our lives aren't tragedies at all, but mechanisms or opportunities by which we can heal ourselves. If there is, for example, a tragic, untimely death in the family, there is also opportunity for healing as well. Often we aren't aware that healing is necessary. We may be going along quite nicely, we feel, until something happens and a crisis results. Then the walls come tumbling down and everyone's vulnerabilities are exposed.

We will get what we need to help us deal with the situation. And as we do, wondrous things are apt to take place, though the result is not always visible to those around us. It may be a personal realization or awakening which comes to us but of which others are unaware. At other times, very evident results occur.

For example, as a result of the death of another, great movements have begun. Funds have been set up and other consciousness-raising ideas have been implemented. In other words, very positive things can come out of our human ability to err or succumb to "tragedy."

As we learn from our mistakes, we benefit. If we do not learn, we continue to set up the same types of situations and conditions in our lives until we do learn.

Repetition is the only answer, because we appear to be slow learners. One day, the light goes on; we see the errors of our ways; and the desire to make a change is planted within us. As this happens, and as we accept the responsibility for who we are, the desire to change our patterns becomes strong within us. Energy follows thought, and, with the help of Divine sources, we begin to set up new conditions which help to guide our way. Then, step by step, we climb out of the hole we are in and help realign the physical, mental, and spiritual aspects of ourselves so that we begin to heal. There need not be fear and judgment associated with our mistakes. The more spiritually developed we become, the more we recognize our place within the universe. We begin to see that our thoughts and acts are not so much good and bad. We are simply out of balance. Without a lot of self-recrimination, we look objectively at our mistakes, make amends where necessary, forgive others, and move on.

We have given up the useless practice of punishing ourselves. Instead, we do what we have to do. We pick up the pieces and go on as soon as possible, without wallowing in self-pity or self- abuse. We need not learn through pain as we once thought. We may, instead, move on without the pain because we have learned the lessons. The important thing is learning the lessons. The reason for the pain that we inflict on ourselves is only to remind us of what we are to learn. We wish to remember the lesson; therefore we inflict pain to insure our experience will not be in vain.

So as we become conscious of making mistakes and as we see the mistakes of others, let's view it all as learning. We are living in a world that is coming into a new age, and we are experiencing growing pains as we emerge from our old system.

On all levels, both individually and, as a society, we are becoming different. We will be positive in our thinking, and love and tolerance will be the rule for all. As we experience our cleansing, let's give thanks to the Creator for the opportunity to learn new ways of approaching life. Let's be grateful for being allowed to be here on earth during this exciting time of growth and change. When we make mistakes, let's learn to be gentle with ourselves as we uplift our fallen spirit and allow ourselves to continue on without guilt or remorse.

Further, let's leave judgments to the universe. Instead of judging, let's promise ourselves to accept God's love and forgiveness as we love and forgive ourselves and all others. As we do this, we will see the world transformed and our lives changed: "sin" and "punishment" will no longer have a hold on us because we will have lost our fear, and love will reign supreme.

ON PRIDE

Excessive pride can get in the way of our ability to heal ourselves, although a certain amount of pride can be looked upon as a positive attribute. We may take pride in our children. We take justifiable pride in a picture we've painted or in a job we've undertaken with success.

But there is another kind of pride that becomes excessive and limits our ability to relate to the world in a way that is honest. As a result, we show a false face to the world. We pretend to be what we're not.

For example, because of our excessive pride, we don't like to let anyone know we are hurting. We'd rather have people think we can take care of ourselves and our life. We want others to see that negative emotions are not part of our experience. We want to pretend to ourselves and to the world that everything's under control and our lives are in order.

Then again, perhaps our pride won't allow us to admit we have a problem or addiction, though everyone knows it. Our pride can thus prevent us from getting the help we need because we can't admit to our weakness.

Maybe we have a problem with power issues and find it difficult to give up control. Perhaps we take great pride in a high position we hold, and find it extremely difficult to pass work on to others: we feel that we have to do it all ourselves. Believing that our way is the only way can limit possibilities, and thus our pride can determine the fate not only of ourselves, but also of others. Great kingdoms and countries down through history have fallen because of the excessive pride and greed of a few individuals. Too much pride has the potential to be seriously damaging to the people affected by this shortcoming one way or another.

For most of us, pride is associated with fear of some kind. Fear of failure might make us show excessive pride in someone's accomplishment. For example, we may see our child's accomplishment as more than it really is for fear that it may not be recognized by others. Fear of loss of status also brings out excessive pride. Fear of criticism of others is likely to do the same.

Excessive pride inhibits us and limits our ability to function in a healthy manner. Because of our need to protect ourselves, we can't relate in honesty to the world or to ourselves. And because of our dishonesty, reality becomes distorted and our perceptions of ourselves and others are not realistic. The truth becomes lost as we find the need to live out our fantasy. Our defense mechanisms go into effect and we put on a suit of armor that disguises our true image or the image of others, and we try our best to fool the world.

Generally, most people see through this, and seldom do we deceive others. Sometimes we can fool people for awhile, but usually not for long. People are usually aware there is something wrong when we are afraid to show love or fear or concern. They know when we have a need to build up ourselves or our children. People recognize our need to display our wealth or demonstrate our power over others. Excessive pride or false pride is recognizable only because at one time or another we've been there ourselves and so we can easily see it in others.

This particular shortcoming is responsible for many unpleasant consequences if we allow it to dominate us. First of all, we lose our contact with our Higher Power because we have assumed the God position. Further, we are playing God in taking credit for our accomplishments because we acknowledge no Higher Power to whom we have turned. We are it. Therefore, in times of trouble we seek only ourselves for answers we do not have. And because we don't have the answers, we become lost in other areas of our lives. We have shut off the Source.

How can we play God and look to God at the same time? When we are assuming the role of perfection, when obviously we aren't perfect, we can't get the help we need. Of course, as we become humble and seek the Higher Intelligence within, it becomes a different matter. But false pride will prevent our being honest with who we are. Moreover, when there are discrepancies within us we have to be careful regarding our judgment of others.

When we recognize that we are lacking in humility and need help with that issue in our lives, we begin to align ourselves with our Creator. And as soon as we do this, we allow the Light to flow in, soothing and comforting our being. It's a struggle to live with false pride, because we always have to pretend, and pretense takes effort. When we give it up, we can relax and become who we really are. We can ask for help when we need it and allow our feelings to show. We can be angry if we need to, but we can apologize when it is appropriate to do so.

When we are humble, we are in balance. Wealth and glitter do not tempt us because we enjoy being who we are as we are in the right relationship to ourselves, to God, and to the world. And if we find ourselves stiffening up in an effort to pretend we're better than, more than, or above the rest of the world, we can be aware of the feeling, relax our mind, emotions, and bodies and ask to be honest. Again, it's fear that drives us to dishonesty; when we see that it's easier to give up the fear than pretend we're more than we are, we'll save ourselves a lot of suffering. Keeping up a false front is not achieved without painful effort!

Humbled before our Creator, we can allow the Higher Intelligence to love and guide us as we gain courage to give up our fear. In its place, we ask for a humble response to the situations and conflicts that confront us. Being able to say, "I don't know," or, "Please help me," and feeling free to express ourselves honestly to those around us will put us at peace. Further, we'll be unafraid to recognize the Source.

Again, as we recognize the Divine within, we will no longer need to pretend that we're something that we're not. We'll feel secure and safe in our honest relationship to life. Others will respond to our honesty and we'll find ourselves in loving relationships with those around us. Further, we'll feel comfortable in our ability to be who we are: unique and divine creative expressions of our Creator.

BOOK FIFTEEN

ON ENCOURAGEMENT

We all need encouragement from time to time. Especially because we are consciously on a spiritual path, we can become discouraged when we see our mistakes and witness our plans not coming off just as we'd hoped.

Because of our limited vision, we don't always know what's right for us. Therefore, at times things are altered according to God's plan, not our own. And sometimes these are in conflict. As we are attempting to trust our intuition, we can become discouraged when we find we have missed a cue, a sign, or guidance that we were counting on. Perhaps we erred in our perception and somehow missed the boat.

We ought to be very gentle with ourselves when this happens. We can't always be perfect. Our intuition is delicate, especially when we attempt to receive answers for ourselves. Our emotions and prejudgments regarding situations in our life can lead us astray. Even as we are aware and attempting as best we can to stay objective, mistakes can be made. Sometimes we overcompensate, causing our intuition to be inaccurate. Whatever the case, we need encouragement to enable us to trust again.

We also need encouragement as our responsibilities increase. As we assume control of our lives and begin to manifest our talents and abilities, more is asked of us. Further, as more is required, we will be doing more work than was formerly expected of us. As we become aware of ourselves and discover all we have to offer, we are encouraged by the universe to use what we have to help ourselves and others.

To give of our time and energy and talent whenever it is needed becomes a way of life. As a result, we need to find balance in our lives. We need to balance work, exercise, play, and relaxation. If we cannot achieve this balance, we become tired.

We begin feeling put upon and can become discouraged as well as drained.

It is at times like this that we need encouragement and wisdom. We need to be told that what we do is worthwhile, but that we ought to take care of our own needs. We must learn to rest and enjoy life as well as keep our bodies healthy through proper exercise and nutrition. We have to take care of mind, body, and spirit if we are to finish this trek up the mountain in good shape. Balance is part of what we need to learn as we make our ascent, but we need encouragement at times to remind ourselves that it is worth the effort to take care of ourselves. It's very easy to get caught up in working too hard and to avoid doing the rest of the things we need to do to stay healthy on all levels.

We also need encouragement to stay focused on our goals as we see that we do not achieve them as quickly as we'd like. Often, when we begin this conscious journey, we imagine great things happening in our lives, and we expect them to occur much more quickly than is ever possible. Spirit will often lure us along, much like a donkey with a carrot dangling in front of him. We will be given a vision, perhaps, of something that will take place in the future, but sometimes we think the future means next month—when actually it may mean a year or two or five down the road.

Therefore, if we are expecting something to happen that does not occur when we think it's supposed to, we can become disenchanted, as well as discouraged with our ability to discern.

Timing, in relation to intuitive thoughts and impressions, is often very vague so we need to be careful when we draw conclusions regarding time. We begin to wonder when the event is going to take place, and then we want to know if it will happen at all. Sometimes we become disheartened to the point of wanting to give it all up. We feel we've been walking this road for a long time. We need a break to restore our enthusiasm.

It is at this point when we feel "at the end" that our Creator gives us something to keep us going. It may not yet be time for the big break we're looking for, but something happens that shakes us out of our blue mood. Sometimes even a compliment from a friend or a pat on the back or recognition for some work done in the past is enough to keep us going. Often it doesn't take much. We need only to feel worthwhile and appreciated for who we are. This can be enough to keep us on track.

We also need to be encouraged to find joy in our lives. As many of us are cleaning up our acts, getting rid of our addictions and watching our diet and nutrition, the old forms of indulging ourselves aren't viable anymore. We have to find new ways to get pleasure out of life. Perhaps taking a long walk or joining a friend for dinner can be stimulating.

Doing some form of exercise is also helpful in restoring one's energy and vitality. And believe it or not, even straightening out drawers and closets can give us a good feeling if we are trying to resist spending money or indulging in buying clothes or whatever appeals to the addictive shopper. Taking care of what we do own, and seeing that things are orderly and in place can be much more productive and satisfying than dragging more stuff into an already messy environment. Sometimes we need to be creative in order to be joyful. Perhaps we crave a malt, but realize that, at this time at least, it's not good for us to have one. If we turn our attention to how good we wish to feel and visualize how we want to look, we can get interested in having something healthy instead. Moreover, a positive result of doing the right thing is that we don't have to suffer guilt.

It's beneficial to follow our intuition regarding our enjoyment of living, and sometimes going off the diet or buying that beautiful coat or dress is the answer. In any case, we need to be encouraged to enjoy our lives, especially as we're working so hard to live up to the high standards we set for ourselves. We are apt to get too serious as we embark on this path, and what a pity that can be. After all, we're simply attempting to live as our Creator intends. The universe didn't plan that we should be sullen, overly serious, and wedded to our work.

We are meant to be fun-loving, balanced, and appreciative of all aspects of life. If we are taking life too seriously, before long someone lets us know. If that "someone" is not a friend or co-worker, somehow the universe lets us know. Somehow we get the message to lighten up. Maybe we read something that we find humorous, and we have a good laugh. And what a relief that can be after we've been spending many hours contemplating the more serious aspects of life.

We also need to be encouraged to speak up—to express ourselves when it is appropriate. This is especially important if in the past we have held back for one reason or another. Often persons who have held back are those who now need to begin trusting more in themselves. Often these are people with highly creative minds, but an inaccurate sense of their intuition. It's time now to begin trusting their impressions and saying out loud what needs to be said.

We can be accustomed to thinking our thoughts without verbalizing our opinions. Perhaps now is the right time to share the thoughts that we have previously held back. Sometimes people aren't aware that they have been holding back until they begin to express themselves. And as they do, more and more ideas develop until a different person starts to emerge.

This all happens because it's time. Things seem to happen in their own good time. There are reasons people spend their childhood as quiet, unassertive little children. And there are reasons why a change takes place somewhere down the road. During our lifetimes, we are all functioning within certain conditions that have purpose. There are conditions beyond our control that we have to endure or be subject to for a period of time, and then these conditions are lifted. As they are, new circumstances take their place. Our situation changes because nothing in the universe remains constant. As a result, we need to be encouraged to "hang in there" if things seem rough, because the tide will change with time. We need, as well, to be encouraged to express ourselves—our needs, desires and opinions.

We receive encouragement from many sources. Friends, family, co-workers, and even people we meet on the street may encourage us. Spirit encourages us as we become discouraged through life's trials. We are given intuitive thought or feeling which tells us to carry on. We are given comfort as we turn within, seeking love, guidance, and wisdom from those in spirit who help direct our lives. Nature, too, can encourage us as we listen to the babbling brook or see a cat with her kittens.

We may be encouraged as we watch a nation set free from oppression, or a small baby being rescued following an earthquake. We may be encouraged as we witness a famous person die bravely and with dignity after a painful terminal illness. We can feel encouraged as we look back to where we began our journey and see our progress. Further, we can be even more encouraged when we look to the future and the promise that it brings. As we are all being prepared for a new time—a new day—we can be encouraged by what that means. A world without war or hunger, chaos, or conflict can promise much to those who anticipate its coming.

A world in which people are free and the environment is clean and safe for all is, indeed, a bright picture. Envisioning an earth where harmony and peace prevail for all gives us hope for the future. Further, because we are the co-creators in making it all come to pass, we may be encouraged to know we have been chosen for such a task.

Therefore, as we play our parts and follow our guidance as best we can, we will be fulfilling our roles in the plan. As we lose our fear of the great power that has been bestowed upon us and as we learn to work in harmony with our Creator, God's divine plan will unfold and manifest a new dawn—a new awakening—as our soul's purpose is fulfilled. So be it!

ON OPPORTUNITY

We tend to see life differently from a spiritual standpoint than from a purely earthly perspective. Our goal, of course, is to base our life on a spiritual foundation—a basis upon which we may establish our values and conclusions. As we see our challenges from an earthly perspective, we tend to immediately feel fear, revulsion, fatigue, rebellion, competition, and other feelings, emotions and attitudes which we associate with the problems confronting us today.

From a spiritual perspective, we may see all challenges in the same way: as opportunities. Every challenge, problem or situation that presents itself to us on any level may be viewed as an opportunity, because, in fact, that is what it is. It is an opportunity to overcome fear. It is an opportunity to gain advancement along one's path of growth. It is a chance to take another step up the ladder. Furthermore, individuals who see their challenges in that light are making great strides and enjoying success.

The minute we start to see the negative side of our life conditions and problems, we invite more negativity. If we insist on seeing our job as troublesome, boring, full of conflict, and demanding, it will not disappoint us. In fact, it will become more of what we already think it is. On the other hand, as we start to think of that same job as an opportunity to overcome our challenges, it becomes something totally different. It becomes a playground or a classroom in which we can become creative and learn much about ourselves and life. It becomes a catalyst for many conditions and situations in which we may choose to improve our lives.

As we learn to deal with the problems with which it presents us, this same job can be responsible for helping us to become something we never dreamed we could be. If we can learn to handle situations which we detest and with which we have to deal every day on our jobs or in our close relationships with significant people in our lives, we find we can master anything.

We have to understand that our lives are a schoolhouse. Our workplace and various relationships represent our classes. Each class has its own challenges, and the problems we encounter point out our weak and vulnerable areas. Some people find one thing challenging in a particular class, while someone else may find another problem. The point is, all our weak areas differ. We are placed in conditions which bring up these weaknesses.

Therefore, if we wish to know what it is we are to learn in this lifetime, we have only to look around us. Our challenges represent what we are here to learn, while our innate abilities and talents are our gifts. If we feel put down by people, our challenge is our self-esteem. If we have a bad temper, we will most likely be placed in a situation with someone or something that will tempt us to become very angry. If we have a tendency to create problems for ourselves or make mountains out of molehills, we will attract situations in which we can do just that. If we have a problem with money, we will be constantly challenged to keep our finances in check.

If we have chosen to work through these lessons on a higher level, we will be confronted with the opportunity to deal with them over and over again until we master our lessons. Once we have truly accepted the necessary learning from what had been difficult for us, we will no longer have to be challenged over and over again. The situation may, however, recur now and again to assure us that we have assimilated thoroughly what we have been taught.

These opportunities often come in different forms. Therefore, we often don't recognize the basic lesson in the experience. Sometimes, after we get home, we say, "Oh, I blew it again!" It doesn't dawn on us that the same lesson is being given. For example, if we discover that one of our lessons demands that we begin asserting ourselves more, we realize that there are many ways in which to do that. We may be confronted with a variety of opportunities, all coming from different directions, which call for our need to be assertive. Usually, we don't have a great deal of time to analyze the situation. All of a sudden the opportunity or challenge is there, and then, just as quickly, it's gone. We have to respond quickly.

This is why it is beneficial to ask for help and Divine Light from our Higher Power as we begin our day. By doing so, we will receive help to say and do the right thing. Our Creator and the spirit forces that work with us know all about us: what our lessons are and when they will be coming to us. Therefore, as we ask for help, it will be there for us.

We can see opportunity everywhere in all that we do. We have the opportunity to heal ourselves in a multitude of ways. As we become alert to our shortcomings, we may also be aware of the opportunities in which we can work on them. Awareness is important. If we are not aware, our chances pass us by and we go on sleeping through our life. Then when we reach the other side following our death, we realize that we've missed the boat entirely, and we wonder what we did accomplish in all our previous time.

As we review our life, we see that opportunity after opportunity presented itself to us to help us get over some weak area we had, and we missed the whole thing. We discover that we spent much of the time blaming others for our unhappiness or refusing to take responsibility for ourselves. We may have simply not even seen the issue, though it had been in plain sight all the while. We chose to overlook it. In any event, we can miss these chances offered to us, and if we don't take them now, we will have to face them later on.

As we put off our challenges, they become more difficult. It is as though the energy is stepped up—the intensity of the problem is increased, so that we will recognize the need to face it. What starts out as a rather small issue can amount to a monumental crisis if we don't take care of the problem immediately.

The universe is relentless, and, like the ocean, it does not forgive those who refuse to take it seriously. Its forces are automatic and without judgment or favoritism. All are treated equally. It doesn't punish or scold. It merely throws back what hasn't been learned to the student who must study it again for another upcoming test. Yet it rewards in equal measure all those who play by its rules.

As a father loves his children, the Lord of the universe loves us. We are encouraged to learn quickly so that the lessons don't have to be harsh or repetitive; however, we are allowed the freedom to take as much time as we feel is necessary to accomplish the task. We are the ones who attract to ourselves what we have not yet learned. And we are the ones who will learn, in whatever way and at whatever speed we choose, because each of us is the captain of our own ship; we are in control. We are responsible for seeing that our homework is done each day. Do we blame the principal when we fail the test? Do we berate the teacher when we forget to bring home our books? And do we blame our friends when we're tired of school and want to play?

Taking responsibility is the key, and watching for opportunities each day can help us greatly to grow and advance. Each time we help someone, we help ourselves. That is the law. Further, each time we say a kind word to another we invite the same treatment to ourselves. And each time we face a challenge squarely, we help ourselves to release the fear it represents. By facing our fears, we see them for what they are: mere shadows, illusions based on false beliefs that don't hold up under close scrutiny. Fears are based on facts we think to be true, but which in reality are not.

Life is a game. If we play by the rules we will see, when it's over, that we have won—perhaps not from the earthly perspective, but from a spiritual perspective. Looking back on this time of plugging away and persevering, learning and giving where we could, we will someday find that we have made progress. Like a sculptor's work of art emerging from a piece of marble, a beautiful form will eventually appear from nothing.

Daring to challenge ourselves in order to move up the ladder, while trusting in our Creator to work with us, and relying on ourselves to take action when called for, we can overcome the most difficult obstacles and climb the most formidable mountain. Why shouldn't we try? Why not go to work on the challenges that we face every day instead of staring at them and wishing they would go away? We stare at our problems, as we might look at dirty laundry, and then look away. Why not tackle them and accomplish something worthwhile? In that way, we can at least say we made the effort. And who knows, maybe we'll succeed. And then, what might become of us if we are successful? That's a whole other story in itself. Will there be more responsibility? More challenges? Harder lessons? Some day it will all be over.

Then we can look back from wherever we are in the spirit world, and say to ourselves, "Congratulations, you stuck it out. You met your worst fears, and you won."

ON UNDERSTANDING AND APPRECIATING GOD'S WORD

For everyone who attempts to understand and interpret God's Word as it has been left to us through the Bible, there will be discrepancies. As we are all individuals and are at different places in our evolution as spiritual beings, we will find different interpretations appropriate to where we are in our growth.

Some of us find literal interpretation of scripture to be the only way to approach the messages the Creator is bringing to us so that we may understand the universe and its laws. There are others who understand the Bible as a symbolic metaphor filled with stories and parables that help us to understand ourselves and bring instruction and guidance at the same time. Further, there are those who feel that much has been lost, not only in the literal, physical sense that was intended, but also through man's translation.

In other words, there remains the question: how accurately did man record? And, given the period in history, how literally can we take what has been written?

Put simply, time in itself can change the meaning of what was originally intended. Man is human and lives in a particular period in time and place in space. Therefore, how he perceives and records could vary with these conditions. Some persons feel that literal interpretation is based on a perception of the truth as it was interpreted centuries ago by fallible men who were products of their time. Other readers who have concentrated on the meaning of The Word have found great help, understanding and knowledge through the hidden translation which they believe was meant to be the true interpretation.

Although there is only one Truth, it seems appropriate to accept both the literal and symbolic meaning of The Word as we humans attempt to understand God. It is necessary to be open to varying interpretations, and the persons who hold them, if we are to live in harmony and peace with each other. If we can't accept another's path to the Creator as their right to explore, we are limiting our own. If we allow others to read and experience what they need to for their growth, we are allowing ourselves the same freedom. If we try to stop or inhibit another's desire to believe what he or she wants to believe, we inhibit our own growth. And if we can't allow others to share their opinions and beliefs, we only stifle ourselves.

As long as we aren't attempting to control others, we ought to be free to share what we believe to be true. However, as we attempt to disallow another's freedom of choice in any way, we are then stepping on toes. We must allow people their right to learn, to explore, and to experience life as long as they aren't impinging on another's right to do the same. What we do to another we do to ourselves—always. If we wish freedom to increase in our lives, we must allow freedom in our neighbor.

How can we say we know what is right for another person? We can't. Therefore, it's best to live and let live and pay attention to the work we have to do within ourselves. It is usually when we have work to do on ourselves that we see the flaws in others most readily. We'd rather look over at the mess in the neighbor's yard than look at our own.

It's easy to find fault with someone else and much more difficult to face our own issues. It takes great courage to look within and take the steps necessary to face and deal with all that is wrong. It's rather like looking in a messy closet. We'd just as soon shut the door and pretend that what we see really isn't there. Facing reality is difficult; it's so much easier to look over at someone else's life and see what they are doing. It's time for all of us to look within, because eventually we will all be forced to deal with our own issues. No longer will we be able to hide.

Illusions are being torn down in society today—witness our public figures. We can bless those individuals whose private lives have been exposed: they are teaching us great lessons through their misfortune. They have agreed—on a higher level—to allow their lives to be an example; we can be grateful for their courage. No matter how these public personalities are viewed, we can thank them for what they teach us as we witness their "fall from grace." For what they experience, we also must experience in our own way as we "clean house."

We are living in a time when we will either have to "shape up or ship out." There is no longer room for the gray area that once was. We can no longer sit on the fence in indecision. It's time we either grow or go. This doesn't mean that all those who have been leaving the earth have decided not to grow. But it does mean that we can no longer be here and not intend to improve ourselves and our lives. It does mean that we must continue to attempt to work in harmony with one another, regardless of the differences between us. For it's only to the degree that we allow others to be themselves that we can grant ourselves the same freedom.

Further, it is only through our tolerance and acceptance of the plight of others that we will receive compassion and sympathy for our own struggles. It is only through accepting the unacceptable in another that we will find ourselves being received into God's kingdom. When we can open our hearts to the less fortunate and find it within us to see that we are, indeed, One, we will find peace. Further, as we each meditate on God's Word, using our heart instead of our intellect to look into the eyes of our neighbor and find ourselves there, we will be on the road to greater understanding.

In the same way, by allowing others to interpret the Word of God in a manner that brings them comfort, we will bring that same sense of spiritual comfort and security to ourselves. While honoring the beliefs and practices of other travelers who are struggling to find their place in the universe, we will find our own place. And as we trust the Light in another, we will begin, also, to trust in the God within ourselves. The knowledge that one day we will all come to the same truth can help us to accept, for the moment, a variety of paths to that truth. And as the higher spiritual forces look down on us and guide our way, we can give thanks for the opportunity to learn and experience all that is appropriate for us.

Therefore, let's give thanks to the Creator who made us, and let's begin to look with acceptance on our neighbor as he makes his way to greater understanding. While refraining from limiting and attempting to control what others believe, think, or feel, we can look forward to the same consideration as we attempt to heal ourselves of the past and move forward into the dawn of a new awakening.

When this new day appears, we will understand that we are One, and no longer will we need to criticize another. No longer will we feel the need to bring others down as we see how we are affected in the process. We will understand the need to allow and accept others as they are. We will comprehend the meaning of love. No longer will we have to read about God's intention for us, because we will be living it. We will be manifesting all that, at one time, we only heard and read about. Further, all that was promised to us will be manifested in our own lives, and we will feel love, peace, and joy in our Oneness.

ON PSYCHIC PHENOMENA

As we develop our intuitive abilities, we open ourselves more and more to the spirit within. While learning to trust the Divine Power as it too grows and expands, a greater awareness of life unfolds before us. As we learn to quiet ourselves and tune in to these forces within which help to teach, lead and guide us forward, we find more and more experiences coming to us that are of a spiritual nature.

It is important, however, that only that which is for our highest good come to us. Gradually, as we learn to walk in the Light and trust the God within, doors that were previously closed open to us. We may receive glimpses of the past or have a certain psychic awareness come to us pertaining to that which is going on in the present.

We may also get a glimpse of a future event: a precognition of what is to be. These occurrences are natural and appropriate, although people sometimes fear these events that appear out of the blue for no apparent reason. As a result, they close the door on their ability to see beyond the threshold. This can be unfortunate, because much can be gained through these channels if the connection to spirit is properly controlled and monitored.

God's gifts don't come to just a few. We all have this ability, but in some the psychic ability is more developed and readily usable. Psychic ability and spiritual awareness are not, however, the same thing. One can have psychic ability without being highly spiritual. And yet a highly spiritual person will have opened the psychic doors as well.

As we grow spiritually, we will begin to open the psychic

senses. As we cleanse the body, mind, and spirit, we prepare the way for a new awakening that gives us greater knowledge of ourselves and the world. This process, however, does not come overnight. It is best not to wait impatiently to have these wonderful and unique psychic experiences, but to allow them to unfold naturally without focusing on the experience itself, but on the growth that helps bring such phenomena about.

In other words, it's best to concentrate on improving oneself in all areas of one's life, including work, relationships, self-concept, faith in self and the Creator, and so forth. It is appropriate, of course, to purify one's heart, mind, and soul in order that spiritual manifestations may come about. God knows when we are ready and can benefit from such experiences. We cannot, of our own ability, control their occurrence. And the more we focus on our desire for psychic phenomena, the less they are likely to happen. We would be wise to forget about that part of our development and focus on the work we have to do on ourselves.

However, one can help to open oneself safely to the spirit world through meditation. As we ask for Divine Light and request that only that which is for our highest good be allowed into our life, we can feel safe and secure in the knowledge that we are being watched over and guided. And as we learn to sit each day for a short period of time, we can benefit greatly as long as we are not in a hurry for results.

Meditation calms us down, and as we learn to trust the spirit within, we learn to trust our process. As we persevere in serious meditation, we will begin to feel comfortable with these moments of silence that we share with our Higher Power. Eventually we get to the point where we are a bit uncomfortable if we miss the time we share with our Creator. We begin to notice how balanced we feel after such communion and how off-center we can feel if we don't take these few moments for ourselves. It becomes a habit—a good habit that, if continued, can bring us much benefit.

We begin to feel comfort and support when we start receiving impressions that appear to guide us gently in a particular direction that turns out to be beneficial to us. Often, as we sit in meditation, this process that unfolds ever so slowly and naturally almost seems to be a non-event. In other words, it feels as if we've always received guidance this way. It's difficult to remember when things were not like this. However, it's also true that many of us have been receiving psychic impressions or thoughts impressed upon us by forces from the world of spirit for a long time, and we're simply not aware of them.

As we develop our psychic abilities more thoroughly, we learn to control these processes. We eventually learn which "channels" or stations to tune in to, and which to avoid. We become aware of the necessity to act responsibly in this area, discerning what is helpful to us and what is not. When we listen to a radio, we don't attempt to hear all of the stations at the same time. We are selective and learn to fine-tune our radio so that we may listen more clearly to that which is appropriate at the time.

At times there are forces which try to get our attention. We may be better off without these forces. Therefore, we need to learn to discern and take care of ourselves as we grow into this fascinating area of psychic development and spiritual awareness. By asking for direction each day, we can enjoy our growth as well as our experiences along the way.

Occasionally, as we are learning and growing, we'll have to deal with forces that appear unpleasant to us. For example, if we fear something or someone, we tend to draw it to us until we release our fear of it. Our negative thoughts will attract that which we fear or despise. It's essential to learn to be aware of our thoughts, trying not to build fear or resentment in our consciousness.

We all experience fear and anger from time to time, but if we continually hold these thoughts in our consciousness, we are forced to deal with what we wish to release. This is the law.

As we learn to send loving thoughts to those we fear and despise, we release the negativity, thus balancing the energy and terminating the need for further learning. And as we learn to talk to people in spirit by mentally picturing them and being open and honest with what we wish to say, we clear the way for healing our relationships. If we remember to be honest without dumping our negative energy onto another, whether in spirit or on the physical plane, we can say we've learned much in communicating effectively with those around us.

As we learn to work with Divine Energy by sending love in all situations, we begin to heal ourselves and our relationship to the world around us. As this healing takes place, we find that spirit is opening itself to us more and more, and we move up the spiritual ladder. By learning to master ourselves and the lower energies, from either the physical plane or the spiritual realm, we gain in mastery over ourselves.

This, of course, is all done with the loving guidance and Divine Light from the Source within and the higher spiritual forces that work with us. The more willing we become, the more help and guidance we receive. God needs workers to help guide us into a new age—a new time of peace and harmony where love prevails as the dominating force. So to the extent that we are eager to learn, our Higher Power will respond with more for us to learn and further manifestations from the spirit world to pique our interest and to let us know that we are, indeed, not alone.

Sometimes it seems as if God reveals His mighty power to us to remind us of what He can do for us and to keep us humble. Let us be grateful for the spirit manifestations or psychic phenomena that have occurred in our life, and ask ourselves in our quiet moments why they occurred and what they were meant to teach us. We're all given our experiences for a reason. Sometimes they come as a spontaneous tuning in to another dimension. We must hold the thought of our experience, and remember them when we begin to feel complacent in our life on earth.

Our routines can become dull, but our spiritual experiences have a way of snapping us out of our daydreams as if to remind us that we are not alone. We are, rather, in the hands of a benevolent force that is powerful beyond words or description. When we realize this fact, we are jarred back to reality with a new sense of respect for life and for our Creator. And as we grow, these tiny flashes of insight continue to remind us of who we are and where we are going.

We help others by sharing what we have received when they ask for it. In so doing, we not only serve those who need assistance, but ourselves as well. For as we give, so also do we receive. Therefore, as we feel comfortable in demonstrating our ability to help another in a manner appropriate to the situation, we begin to act as the channel we were meant to be.

Further, as we purify ourselves, our light becomes brighter and our love stronger, until one day we will appear as a great beacon of light to which others will turn for support and direction. So let's be patient with our growth as we sit in the silence, learning to trust the God within to light the way.

Seek for Fulfillment

Release your doubt.
Release your fear.
Enjoy the earth
While you are here.

Follow your heart
And follow your dreams,
You may be surprised—
Life's not what it seems.

For the way is prepared
When you follow your light.
As angels go first,
To make your path bright.

And be not discouraged
Should you make a mistake,
For experience is gathered
On each road we take.

And who is to say
If one has erred?
Do not be afraid,
Do not be scared.

Perhaps your adventure
Was needed, you see,
To help with your goal
To be all you can be.

So, judge not your past
And live for today.
Take in each moment
And go on your way.

Look for your essence,
For that which is you.
Seek for your spirit
In all that you do.

This brings you to balance,
To that even place...
This brings you to peace,
To that sacred space.

From where we make choices
That keep us on course,
And opens our hearts
In love, to the Source.

—Jill Downs

About the Author

Jill Downs has a BA in sociology and has worked as a licensed practical nurse; facilitated family groups in recovery; has experience working with the elderly in nursing homes and the dying in hospice. She has served as board president of the Lake Superior Interfaith Community Church and was instrumental in creating a learning center there. Her intuitive skills were developed through work in spiritual counseling and teaching meditation classes in the community. Her spiritual growth and development has included a significant spiritual awakening with profound journeys into consciousness and intensely challenging work in the inner planes. At present she conducts workshops on personal and spiritual growth. She lives with her attorney husband on the shores of Lake Superior in Duluth, Minnesota. Their two daughters live in Duluth and Colorado. The author maintains that a spiritual journey begins by learning about and accepting the depth, potential and capabilities each of us has. She feels this journey is enhanced by the insights and views shared by others. These essays are her way of helping every reader become fully human, fully conscious and engaged in this wonderful journey called life. *The Awakening of the Heart* is her first book.

Index

BOOK ONE

BOOK TWO

BOOK THREE

BOOK FOUR

Index Con't.

Index Con't.

Index Con't.

Other Savage Press Books Available

Appalachian Mettle by Paul Bennett

Hometown Wisconsin by Marshall J. Cook

The Year of the Buffalo, a novel of love and minor league baseball by Marshall J. Cook

Treasures from the Beginning of the World by Jeff Lewis

Stop in the Name of the Law by Alex O'Kash

Something in the Water by Mike Savage

Widow of the Waves by Bev Jamison

Dare to Kiss the Frog by van Hauen, Kastberg & Soden

Voices from the North Edge by St. Croix Writers

Gleanings from the Hillsides by E.M. Johnson

Keeper of the Town by Don Cameron

Thicker Than Water by Hazel Sangster

Mystic Bread by Mike Savage

The Lost Locomotive of the Battle-Axe by Mike Savage

Moments Beautiful Moments Bright by Brett Bartholomaus

Beyond the Mine by Peter J. Benzoni

Some Things You Never Forget by Clem Miller

Superior Catholics by Cheney and Meronek

Pathways by Mary B. Wadzinski

SoundBites by Kathy Kerchner

Treasured Thoughts by Sierra

In the Heart of the Forest by Diana Randolph

Canoe & Kayaker's Floating Log Book by John Handy

The Duluth Tour Book by Jeff Cornelius

Burn Baby Burn by Mike Savage

To order additional copies of

The Awakening of the Heart

or receive a copy of the complete
Savage Press catalog,

contact us at:

Phone Orders: 1-800-732-3867

Voice and Fax: (715) 394-9513

e-mail: savpress@spacestar.com

Visit online at: www.savpress.com

Visa or MasterCard accepted

Savage PRESS

Box 115, Superior, WI 54880 (715) 394-9513